Cloth, Dress and Art Patronage in Africa

Dress, Body, Culture

Series Editor **Joanne B. Eicher,** *Regents' Professor, University of Minnesota*

Advisory Board:

Ruth Barnes, *Ashmolean Museum, University of Oxford*
Helen Callaway, *CCCRW, University of Oxford*
James Hall, *University of Illinois at Chicago*
Beatrice Medicine, *California State University, Northridge*
Ted Polhemus, *Curator, "Street Style" Exhibition, Victoria & Albert Museum*
Griselda Pollock, *University of Leeds*
Valerie Steele, *The Museum at the Fashion Institute of Technology*
Lou Taylor, *University of Brighton*
John Wright, *University of Minnesota*

Books in this provocative series seek to articulate the connections between culture and dress which is defined here in its broadest possible sense as any modification or supplement to the body. Interdisciplinary in approach, the series highlights the dialogue between identity and dress, cosmetics, coiffure, and body alternations as manifested in practices as varied as plastic surgery, tattooing, and ritual scarification. The series aims, in particular, to analyze the meaning of dress in relation to popular culture and gender issues and will include works grounded in anthropology, sociology, history, art history, literature, and folklore.

ISSN: 1360-466X

Previously published titles in the Series

Helen Bradley Foster, *"New Raiments of Self": African American Clo in the Antebellum South*
Claudine Griggs, *S/he: Changing Sex and Changing Clothes*
Michaele Thurgood Haynes, *Dressing Up Debutantes: Pageantry a in Texas*
Dani Cavallaro and Alexandra Warwick, *Fashioning the Frame: Boundaries, Dress and the Body*

Cloth, Dress and Art Patronage in Africa

Judith Perani and Norma H. Wolff

Oxford • New York

First published in 1999 by
Berg
Editorial offices:
150 Cowley Road, Oxford, OX4 1JJ, UK
70 Washington Square South, New York, NY 10012, USA

Berg is an imprint of Oxford International Publishers Ltd.

Library of Congress Cataloging-in-Publication Data
A catalog record for this book is available from the Library of Congress.

British Library Cataloguing-in-Publication Data
A catalogue record for this book is available from the British Library.

ISBN   1 85973 290 9 (Cloth)
       1 85973 295 X (Paper)

Typeset by JS Typesetting, Wellingborough, Northants.
Printed in the United Kingdom by Biddles Ltd, Guildford and King's Lynn.

Contents

Acknowledgements

Cloth, Dress and Art Patronage in Africa examines African cloth and dress traditions from the perspective of the art patronage process. Our interest in art patronage in Africa initially developed as a result of early field work among the Nupe and Yoruba and was further pursued with later field work among the Hausa, Nupe and Yoruba peoples of Nigeria. We wish to recognize the support of various agencies and institutions which allowed us to conduct field work in Africa. Perani: Fulbright-Hayes grant for doctoral research, 1973; Social Science Research Council postdoctoral grant for International research, 1980; Ohio University Research Council grant, 1981; Ohio University Baker Award, 1990. Wolff: Fulbright-Hayes grant for doctoral research, 1972–1973; Social Science Research Council postdoctoral grant for International research, 1980; Sigma Xi grant-in-aid of research, 1982; Institute for Advanced Studies, University of Iowa, 1993; U.S.A.I.D. Iowa-Nigeria Universities Development Linkage Program, 1993, 1995; Iowa State University Council on International Programs Internationalization, Globalization grant, 1997.

There are a number of individuals who offered various types of support for our research over the years. In particular, we wish to thank Renee Boser, Joanne B. Eicher and Roy Sieber for encouraging our research on African cloth and dress traditions. There are several individuals in Nigeria to whom we are especially grateful for providing data and assisting us with our fieldwork. We especially wish to thank Yahaya Shehu, Idris Ibrahim, the late Alhaji Bayero, former Head of Bichi District in Kano State, the staff of the now defunct Kano State Arts Council and Bolanle Wahab of The Polytechnic, Ibadan. Thanks also go to Jennifer Bryne and Katie Kempton for editorial assistance with the manuscript. We especially appreciate the generosity of the following individuals and institutions for making their photographs available: Tavy Aherne, Eli Bentor, Al Brooks, Alice Burmeister, Joanne Eicher, Stephen Howard, William Siegmann and the New Orleans Museum of Art. Finally, we wish to recognize Joanne B. Eicher, editor for the *Dress, Body, Culture* series for suggesting that we submit our manuscript for consideration and for her ongoing support and insightful suggestions throughout the production process.

Introduction

'Cloth is the center of the world' (From the Dogon creation myth, Griaule and Dieterlen 1954)

One cannot work in West Africa for long without noting the cultural importance of cloth and clothing. Yoruba axioms, for example, include 'Cloth only wears, it does not die,' 'We have always been born clothed,' and 'My family is my cloth,' expressing the Yoruba love of cloth and clothing (Renne 1995; Cordwell 1983; Wahab 1997). This book contributes towards understanding cloth and dress in the African context through an examination of the dynamics of cloth production, patronage, consumption and the social significance of dress.[1] Approaching the study of cloth and dress from the standpoint of art patronage recognizes that certain artifacts are key to the expression of culture both as aesthetic products and as consumer goods.[2] Beyond the initial production and consumption processes, cloth as dress gains meaning as part of the culturally-constituted body. The clothed body is essential to the projection of the social self by expanding the 'vocabulary' of the body and visually reinforcing social roles. By extension, cloth draws boundaries between the cultural and natural worlds in social and ritual contexts.

Focusing on cloth and dress, this book explores the most basic processes of artistic production – innovation and change, continuity and the efflorescence or decline of art traditions. Our processual approach, which considers the life history of art objects, ties artist, product, patron or consumer and audience together in an alliance marked by dynamic transactions. By emphasizing the processual nature of art patronage, we open up the contextual perspective to follow the full life history of cloth and dress in particular social and economic environments. The patron's demand and use of cloth in dress and other contexts is important to understanding the full significance of textiles and dress in cultural context.

Definitions

In the early 1970s Roy Sieber curated an exhibition entitled 'African Textiles and Decorative Arts' for the Museum of Modern Art, in which 'a wide variety of objects usually viewed as ethnographic material culture, of interest only to an anthropologist, became accepted as art' (Thieme and Eicher 1985: 1). Since then, studies of African cloth have been undertaken by a number of art historians and anthropologists.[3] Voicing the concerns of many scholars, John Picton asserts that 'it is impossible to consider life and art in Africa in the absence of textiles' (1995b: 11). African dress has received even less attention, although interest has grown steadily since Joanne Eicher's pioneering work in the 1960s.[4] Eicher and Thieme have urged scholars to consider dress as 'an integration of form, activity, and meaning and [as] a vehicle for the display of human behavior' (Thieme and Eicher 1985: 5). In the 1990s the relationship of 'human agency' to the nature of material culture – including cloth and dress – has received attention, with cloth being 'critical in the representation and reproduction of society [and] often a critical link between social groups across space and through time'. (Hendrickson 1996: 8)

Dress has been defined as 'an assemblage of body modifications and/or supplements displayed by a person in communicating with other human beings' (Eicher and Roach-Higgins 1992: 15). This encompassing definition considers the full range of body supplements as well as the social aspects of dress, addressing the importance of the total process of covering the body. According to Thieme and Eicher, dress involves 'obtaining, manufacturing, and preparing items of dress; donning, wearing, . . . and storing or maintaining items of dress and adornment between wearings' (1985: 3). Such a broad-based concept of dress is particularly useful for our study of cloth and dress from the perspective of art patronage. The processes of 'obtaining' and 'manufacturing' emphasize the 'why' and 'how' of cloth production and cloth acquisition. Also, a distinction between dress and costume is necessary; costume is a sub-category of dress restricted to specific occasions. Often costume conceals the identity of the wearer, such as that worn by masqueraders, with the aim of projecting a different persona.

Discussion of dress must consider the body. Eicher and Roach-Higgins have argued that

> the dressed person is a 'gestalt' that includes body, all direct modifications of the body itself, and all three-dimensional supplements added to it . . . only through mental manipulation can we separate body modifications and supplements from the body itself – and from each other – and extract that which we call dress. (1992: 13)

By focusing on the art patronage process affecting dress, we draw upon Eicher's and Thieme's idea:

> Ultimately, the factors that underlie the act of dressing the body in specific ways and at specific times, are more important for understanding the meaning of dress than is identification of the material forms themselves. (Thieme and Eicher 1985: 4)

Addressing 'the act of dressing the body' and the social self from the perspective of art patronage reveals a larger system, in which the culturally-constituted body intersects with the production and consumption of cloth and dress.

Another Western term needing re-examination is 'Art'. Roy Sieber has argued that 'if . . . we are at all concerned with the larger problems of artist, art, and aesthetics and attempting to view them cross-culturally, we must re-examine our ground rules, [and consider] the possibility of more open-textured definitions of art, or a cluster of concepts, as a working basis for further research' (1973: 426). Historian Jan Vansina has noted that

> art is a term of western culture but a very inexact one. The threshold between what may be judged a work of visual art and another kind of man-made object is often a matter of dispute. (1984: 1)[5]

A further problem is the tendency for scholars to label only certain types of African handmade objects as 'art' and dismiss the rest as 'crafts'. This art/craft dichotomy is a relatively recent western art historical construct. In the Italian Renaissance period, for instance, there was no distinction between the 'decorative arts' and 'figurative painting' (Cole 1983: 16). The art/craft dichotomy has little applicability to the arts of Africa, where the hierarchy of values attached to different media varies from society to society. The Western separation of art and craft has a connotation of an 'unpredictable, culture-transcending element of creativity in artistic production', while craftwork is characterized as being 'predictable, traditional, competent but limited by precept and technique' (Siroto, cited in Polakoff 1978: 22).

Commenting on the sculpture-centric research interests of many African art scholars, John Picton notes that 'most scholars agree that sculpture has for too long dominated African art studies' (1992: 44). While sculpture constitutes a very important category of African art, it excludes the creative diversity found in other media. In this study we reject the art/craft dichotomy and refer to producers of handmade objects made with aesthetic intent as artists. To regard cloth and dress as anything but art is to deny the vital role they play in expression of cultural values in utilitarian and ritual contexts. In the end, however, any efforts to answer the broader question 'What is Art?' remain as elusive as the deconstructivist's view of meaning.

Chapter Summaries

Part I (Chapters 1 through 4) broadly deals with the impact of art patronage on African arts, particularly cloth and dress. Chapter 1 establishes the book's themes, their theoretical roots, and presents a framework for examining the components of art patronage. Chapter 2 focuses upon the importance of cloth and dress in the African context, introducing the mediating functions that fuel acts of patronage for the textile arts. The chapter surveys the secular and religious contexts of cloth, while exploring its mediating functions in a variety of contexts. Chapter 3 examines the nature of art patronage in Africa. Using a full range of art traditions, the chapter presents a discussion of patron roles and art patronage transactions. Chapter 4 focuses upon the relationship between leadership arts and power in African state societies.

Part II (Chapters 5 through 8) provides in-depth case studies of art patronage and trade from the Hausa, Nupe and Yoruba state societies of Nigeria, linked by geography, history and culture. The choice of these cultures for in-depth scrutiny results from the authors' field, museum and archival research over the past twenty-five years: Perani has worked with the Nupe since 1973, Wolff has focused on the Yoruba since 1972 and both authors have conducted joint research among the Hausa since 1981. Chapter 5 situates the Hausa, Nupe and Yoruba states historically so that the art patronage-related issues associated with cloth and dress can be examined in Chapters 6 to 8. The chapter presents a brief overview of the historical development of the Fulani Sokoto Caliphate and the Yoruba Oyo Empire that facilitated intercultural contact between the Hausa, Nupe and Yoruba states. Chapter 6 explores the cultural linkages between the Hausa, Nupe and Yoruba in the production and use of luxury cloth. The interrelationship of leader patronage and market demand and their importance in shaping luxury traditions of 'caliphate cloth' (produced in all three societies) and Hausa *yan kura* cloth is a focus. Chapter 7 continues the examination of intercultural linkages by assessing the impact of large-scale sociopolitical and economic change on Nigerian cloth production in the twentieth-century colonial and independence periods. The chapter focuses on continuity and innovation in cloth traditions among the Yoruba and Hausa. Chapter 8 considers the continuing vitality of Yoruba cloth and textile arts in the late twentieth century, in contrast to the decline found in the Hausa and Nupe traditions. The chapter considers the contemporary Yoruba milieu where indigenous handwoven and dyed cloth have successfully competed with imported and factory-manufactured cloth in a dynamic fashion world of clothing.

Notes

1. In this book 'Africa' is used to refer to Africa south of the Sahara.

2. Grant McCracken has made this point clearly. ' . . . Without certain consumer goods, certain acts of self-definition and collective definition . . . would be impossible' (1986: 71).

3. These scholars include, but are not limited to, John Picton, Joanne Eicher, Lisa Aronson, Elisha Renne, Sarah Brett-Smith, Joseph Nevadomsky, Bernhard Gardi, Renee Boser-Sarivaxevanis, Peggy Gilfoy, Venice and Alastair Lamb, Jean Borgatti, Patricia Darish, Duncan Clarke, Kris Hardin, Judith Perani and Norma Wolff. See Plumer (1970) for early work on African textiles.

4. Those concerned with African dress include Joanne Eicher, Tonye Erokosima, Susan Michelman, Tunde Akinwumi, Fred Smith, Mary Jo Arnoldi, Christine Kreamer, Herbert Cole, Doran Ross, Hildi Hendrickson, Perani and Wolff. See Eicher (1969) for early work on African dress.

5. Vansina goes on to extend his definition to fit the African context. 'Any man-made object studied from the point of view of form may be an art object, and form is a major concern of any study of the arts, whether or not the objects will be lasting, whether or not the object was made just to express form, whether or not the object is a man-made thing or merely an embellishment of some other object, such as painting on the human skin' (1984: 1–2)

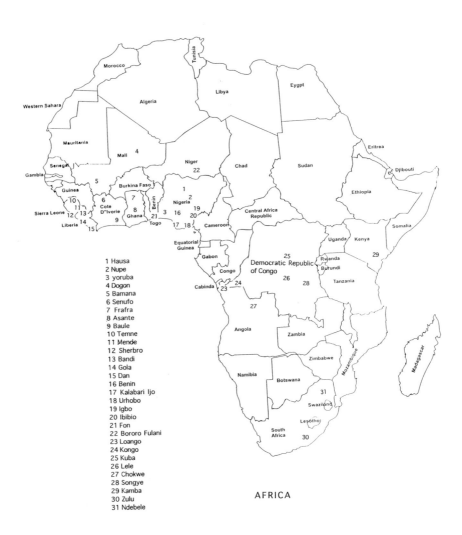

1 Hausa
2 Nupe
3 yoruba
4 Dogon
5 Bamana
6 Senufo
7 Frafra
8 Asante
9 Baule
10 Temne
11 Mende
12 Sherbro
13 Bandi
14 Gola
15 Dan
16 Benin
17 Kalabari Ijo
18 Urhobo
19 Igbo
20 Ibibio
21 Fon
22 Bororo Fulani
23 Loango
24 Kongo
25 Kuba
26 Lele
27 Chokwe
28 Songye
29 Kamba
30 Zulu
31 Ndebele

AFRICA

Figure 1. Map of Africa. Source: Judith Perani and Norma Wolff.

Part 1

The Impact of Patronage on the Arts of Africa

Art Patronage as a Generator of Cloth and Dress

The Relationship of Art Patronage to Cloth, Dress and the Body in Africa

Cloth, as a valued cultural artifact, is involved in every aspect of African life, playing an essential role in marriage, political and ritual exchanges. (see Chapter 2) As dress, cloth reaches its most culturally meaningful form. A clothed body is essential to complete human identity, setting apart the cultural self from the unclothed 'natural' body. Depending upon cultural precepts, minimal dress in some societies may make the body very visible, while in others the body is fully concealed and physically enlarged by accumulative dress. In all cases, as a kind of cultural or social skin, cloth layers the body with meaning (Turner 1980). Culturally significant body postures and gestures are emphasized by dress ensembles tied to a society's important political, social and religious institutions. When the body of a political leader is covered with layers of draped cloth or opulent tailored garments, dress expands and enlarges the body, projecting high social status and political power. On the other hand, when a member of a religious association dons a mask and costume, dress conceals and denies the wearer's human body. Thus:

> the surface of the body, as the common frontier of society, the social self, and the psycho-biological individual, becomes the symbolic stage upon which the drama of socialisation is enacted, and bodily adornment . . . becomes the language through which it is expressed. (Turner 1980: 112)

While focused on hats and hairstyles, the following insights apply to larger dress ensembles:

> People use hats and hair styles to express and explore shared and deeply held cultural beliefs and values towards ethnicity, gender, life stages, status and authority, occupation, and social decorum. As a material 'language' hats and hair styles can

be put on, and taken off, manipulated, and invested with an aggregate of meanings depending on how and in what contexts they are put into play. (Arnoldi 1995:45)

Functioning as a moveable armature that gives form to dress, the dressed body encodes and communicates culturally important beliefs and values tied to a society's political, social and religious institutions.

Like all cultural artifacts, cloth has a life history. Depending upon the particular life history phase, the cultural value of cloth at any specific moment may lie primarily in either an aesthetic, social or economic function. 'A textile is a context of ideas-and-practices that is both prior to and not necessarily dependent upon subsequent usage' (Picton 1995: 13). A full life history of cloth and dress must consider the individual and group behaviors influencing production and consumption processes. An investigation of the production and function of cloth and dress traditions from the vantage point of the art patronage process reveals the dynamic links between artists, patrons, products and audience in ongoing social interactions. These social actors and their transactions provide a lens through which to view the history of cloth use in Africa.

In this volume, starting from the perspective of art patronage, important questions about the development, continuity and integration of cloth and dress in social context are addressed: Why and for whom are cloth and dress created? What kind of social feedback from patrons affects the production behaviors of textile artists? How does innovation enter into a cloth or dress tradition? How do cloth and dress create and reflect their sociocultural contexts? A consideration of the art patrons, those individuals or groups who commission, purchase or use items of cloth and dress, provides some answers.

Affecting continuity and change in any art tradition, patrons encourage production through direct request, as well as through anonymous consumption. Additionally, they introduce the completed work into the broader social environment, where it functions and is evaluated by the larger community. While the artist is 'a mediator ... between the collective and individual striving for expression' (d'Azevedo 1973b: 13), the patron mediates between the artist and the larger community. Although creative innovation may originate with the artist, the patron ultimately approves and supports the artist's interpretation. The final art product becomes a tangible embodiment of the interaction of patron demand, individual artistic creativity, and existing prototypes. By addressing the clothed body and the social self from the perspective of art patronage, the larger system in which the culturally-constituted body intersects with the production and consumption of cloth and dress in society becomes apparent.

Art Patronage in the West and Africa

Fundamental differences affect the study of art patronage practices in Western societies and Africa. Mainly, the nature of the evidence differs. Patronage practices for the Italian Renaissance period, for example, are well-documented with written records.[1] While Renaissance artists might stockpile a few small paintings for sale, the vast majority of works was made to order (Cole 1983: 51). Written documentation exists in the form of contracts, letters and shopbooks recording daily business transactions. The contract often high-lighted the economic and legal circumstances as well as giving instructions on type, size, subject, materials and payment arrangements. An excerpt from a 1473 contract between the Sienese painter Matteo di Giovanni and the Siena bakers' guild was typical of the period.

> Antonio da Spezia and Peter Paul of Germany, bakers, . . . elected and deputed . . . by the Society of St. Barbara . . . for the work on the painting . . . ordered and commissioned Matteo di Giovanni . . . to make and paint . . . an altarpiece for the chapel of St. Barbara . . . with such figures, height and width, and agreements, manners . . . (cited in Cole 1983: 52)

The contract included a detailed discussion of size, iconography and material specified by the patron:

> In the middle of the aforementioned panel the figure of St. Barbara is to be painted, sitting in a golden chair and dressed in a robe of crimson brocade . . . Item, that the said master Matteo has to have this panel of wood made to the measurements mentioned, at his own expense, and have it painted and adorned with fine gold, and with all the colors, richly . . . (Cole 1983: 52–4)

Frequently, contracts contained lengthy sections concerned with the payment schedule:

> And all these things for the price of ninety florins . . . at the end of the time, and when the said master has completed the painting in every degree of finish, and placed it on the said altar. (Cole 1983: 54)

In contrast to the Italian Renaissance period, written contracts between African artists and their patrons are extremely rare; instead, transactions are normally verbal and generally less specific. While some acts of leadership patronage have been recorded, African art patronage practices still need extensive documentation. As already suggested, evidence for art patronage in the African context must be sought in the broader context of material culture, production and use. The historian Philip Shea, on the basis of his Hausa textile research, argues that we must consider

> who produced what, when they produced things, why they produced them, and for whom they produced these things . . . In addition to examining the technology and processes of production, we must also look closely at the set of relations which existed between and among the various direct producers, those who organised and controlled production, and the ultimate consumers. (1983: 94)

Jan Vansina and Suzanne Blier have emphasized the importance of the patron. Vansina stresses the patron's importance to the creative processes of artists.

> The creative process turned around three main pivots: the patron, the artist, and the products. However important the influence of the mental images of patron and public were, they only set limitations or requirements on the creation of acceptable art. The artist was the person who turned a mental image into matter. (Vansina 1984: 136)

Blier, on the other hand, emphasizes the role that patrons play in monitoring the artistic process.

> Artists or architects . . . are far less knowledgeable when it comes to the underlying meaning of a work or its symbolic grounding than are others in the society, such as priests and geomancers . . . Patrons . . . generally knew when and for what purpose a work was commissioned. They also were informed about the context of the work with regard both to the significance of its setting and the identities and roles of various other objects that were positioned near the work. (1988: 80)

For the purposes of our analysis of African cloth and dress traditions we broaden the definition of 'art patron' to include all those individuals or groups who commission, consume, and/or use art products. Members of audiences who react to art products when displayed in public contexts are also art patrons. Compared to definitions of art patrons generally used in Western art history, this definition is more fluid and open-ended, taking into account that the art product has a full life history and that the interaction between an art product and art patron continues well beyond the creation stage (Perani and Wolff 1996).

Process and the Life History of Art Products

Acts of patronage occur within the larger context of the 'artistic process.' An analysis of the impact of patron demand on an art tradition requires a processual approach stressing the dynamic nature of the artistic process and the interaction between patron, artist and art product. A processual approach emphasizes fluidity, viewing culture as a web of meaning which is continually emerging in the present. Social reality is a place where 'cultural change, cultural continuity, and cultural transmission all occur simultaneously in the experiences and expressions of social life' (Bruner 1986: 12).[2]

The necessity for a theoretical approach integrating art products and the contextual behaviors that give them cultural meaning was recognized by anthropologists Warren d'Azevedo (1958, 1973) and Alan Merriam (1977). D'Azevedo first called for an approach to distinguish between artistic and aesthetic behaviors. To understand the nature of art, d'Azevedo suggested a focus on 'artistry,' describing art as:

> a way of doing, a way of behaving as a member of society, having as its primary goal the creation of a product or effect of a particular kind . . . giving emphasis to persons and social events rather than to artifactual objects abstracted from either the processes of production or consumption. (d'Azevedo 1973: 6–7)

The primary actors in aesthetic actions are knowledgeable beholders or appreciators, while artists are the creators of new art forms in acts of artistry that express both individual and collective expression (d'Azevedo 1973: 6). Merriam's approach focused on the cultural feedback between artist, product and production behaviors. He stressed the indivisibility of behavior and product as follows:

> Behavior . . . is separable from the product analytically, but in reality it is inseparable, because no product can exist except as the result of the behavior of some individual or individuals. Similarly, behavior is always underlain by a series of conceptualizations which concern the product, the behavior that goes into making the product, the role played by the product in the society, and so forth. (Merriam 1977: 336–7)

While Merriam does not mention patrons, the importance of feedback from direct or indirect patronage cannot be denied. The art object results from a social act of production; its attributes reflect the idiosyncracies of the producer(s) and the social influences of patrons and other significant persons.

More recently scholars have drawn upon contemporary practice-oriented theorists such as Giddens (1976) and Bourdieu (1977) to inject the concepts of human agency, social reproduction and patterns of action that are at work in the continual recreation of culture.[3] Modern practice theory links culture and behavior by recognizing that the social system places powerful constraints on behavior and yet 'that system can be made and unmade through human action and interaction' (Ortner 1984: 159). The concept of 'human agency' suggests that individuals as 'social actors' are decision-makers who with intent and consciousness of action choose between alternative actions. According to anthropologist Sherry Ortner:

> History is not simply something that happens to people, but something they make – within, of course, the very powerful constraints of the system within which they are operating. A practice approach attempts to see this making, whether in the past or in the present, whether in the creation of novelty or in the reproduction of the same old thing. (Ortner 1984: 159)

Art products, therefore, must be understood as 'things-in-motion' as they move through their life histories in a specific or a series of sociocultural contexts (Appadurai 1986: 5).[4] From the perspective of art patronage, an art product passes through several stages of life history, and only when it is in the possession of an art patron/consumer does it become imbued with full sociocultural meaning. It is the patron/consumer who makes decisions that enhance or decrease the product's cultural and social value throughout its life history. While 'the art forms belong to the artist, the meanings belong to the broader community that makes the demands, sets the patterns, and then uses what the artists are able to produce' (Biebuyck 1969: 11). In this process,

> the original work is fully endowed with intention by its creator as well as by its patrons, but the successive meanings an object is given are fluid and negotiable, fragile and fully capable of erasure as it passes from hand to hand. (Kasfir 1992: 47)

Cloth as a focus of study demonstrates this flexible character. With recontextualization, it is not uncommon for cloth to undergo transformation in value and meaning during its life history. For example, most cloth made for sale is treated as an economic commodity during the production process. At this point, the impersonal economic forces of the marketplace play a critical role in influencing artistic decisions. When purchased by a consumer-patron, it is often used to construct a dress ensemble, gaining new aesthetic significance and social meaning. The processual approach, which an art patronage perspective offers, integrates the entities of artist and patron as it reveals patron-artist transactions activated by dynamic reciprocal feedback. It is through the actions of both artists and art patrons that cloth and dress traditions unfold.

A Framework for Analysis

The five-part analytic framework presented here directs attention to the significant components of art patronage necessary for understanding the processes involved. In Part I, the major *persona* or actors in the artistic process are introduced. The key roles of artist and patron, and the social factors that influence their roles, are discussed. Part II deals with the special nature of art *products* as aesthetic objects and their relationship to commodities. *Processes* linking artists, patrons and art products during and after artistic production are the subject of Part III. Part IV, a consideration of *place*, examines the importance of the sociocultural context of patron-artist inter-actions by focusing upon two types of space – physical and social. Finally, in Part V, the concept of *practice*, a broader theoretical framework linking players, processes, products and place into a single analytic model is presented.[5]

Persona   The key players in the artistic process are the artist and the art patron.[6] The *artist* is an individual who creates art products, or artifacts of material culture, which may be subject to aesthetic judgement. Artists can work individually or collaborate in a workshop, caste, kin group, ward or slave group. They carry out the creative process necessary to bring an art product into existence, giving material form to cultural mental prototypes that fuel the art tradition.[7]

Defining the art patron necessitates a broader perspective. Patronage is critical in activating the artistic process; the demand for art products must exist for production to be initiated and for it to continue. As earlier stated, art patrons influence artistic production through commissioning, consuming and instilling meaning into art products. An *art patron* acts individually or as part of a group to commission art products directly from the artist, or alternatively to purchase and use art products while remaining anonymous to the artist.[8] Members of audiences who react to art products when displayed in public contexts also constitute patrons. Through their approval or rejection as critics, future artistic production can be influenced.[9] Whether in a direct face-to-face interaction or through indirect feedback, it is the demands and opinions of art patrons that influence the production acts that encourage continuity or change in artistic traditions. Both artists and art patrons are decision-makers, influenced by their particular life circumstances and the cultural constraints that guide behavior.

Acts of patronage are carried out by people who are playing out particular roles associated with their social identity or status.[10] Roles provide order in the social structure by allowing one to predict the action of others; that knowledge can be used to choose a course of action which will maximize one's own personal goals in a transaction. All individuals can play a number of different roles, but in any specific interaction one role dominates and directs behavior. However, there is often a kind of role feedback from other roles which infringes upon the business at hand. There are normally built-in assumptions about the allocation of power in role transactions. In each interaction, one status is normally ranked higher, so that patterns of deference and dominance are evident in the role behaviors. In such situations, role behaviors tend to be stereotyped and formal. While actors are expected to adhere to socially predictable role behavior, all roles can be manipulated within culturally understood acceptable boundaries.

While it is possible to identify role behaviors of art patrons in Africa, it is an analytic distinction. The identification of a person as 'art patron' in the Western sense probably does not exist in African societies. Rather, art patronage behaviors are incorporated into more comprehensive roles in which the consumption of culturally-valued objects is required or desirable. In an act of patronage, the rights, prerogatives, obligations and customary behaviors associated with such comprehensive roles motivate a person to act in culturally approved and predictable ways. Major categories of such roles are identified in Chapter 3.

Products The art product[11] is a tangible artifact created by human labor in response to cultural demand, i.e. patronage. It is a material manifestation of an artist's creative behavior based on mental images associated with definite meanings (Vansina 1984: 101). As art, it is subject to aesthetic evaluation and can be judged in terms of quality by indigenous and Western standards. The meaning of the art product is inherent in its form (endowed by society on the basis of its membership in an artifact class), its function (as prescribed by its artifact class and expected social utility), and its trajectory or life history in social context (Appadurai 1986: 5). Once created, the art product enters into a social world where it is subject to possible recontextualization and redefinition.[12]

When considering the function and life history of an art product, it is crucial to realize that it is not only an aesthetic form but also a kind of commodity, a product created principally for exchange. Ultimately, all art products are commodities in the context of art patronage. Both patron and artist are concerned with negotiating value, whether it is an exchange of tangible wealth or intangible prestige or political value. 'Commodity-hood' is bestowed on a thing when exchangeability for another thing is its most important social characteristic (Appadurai 1986: 13). Subject to possible recontextualization in the social world, an art product can move in and out of commodity-hood during the course of its life history (Kopytoff 1986). Assignment to commodity-hood can be the norm for a certain type of object, that is, if it is made with economic exchange in mind, or the original creative intent may have specified a different life trajectory, such as that of a ritual power object.[13] For example, cloth may be produced as a market commodity, while a masquerade costume once used in ritual and later sold to a European acquires commodity-hood in a context unanticipated by the original patron and artist responsible for its creation. Whatever its function, the art product as commodity possesses a degree of economic value as a product of human labor, gaining 'use value' in the course of its life history.

The life history of an art product can be divided into two phases: production and social use. The production act involves the initial creation of the product guided by transactions between the artist and patron or the artist's perception of anonymous patron demand. Even before production begins, social understandings between patrons and artists about a proposed product's future function put limitations on the form to be created and determine how it will be treated during the production process and afterwards. Whether the art product is perceived as a utilitarian, prestige, trade or ceremonial good will influence every aspect of production, as well as the agreed upon contract and its future life trajectory. While the artist, with the input of the patron, initially instills the art product with form and cultural meaning, the object gains additional social meaning through use. It is those human transactions, attributions and motivations directed toward an art product in the course of its life trajectory that give it full meaning (Appadurai 1986: 5).

Processes The concept of *process* calls attention to the transactions between artists and their patrons and the impact of these interactions on art products as well as the larger art tradition. It is here that human agency enters in as patrons play out their roles to initiate production through direct contact or indirect feedback to creators. As earlier mentioned, art as culture is always in a state of becoming. A particular art tradition, be it cloth, sculpture or pottery, is recreated with each production act.

An *art patronage system* situates the patron-artist interaction in the broader sociocultural context where artist-patron transactions and the use of art products take place. The system links producers, products and consumers in dynamic interactions that contribute to continuity and change in the art tradition. In the continual recreation of art traditions in response to patron demands, 'drift,' gradual and unpredictable modifications in the formal attributes of artform types or 'icons,' takes place (Anderson 1989: 160–1; Vansina 1984: 145–8). 'Every icon is both a replica and an innovation, never wholly original, rarely a totally slavish copy' (Vansina 1984: 154). Artistic change constituting a break in a tradition may involve abrupt shifts in production behaviors or attitudes bringing about modification of existing artforms or the emergence of new forms and meanings. The source of such change must be sought in the art patronage system.

The actions of patrons and artists in the preproduction period as manifested in *patron-artist transactions* are of particular importance to understanding the dynamics of art patronage systems. A 'transaction'[14], is a social interaction involving exchange of valued material (art objects, labor) or immaterial items (status, power) between individuals or groups, in this case patrons and artists or their agents. Transactions involve reciprocal negotiation and feedback in culturally-specific contexts which pattern the behavior of the participants (Kapferer 1976: 1). While transaction theory emphasizes the economic aspects of production and distribution, transactions also have a psychological component (Scheflen 1974) which engages people in goal-oriented customary behaviors that evoke cognitive images shared by other individuals. Ordinarily, transactions allow for a range of alternative outcomes and behavioral variations, but some may be rigidly programmed. 'Institutional transactions' are highly structured events in which the place, sequence of events and performance styles of the players allow little variation. Such transactions have a cultural 'set of rules for decorum and procedure and some system of values and rationalizations' which predict the outcome (Scheflen 1974: 90). Patron-artist institutionalized transactions, such as those between religious functionaries and artists, tend to be governed by rules of procedure and production that encourage artistic change only within strict limitations. 'Exploratory transactions,' on the other hand, are less rigidly programmed. Although they are still affected by expectations about proper role behaviors, the sequence of events and the outcome are not predetermined. There is more opportunity for innovation and change in production and product. Such exploratory transactions are common when artists deal with outgroup patrons from different ethnic groups whose cultural understandings and expectations may differ. Applied to patron-artist interactions, the concepts of institutionalized and exploratory transactions call attention to the importance of examining the nature of the roles being played out by patron and artist, the idiosyncrasies of producer and consumer, the social context of production, and the influence of the social milieu.

For Africa we distinguish four major forms of patron-artist transactions.[15]

1. *Contractual transactions* involve a commissioning process which also entails face-to-face interactions between patron and artist. A verbal or written contract designates the terms of production. While the verbal contract is most common, the use of a written contract has become

frequent when art products are produced in large numbers as commodities for resale. Whether verbal or written, the contract is an order for production, designating the quantity and quality of the art products, formal characteristics, materials, iconography, production timetable and payment arrangements. The transaction ends when the product is turned over to the patron who pays or rewards the artist.

2. *Cliental transactions* are long-term patron-client relationships where patron and artist-client are linked in a set of ongoing reciprocal services and obligations.[16] Cliental relationships, common in state societies, may involve individuals in binding, lifelong bonds, characterized by social inequality and differences in power. The patron's political and economic power allows access to means of production, major markets, and political influence. The relationship between patron and client is based on reciprocity in which the client offers the patron services and loyalty in exchange for security and access to desired resources (Eisenstadt and Roniger 1984: 48–9). The patron then controls distribution of the products. For example, kings and chiefs often saw to the basic subsistence needs of artists whose output they controlled (see Chapter 4). Long distance traders also frequently supported artists to ensure quality commodities.

3. *Marketplace transactions* are removed from the production arena. Such transactions occur when a seller and patron engage in direct face-to-face interactions to negotiate the value of stockpiled art products. Price is the primary focus of the transaction. In this context, the art product's primary identity is that of commodity, subject to the 'market principle' where prices are determined by the forces of supply and demand. Marketplace transactions, common to large state societies, are at the core of complex trade networks as art products move from hand to hand.

4. *Introspective transactions*, which have no patron present, involve artists in internal dialogues in which art products are created for self consumption or on behalf of a spirit entity. Artists look inwardly for inspiration rather than negotiating form and subject matter with external patrons. In some cases, artists may be motivated by a desire to demonstrate artistic virtuosity. Acting as their own patrons, these artists, unfettered by patron demands, are more likely to innovate and expand the boundaries of an art tradition. Art products resulting from such introspective transactions tend to be influential only if patrons see the work and request replications.

Place 'Place' refers to the cultural arenas or social contexts through which art products pass in their life histories. *Objective or physical space* is the actual perceivable geographical place in which patron and artist interact and where the art product is created and used. Concern with the physical setting draws attention to: (1) where is it considered proper for transactions between patron and artist to be conducted? (2) where is art production 'expected to take place? (3) in what contexts are art products used? and (4) do these physical contexts affect patron-artist transactions and the life history of the art products?

Examining the impact of physical context on art patronage systems reveals the importance of a second kind of space – *subjective or social space*, which places the artistic process in specific cultural contexts.[17] Social space alludes to the sociocultural (economic, sociopolitical, and ideological) influences that shape behavioral acts. The importance of social space is evident, for example, in special rules of production, or in the use and access to art products surrounding leadership and ritual arts, as opposed to those meant for the market. It is also a key to understanding the type of transaction occurring with outgroup patronage where cultural expectations of patron and artist do not coincide.

The concepts of physical and social place are particularly useful in examining the life history of art products and their changing meanings. While some art products will function throughout their existence in the well-understood utilitarian, ritual or prestige contexts for which they were made, others move through different physical and social spaces. The movement in and out of 'commodity-hood,' for example, involves a series of redefinitions of the art product by patrons.

Practice 'Practice theory'[18] brings together players, products, processes and place by examining social action as carried out by individuals as they interpret, manipulate and reproduce the cultural structures of their social world. Practice calls attention to human agency and culturally mediated behaviors in sociocultural contexts. It also allows for a melding of the influences of pre-existing culture and the existing social context to reveal how art patronage systems influence continuity or change in art traditions.

To examine art patronage practices, the concept of 'habitus,' formulated by French anthropologist Pierre Bourdieu, provides a useful starting point[19]. Bourdieu is concerned with the visible everyday actions of individuals (practice) and their relationship to underlying cultural structures. Practice, according to Bourdieu, is a system of structured and structuring 'dispositions' that generate and pattern social actions and strategies (Bourdieu 1980: 52). It is a product of 'habitus' or culture.

The *habitus*, a product of history, produces individual and collective practices . . . in accordance with the schemes generated by history. It ensures the active presence of past experiences, which, deposited in each organism in the form of schemes of perception, thought and action, tend to guarantee the 'correctness' of practices and their constancy over time, more reliably than all formal rules and explicit norms. (1980: 54)

Unlike cultural 'rules,' dispositions allow for a range of behavior in the form of habits or tendencies to act in certain ways, either consciously or unconsciously, but always influenced by the social context of the players' behavior and history. Habitus can be seen as an agent of continuity but also as a context for decisions promoting change.

The theoretical framework of practice and habitus provides insights into the structured yet dynamic processes that guide patron-artist transactions. Applied to acts of art patronage and production, it offers an opportunity for conceptualizing each transaction and act of artistic production as a process of creative transformation growing out of the practices of daily life.[20] Patron-artist transactions, as practice influenced by habitus, are products of specific social conditions. They reflect the result of current circumstances, but are constrained by largely unconscious inputs influenced by the personal histories of the participants.

As a prelude to further consideration of the nature of art patronage and patron roles in Africa we focus in Chapter 2 on cloth and dress as important art forms and major cultural signifiers in an examination of the many functions that cloth and dress play in the African context.

Notes

1. See Haskell (1963), Chambers (1970), Baxandall (1972), Cole (1983), Kempers (1992).

2. In contrast to the processual approach, many theories of culture and society do not provide for the dynamics of the interrelationship between the arts and the actions of individuals, such as art patrons. The influential theories of functionalism, structuralism and cognitive anthropology treat culture as shared rights and obligations, a set of rules, recipes for behavior or cognitive blue-prints which have a deterministic effect on the behavior of culture bearers. They provide basically static models of culture which underlie social life, offering the incentives and constraints that determine how individuals play out their life roles.

3. See Arnoldi, Geary and Hardin (eds) (1996) for examples of studies which incorporate this paradigm.

4. The concept of 'the life history of things' in which artforms undergo recontextualization in their lifetimes is also implicit in the work of d'Azevedo and Merriam.

5. The term 'practice' (or 'praxis') is used in anthropology to refer to human actions that are produced by and in turn reproduce cultural structures, rules and institutions (Ortner 1984; Bourdieu 1980).

6. The term 'art patron' as used here is not always equivalent to the concept of 'patron' as used to describe patron-client relationships in African societies.

7. See d'Azevedo (ed.) (1973) and Abiodun, Drewal & Pemberton (1994) for discussions of the nature of the African artist.

8. Those anonymous consumers who influence the artist through their purchases of art products are called 'unknown patrons' by Vansina (1984: 45). In discussions of economics and trade they make up the 'impersonal market'.

9. From the viewpoint of art history, audiences who react to art products on display in public contexts are regarded as 'art critics' as opposed to 'art patrons' who take an active role in the creation of the art product. Our more inclusive definition of 'art patron' stresses the importance of looking at the total life history of art products and the feedback that influences further production of similar products.

10. 'Social status' is used here in the anthropological sense to refer to social positions or identities as opposed to only relative social hierarchy. 'Roles' refer to the behaviors appropriate to particular social statuses.

11. The quality of the workmanship, the intent of the maker, the use to which the objects are put, and the social attitude toward the objects by the group that uses them are all taken into consideration in assigning them to the category of 'art'.

12. Following Appadurai, this represents a break from the 'production-dominated Marxian view of the commodity' by focussing on a thing's 'total trajectory from production through exchange/distribution, to consumption' (Appadurai 1986: 13).

13. Appadurai has defined four types of commodities: (1) commodities by destination, objects intentionally produced for exchange; (2) commodities by metamorphosis, initially produced for non-commodity uses but later diverted to commodity candidacy; (3) commodities by diversion, a type of 'commodity by metamorphosis' where objects are originally protected from commodity status but later are placed into it; and (4) ex-commodities, objects taken temporarily or permanently from the commodity state and placed into a non-commodity context (Appadurai 1986: 16).

14. The concept of 'transaction' as used here draws upon anthropological exchange theory (Kapferer 1976) and the literature of psychology and psychiatry (Scheflen 1974).

15. The distinction between 'contractual' and 'cliental' draws upon Dilley's discussion of relations between Tukulor weavers and their patrons (Dilley 1986: 130).

16. This type of social interaction engages patron and artist in 'patron-client' political relationships as described by social scientists (Eisenstadt and Roniger 1984: 48–9).

17. Helen Callaway (1981), in a discussion of Yoruba women's use of space, describes social space as an analytical concept that reflects the influence of kinship structure, social and economical organization and gender.

18. The 'practice-oriented approach' or 'practice theory' is an amalgamation of theory from several different disciplines. It is particularly associated with the work of Pierre Bourdieu (1978; 1980) and Anthony Giddens (1979).

19. In determining the applicability of Bourdieu's theoretical model to art patronage, articles by Mahar (1992), Schiltz (1982) and Turner (1993) which applied the theory to field data were particularly useful.

20. The term 'creative transformation' was suggested by Cheleen Mahar's study of the habitus of Latin American squatter settlements in Oaxaca, Mexico (Mahar 1992). Mahar draws upon Bourdieu's practice theory to conceptualize the daily strategies of individuals, influenced by habitus and social space, as a process of ongoing creative transformation accounting for the way that human agency brings about culture change (1992: 275–81).

Cloth and Dress as a Mirror of Culture in Africa

In the mythology of the Dogon people of Mali weaving is one of the primordial crafts invented by *Nommo*, the son of God who split into male and female the 'egg of the world', creating humankind and culture. *Nommo* used his jaw-bone for a loom and his tongue for a shuttle to weave together the four elements (air, fire, water, earth) to create the universe. The patterns he wove into cloth strips correspond to the twenty-two categories of the primordial universe which symbolize the origin of all things. To wear or possess a blanket with one of these patterns is to be 'in harmony with the rhythm of the universe' (Griaule and Dieterlen 1954: 107).

The Dogon are not alone in the importance that African people attach to cloth. Everywhere, Africans use cloth to dress themselves and things important to them. Cloth, the most important two-dimensional artform in Africa, possesses qualities which encourage a multitude of usages. Being flexible and portable, it enfolds, wraps and encloses. Cloth invites decoration and through color and pattern carries a rich symbolic message. As a product of human culture, cloth dresses the body, packages artifacts and defines space to impart cultural meaning. The importance of cloth is reflected in commissioning and production practices, in distribution and consumption patterns, and in meanings it acquires through use. As a mediator of cultural meaning, cloth has overwhelming significance at the individual, group and societal level. The relationship of cloth to cultural expression is clearly seen in its use to express 'boundedness' or 'containment,' particularly as dress.

> Things that have to be protected must be contained, and things that must be controlled should be contained. Cloth, once it is made into a garment, does both. There are certain kinds of clothes, such as warriors' and hunters' shirts, that are particularly known for their abilities to contain and protect. (Hardin 1993: 140)

In cultural context cloth serves basic needs as clothing and shelter, defines ethnic identity and social status, articulates sacred and secular boundaries, and acts as a measure of value. In its many forms it is an important indicator of cultural change.

Characteristics of African Cloth[1]

Cloth in Africa is created from a range of indigenous and imported materials. Cotton, local silk, bark, bast, goat's wool and raffia are indigenous materials commonly used in weaving, along with imported silk, rayon, wool, lurex and cotton threads. While felted barkcloth is probably the oldest form of indigenous African cloth, woven cotton fabrics dating to the eighth century have been found in burials in Niger (Clarke 1998: 18), and fragments of plain and patterned strip cloth dated to the eleventh century from Tellem cave burials in the Dogon region of Mali provide evidence of a long-standing aesthetic tradition (Bolland 1992).

Two types of looms are commonly used to weave cloth. The upright single-heddle loom has a fixed vertical frame upon which the warp is held under tension to weave cloth of a pre-determined length. It is commonly used by women to weave broadcloth (20 to 30 inches wide); two or three cloths are stitched together for clothing. In some regions men use a similar upright loom to weave cloth from raffia fiber. The double-heddle loom, with the unwoven warp yarns stretched out several yards in front of the weaver with a heavy sled to maintain tension, is used primarily by men to weave narrow strip cloth several yards long. The strips are cut and edge-stitched together to make larger pieces of cloth for clothing and blankets.

Design Techniques

African textile artists use numerous design techniques to enhance the attractiveness and value of their products. The primary methods involve woven patterns that produce variations in surface structure and the dyeing of yarns and whole cloths.

Woven Patterns African weavers have developed a number of ways to enhance the decorative effect of woven cloth. Varying the size, material and thickness of weft yarns alters the surface, while differences in the colors of warp and weft yarns create contrasting patterns.[2] Colored stripes are common in both broad and strip cloth in Africa. By combining different colors of both weft and warp yarns at regular intervals, checks or plaids result. Stripes can take on added visual interest by using an *ikat* technique in which bundles of resist-dyed warp yarns produce variegated stripes that fade from one color into another at regular intervals.

The insertion of supplementary weft threads, caught by warp yarns at regular intervals to create patterns that 'float' on the surface of one side of plain-weave cloth, is a technique used by broadcloth and narrow-strip weavers throughout West Africa.[3] Float designs are achieved by using supplementary heddles or by inserting non-structural weft threads into the warp by hand. A shag effect can be created by pulling out loops of the inserted weft to extend above the cloth face. In an openwork technique found primarily in the Yoruba area, supplementary weft threads are used to bind a group of warp yarns together, creating a series of holes across the width of the cloth. The supplementary threads, floating over the surface of the cloth to the point where the next row of holes begins, create a pleasing pattern.

Dyed Patterns Indigo dyes obtained from wild and cultivated forms of the *Indigofera* plant are ubiquitous in West Africa. Specialist dyers, utilizing indigo and other natural coloring agents, including mud, use pattern dyeing methods to add designs to cloth surfaces. In the tie-dyeing technique, areas of the cloth are wrapped or folded and tied to prevent the dye from penetrating. In a related technique, sections of the cloth are tightly stitched before immersion in the dye vat. In resist-dyeing, painted or stenciled starch or wax patterns are applied to one surface of the cloth prior to dyeing.

Painted, Drawn and Stamped Patterns A few African textile traditions involve applying paints to the surface of the cloth either through freehand drawing and painting (Bamana and Senufo mud cloth in the Western Sudan and painted bark cloth in Central Africa) or the use of stamps (Asante *adinkra* cloth in Ghana).

Embroidered Patterns Most embroidered patterns are applied to garments and saddle blankets. Using a variety of stitches, ornamental needlework in matching or contrasting colors is applied to the surface of woven cloth by specialist embroiderers to create decorative patterns. Today, embroidery is done both by hand and sewing machine, using cotton, silk, synthetic and metallic threads in West Africa and raffia in Central Africa.

Appliquéd Patterns Appliqué designs are made by adding decorative cutout shapes, stitched or glued onto a cloth or leather surface, particularly in West Africa.

Surface Attachment Patterns The attachment of elements such as beads, cowries, seeds, mirrors, leather amulets and animal parts to the surface of cloth is a widespread African practice. Often such attachments denote economic, political or spiritual power. For example, the application of glass beads and cowrie shells, producing a rich surface texture, distinguishes the clothing and regalia of kings and chiefs throughout the continent while protective charms and amulets are added to the garb of hunters and warriors.

Alteration of Pre-patterned Factory Cloth The ingenuity of African textile artists is further demonstrated by traditions which modify the structure of factory-made cloth to create a totally new look. Best known is the unique *pelete bite* drawn-thread cloth of the Kalabari Ijo people of Nigeria, in which the surface texture and design of the imported cloth is altered through the technique of cut and drawn thread work. Threads are clipped and removed from the cloth to create geometric designs which contrast with the background cloth (Eicher and Erekosima 1981).

The Importance of Color

A basic feature of cloth is color. While color results from available dyes and materials, everywhere it is grounded in deep cultural meaning. In Africa the triadic color scheme of white, red and black plays a particularly important symbolic role, enhancing the meaning of clothes and furnishing cloths used in ritual and leadership contexts. Red cloth, often associated with political and supernatural authority, not only projects power but also suggests danger. White projects a more benign message associated with purity and links to the spirit world. Black, on the other hand, is associated with the darkness of the unknown and death in many societies.[4]

Mediating Functions of Cloth and Clothing

African peoples have developed rich textile traditions and distinctive forms of dress to communicate and enhance cultural meanings. In any one cultural context, a particular type of cloth or dress item can be a visible sign, clearly signaling gender, social status, political office, allegiance to a deity or personal prestige. Cloth and clothing can also convey esoteric symbolic information understandable only to initiates. Whether sign or symbol, this ability to transmit information and mediate meaning through shared understandings in sociocultural contexts is a primary characteristic of cloth.

A cloth's mediating functions are determined by art patrons who commission, purchase and use it. A single type of cloth can serve many functions. While producers and patrons usually share expectations about a range of culturally appropriate ways in which a cloth may be used, patrons inject it into social contexts, thereby manipulating meaning. The ingroup patron buys cloth in the market for clothing; the same cloth may be bought by a European outgroup patron to hang on the wall for decoration. Patron perceptions of the ultimate use of the cloth will influence the commissioning process or the choices made in the marketplace. Patrons are also instrumental in changing the mediating functions of a single piece of cloth during its life history. A prized woman's wrapper can be presented by a grateful supplicant to decorate the altar of a deity. Whatever use the patron makes of the cloth, it serves a mediating function as a bearer of cultural meaning.

Beyond basic roles in shelter and protection, cloth and dress have overlapping mediating functions including (1) expression of self and personal worth; (2) indicator of occupation; (3) measurement of social value; (4) standard of economic value; (5) identification of gender role; (6) marker of progression through the life cycle; (7) definition and negotiation of political power; (8) religious signifier and repository of supernatural powers; (9) delineator of social space; and (10) indicator of culture change.

Mediation of Self and Personal Worth

Clothing the body is a part of the 'bodily practices [that] mediate a personal realization of social values' in society (Lock 1993: 137).

> The body is perhaps the quintessential subversive object sign, since it refers almost inevitably to individual as well as to group intentions and identities, which are always at issue – and at risk – in a changing, plural, social and cultural world. (Hendrickson 1996a: 15)

While culture dictates 'proper dress' for every social occasion, there is room for personal choice, so that clothing reflects a conscious projection of individual self. In the presentation of self in public contexts, there is always an element of 'impression management' involving deliberate behavior on the part of an individual to project a desired persona (Berreman 1962). Putting on cloth involves intent; the individual enters the social arena dressed to achieve certain perceived goals. In the quest to express one's personal worth, an individual can draw upon a rich vocabulary of cloth and clothing to express prestige, proclaim group membership or challenge tradition.

In many African contexts, expressions of self are tied to group membership. Pride of family, political affiliation, social club association and even friendship can be demonstrated through wearing identical dress to show group affiliation (*aso-ebi*). (see Figure 5.2)

An example of a decent *aso-ebi* showing was when Patrick and Janet, both middle-level public servants, were married in Lagos, Nigeria in 1991. Guests counted 15 different *aso-ebi* worn, representing different affiliations, with the groom or bride . . . The immediate families of the bride and groom wore *aso-ebis* of fuchsia and green silks respectively. Patrick's mother and each of his sisters brought their friends who showed their support by dressing in varied colored *aso-ebis*, expressly selected by the family. (Ugwu-Oju 1997: 13)

One way to express individual concepts of self and personal worth is through headgear. 'The head, high and center, is an ideal site for the aesthetic and symbolic elaboration of the body' (Arnoldi 1995: 9). Men's caps, for example, communicate messages of self-esteem. The cap, a modestly priced accessory, allows a man to alter his dress according to the occasion. The cloth cap worn by Yoruba men signals both blatant and subtle messages. For example, in Lagos society of the 1990s, men may indicate group affiliation by wearing matching caps alone. The basic soft high-crowned man's cap can also be manipulated in a number of ways to express individual inclinations. Young men who want to look particularly 'dashing' pull the crown to the front, twisting it into a forward-thrusting peak. The cap and the cloth from which it is made can also be used to indicate individual wealth and status. In a Yoruba proverb the cap becomes a metaphor for personal ambition: 'He who is destined to wear a cloth cap aims at wearing a velvet cap; one who is destined to wear a velvet cap aims at wearing a crown' (Borgatti 1983: 32). This proverb suggests that in a society where personal achievement is linked to the accumulation of wealth, the danger of overreaching one's station is always present.

Another way of making personal statements with cloth involves the use of factory-printed wax prints or fancy prints imprinted with designs, mottos and proverbs referring to contemporary social and political happenings. Specially printed commemorative cloths allude to a huge variety of different events and persons: independence anniversaries, visiting dignitaries, government educational and health programs, art festivals, popular musicians and even birthday celebrations of wealthy individuals (Spencer 1982, Akinwunmi 1990). To wear a commemorative cloth is to visually communicate that one has either a relationship with the person or event or identifies with the subject of the cloth's design. In a 1990 remembrance day celebration attended by the authors in Nigeria, the extended family, close family friends, cooks and helpers and guests from the USA wore matching t-shirts printed in the USA with pictures of the deceased parents of the host. Mottos on factory cloth also can be used to mediate personal relationships. For example, in Côte d'Ivoire, married women wore cloth with mottos such as 'Darling, don't turn your back on me' and 'Condolences to my husband's mistress' to send silent but potent messages to husbands and rivals (Domowitz 1992).

Mediation of Occupational Status

While occupational or subsistence activities may be signaled by no more than so-called 'everyday dress,' often old and ragged if tasks demand physical labor, certain occupations are signaled by distinctive clothing. The special garb of hunters, regarded as extraordinary beings, is an example (see Chapter 3). Religious specialists often wear distinctive clothing and carry accessories to impress clients with their control over supernatural powers. Among the Kongo in the Democratic Republic of Congo, a diviner (*nganga*) wears a costume covered with wild animal skins, bird feathers, dried plants, leopard teeth, bells and 'anything else that is unusual and wearable' (Weeks 1914, cited in MacGaffey 1993: 51). The multivocal message of inherent power projected by a *nganga*'s dress, made from a dangling piece of India trade cloth, is described as follows:

> The unknown *nganga* . . . must have been delighted to come across the piece of Indian trade cloth showing an elephant on a red background. He would have flaunted it as a wordless assertion of the kind of powers that, as *nganga*, he mediated. Red is itself the color of danger, of transition, of the intervention in ordinary life of unseen powers. (MacGaffey 1993: 54–5)

Dress signaling occupation is also seen in leadership contexts in the attire of servants and office holders. In nineteenth-century Nigeria, the Oba (king) of Benin's soldiers were distinguished by special dress:

> When the noblemen go to war they dress in scarlet cloth, which they buy from the Dutch . . . Common warriors go with naked upper body. They wear a cloth as fine as silk wrapped around their hips. (Dapper 1868, cited in Spring 1993: 49)

Mediation of Social Value

As a measure of value, cloth plays a vital role in social reproduction through recurring acts of exchange that encourage both cultural continuity and transformation. Due to its multitude of cultural uses, cloth is always perceived as a social valuable – whether that value is linked to individual survival, symbolic support of a culture's ideological system, or individual and group social rank. A Dogon proverb, 'To sell the family's cloth is to sell the family's value' (Guimbe 1997), clearly addresses cloth's importance in mediating social value. Entering into every aspect of life, cloth circulates in arenas of value[5] where valued goods are exchanged and shared understandings concerning outcomes exist. As a repository of wealth, cloth can be accumulated for exchange, providing visible evidence to support claims of social power. Gifts of cloth and clothing are often used to solidify marriage and political alliances. Cloth is a suitable tribute payment to a leader, and as a valued good, an appropriate gift or sacrifice to the deities. For these reasons, cloth and dress are treated as stores of wealth and valued as inherited goods. To possess cloth and dress in quantity, to display it in a culturally appropriate way, and to control its allocation, are markers of wealth and prestige. Among the Mende of Sierra Leone, the affluent, including paramount and lesser chiefs, preserve large collections of cloth passed on through several generations as stores of wealth (Edwards 1992: 148). Yoruba families also pass prestige clothing from generation to generation to be worn on special occasions. In this way, the display of cloth is a display of family wealth.

African funerals are often arenas of value where cloth is displayed and exchanged to mediate existing social ties and forge new ones. At funerals for adults, rituals must provide symbols of continuity to deal with the social disruption that occurs at the death of a socially important individual. As Victor Turner has suggested, 'celebration of the dead in most societies is also celebration of the survivors' (Turner 1982, cited in Smith (1987b: 46). A function of African funerals, exemplified by the Frafra in northern Ghana, is the re-establishment, reorganization and revitalization of ties among the living and between the living and the ancestors – a process critical to maintaining the sociocultural system (Smith 1987b: 51). Funeral clothing and cloth worn by participants and the deceased express 'values of identity and incorporation' (Smith 1987a: 28).

Among the Senufo in Côte d'Ivoire the exchange of cloth at funerals mediates social relationships in family and community, ensuring the continuing social integration of the village (Glaze 1981: 158–93). Prior to burial, the body of a male elder who was a member of the Poro secret society is shrouded in multiple pieces of strip cloth chosen for their beauty.

> A few initiates and relatives carry the body outside . . ., placing it on the stack of thirty-five cloths chosen for burial. Each cloth is carefully wrapped around and sewn in place, creating a smoothly molded form made aesthetically pleasing by the vivid colors and patterns of the outer cloth. A bright red Poro elder's cap is fastened at the head of the form, partially hidden by the layers of cloth. (Glaze 1981: 186)

Preceding this shrouding, guests presented burial cloths as expressions of social relationships; the closer the relationship, the greater the number of cloths expected (Glaze 1981: 159, 166). An important part of the funeral observances was the counting and distribution of the burial cloths.

> Each cloth is subjected to comments and judged for its size and beauty. Small cloths are laughed at, whereas others that reach extravagant lengths of fifteen feet or more occasion laughter of quite a different nature in response to the speaker's exclamations on the good fortune and importance of the dead one (Glaze 1981: 184).

Through their judgements of the burial cloths, this Senufo audience as patron contributes to the continuity of the textile tradition.

The Kalabari Ijo of Nigeria display heirloom cloth in funeral context to enhance kin group status. While not producing cloth themselves, the Kalabari draw on a range of commercial and handcrafted textiles to wear, display and store as repositories of personal and family wealth. Stored in family 'cloth boxes,' the heirloom textiles are cared for by the eldest family woman who knows the history of each cloth (Eicher and Erekosima 1989: 202). These cloths are brought out for funerals of elderly and respected individuals to dress the space surrounding the deceased. The walls and ceiling of one to three or more rooms in the family house are draped with cloth as backdrops to funerary activities. When multiple rooms are used, the final room exhibits the most expensive cloth owned by the family. The 'state-bed' where the corpse is displayed is a particular focus of decoration, with the body surrounded by a variety of textiles folded in aesthetic arrangements of pattern, texture and color (Eicher and Erekosima 1989). (Figure 2.1)

Mediation of Economic Value

In contrast to cloth exchanges done with the expectation that prestige and social ties will be enhanced, there are also exchanges strictly for money or goods of equivalent worth. In most cloth-producing areas, surpluses are regularly created for barter or sale; cloth becomes a market-driven commodity and has standardized monetary values attached. Producer, trader and consumer share understandings about monetary equivalents which shift according to factors of supply and demand. As a market-driven commodity in the context of local markets and long-distance trade networks, cloth becomes a 'quintessential commodity' where its exchange for other goods of equal value becomes its defining function (Appadurai 1986: 15). Cloth that enters into this state is not consumed for household or personal use, but is used exclusively in economic exchange, that is, it becomes a kind of currency (Johnson 1980: 193).

Figure 2.1. Kalabari Ijo Funeral Room. Kalabari women completing bed decoration with Igbo *akwete* cloth in the form of a 'masquerader's hat'. The walls of the room are draped with George cloth, Buguma, Nigeria. Source: Joanne B. Eicher.

Prior to the introduction of money, cloth was the 'most common kind of currency for ordinary marketing' in West Africa (Bohannan and Curtin 1988: 186–7). In marketplace transactions cloth measured the value of other commodities and services. Among the Tiv of Nigeria:

> You could buy one iron bar (*sokpo*) for a *tugudu* cloth [a large white cloth]. In those days five *tugudu* cloths were equivalent to a bull. A cow was worth ten *tugudu*. One brass rod (*bashi*) was worth about the same as one *tugudu* cloth; thus five brass rods were worth a bull. (Bohannan 1968: 229)

Generally, cloth made a suitable currency. Taking the form of standardized wheels of cotton strip cloth in West Africa and bundles of raffia palm cloth in Central Africa, it was easily transported and stored. It was always valuable because of its subsistence and social importance. In its life history, 'money cloth' could be removed from currency status. When used as clothing, implications of value were retained so that 'it was possible to wear one's fortune and save it at the same time' (Johnson 1980: 194). In currency status, cloth surpluses played an important role in long-distance trade exchanges for essential goods. The Baule of Côte d'Ivoire for example, traded cloth to the neighboring Guro peoples for iron and cattle, as well as for Guro-produced cloth (Etienne 1980: 221, 236). They also, like most inland cloth producers of West Africa, traded cloth with coastal peoples who exchanged directly with the Europeans for guns, gunpowder, and salt (Etienne 1980: 221).

European traders regularly used cloth and items of clothing as trade commodities and currency. Samuel Baker, writing about his 1860s expedition to the headwaters of the Nile, noted the advantage of cloth and clothing as items of exchange in an area where people were still wearing leather and barkcloth clothing.

> Clothes of all kinds are in great demand here, and would be accepted to any amount in exchange for ivory. Beads are extremely valuable, and would purchase ivory in large quantities . . . Clothes being perishable articles would always be in demand to supply those worn out; but beads, being imperishable, very soon glut the market. (Baker 1892: 283)

Mediation of Gender Roles

Gender dictates basic male and female clothing styles. The structure of the garments, the parts of the body covered, the accessories thought necessary, and sometimes the type of cloth, differ according to gender. These gender-specific clothing styles provide a base on which variations tied to activities, life stage and status are built. Among the Asante of Ghana the dress of boys and girls is differentiated from birth. For females, the most fundamental item of dress is waist beads worn throughout life, with the sequential addition of clothing items. At the age of five or six sexual modesty demands the addition of a strip of red cloth to cover the genitals. At seven or eight a wrapper is added to cover the body from waist to knees. As the girl nears puberty a white undercloth replaces the red strip so that first menstruation can be monitored. In the past the wrapper, undercloth and additional waist beads made up a young woman's everyday dress. At marriage, women added a second piece of cloth to secure infants carried on their backs. Elderly women usually wore this baby tie folded over their left shoulders, indicating their status as mothers. Young boys wore a loincloth like adult men, and at the age of eight added a rectangular cloth wrapped around the body and tied behind the neck. The tied style of boys' dress, marking position in the life cycle, differed from the toga-like men's dress where the cloth is thrown over the left shoulder and upper arm (McLeod 1981: 145). (see Figure 4.1) Among the Ndebele of South Africa boys and girls start life wearing the same dress, a loin covering made from leather with fringe and decorative beading (*gbahi*), but as they mature gender distinctions in dress are imposed. While older boys wear western-styled trousers, girls first wear a larger loin covering and at marriage adopt the *jocolo*, a five-paneled beaded apron, worn thereafter as special occasion dress (Priebatsch and Knight 1978: 24).

Another function of gendered dress is to mediate temporary gender reversal and ritual transvestism. Among the Hausa, where gender differences are reinforced by purdah (female seclusion), under special conditions a woman wears male dress. A bride, for example, may wear a man's gown and trousers when she enters her husband's house and a daughter of the nobility may wear the royal *alkyabba* cloak, usually restricted to male leadership dress, when she leaves the palace for her husband's house upon marriage. Ritual transvestism, a common feature of African masquerade traditions, is also facilitated by dress. Among the Yoruba, masqueraders appear at funerals and annual festivals to honor the ancestors and to praise and punish social behaviors. In one type of *Egungun* masquerade, male performers portray women in unflattering ways. In the town of Abeokuta, masqueraders parody overly-proud women by dressing in the current feminine height of fashion. In another context, Yoruba male Shango priests, coiffed in female hairdos, honor the male thunder deity by cross-dressing in women's wrappers and blouses, visually demonstrating their social relationship of 'wife' to the husband, Shango.

Mediation of Life Cycle Stages

As we have seen, dress signals status changes and accumulation of social power throughout the life cycle. Sexual maturation, parenthood and full adulthood, marked by elder status and the accumulation of knowledge, are all valued in African societies. As individuals move beyond childhood to adulthood and positions of social power 'increasingly greater amounts of the body are covered with cloth and adornment' (Michelman and Erekosima 1993: 164).

The relationship between dress and recognition of adult accomplishment has been well-documented for the Kalabari Ijo people of Nigeria who pass through a series of hierarchically recognized statuses in their lifetimes (Eicher and Erekosima 1993, Michelman and Erekosima 1993). For women, status changes are based on biological and moral maturation; for men, the stages are associated with economic, political and personal achievements that accrue with age. The admired Kalabari person achieves success in life in part through 'correct comportment' displayed as good taste and upbringing shown in a person's speech, behavior and personal appearance (Eicher and Erekosima 1993: 38).

There are four recognized status levels for Kalabari males associated with political power; each stage is marked by distinctive dress (Michelman and

Erekosima 1993: 171–4). *Asawo*, 'young men that matter', carry out civil community projects wearing cotton wrappers with light-weight European-style shirts (*etibo*). Older adult males, *Opu awawo*, 'gentlemen of substance,' wear longer embroidered shirts (*woko*) with wrappers or trousers, adding walking sticks and English-style top-hats. The *Alapo* chiefs wear the longest shirts (*doni*), reaching to the ankles. A hat, walking stick, fan, elephant tusk and necklaces complete the ensemble. The ruler and most esteemed chiefs wear wrappers with a sleeveless long flowing robe with a distinctive square-shaped collar made of imported Indian madras (*injiri*). Few accessories are worn, so that attention focuses on the beauty of the cloth.

The importance of dress in signaling changing status is clear in the labels given to the stages of Ijo women's lives. When a girl's menses start, she enters the *bite pakiri iwain* stage('tying half the length of a piece of cloth'), and she begins to wear a small cloth pubic covering. After the breasts become prominent she enters the *ikuta de* ('bead display') stage, when she wears an ensemble of four short wrappers layered to increase her feminine bulk, a blouse and coral jewelry. (Figure 2.2) The transition to full adult clothing occurs in the *bite sara* stage. At this point the young woman begins to wear a 'down' wrapper reaching to the ankle, covered by a second 'up' wrapper extending to the knee. A blouse (preferably of imported lace or beaded), costly jewelry, fashionable shoes and purse, and a choice of headdress complete the ensemble. A final form of adult female attire marks the *iriabo*, a celebration of motherhood following the birth of a child where multiple wrappers worn to the knee emphasize the fully rounded body as 'the ultimate expression of femaleness' (Michelman and Erekosima 1993: 174–5).

When the onset of puberty is ritually managed in African societies, boys and girls are often separated from one another and isolated away from the community in initiation camps where special dress mediates the life cycle transition. Clothing, or lack of it, emphasizes the initiates' liminal identity. Initiates are neither children nor adults, but exist 'betwixt and between' cultural statuses; they have left childhood behind but are not yet integrated into society as functioning adults. When the initiates have passed through liminality and are ready to rejoin the community, adult clothes are presented to them to underscore the new status. Among the Urhobo in Nigeria, girls are circumcised at puberty to mark their transition to adulthood and readiness for marriage. Circumcision is followed by a 'Sitting-Down Celebration,' a public declaration of a girl's entrance into the privileges of womanhood in which young women, beautifully and richly dressed in adult attire, receive guests (Foss 1979: 45).

In Temne initiation rites in Sierra Leone, the color of the garments provides important mediating functions (Lamp 1978). Male initiates sequestered in

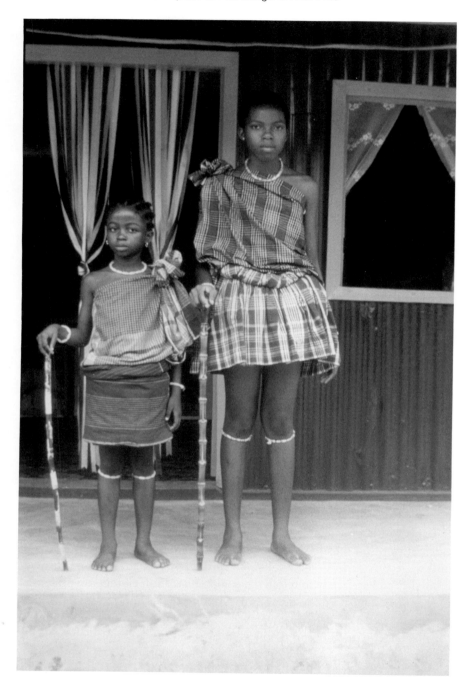

Figure 2.2. Kalabari Ijo girls wearing ceremonial dress marking life cycle transition, Buguma, Nigeria. Source: Joanne B. Eicher.

the camp must be protected against harmful forces during this liminal period. Because witches fear fire (and the colors of fire), boys wear long red camwood-dyed robes and caps designed to frighten away any witches who seek to abduct them. At the end of the initiation cycle, boys are ritually bathed 'to cleanse them finally of their film of metamorphosis' and dressed in new clothes for their introduction into adulthood (Lamp 1978: 49). Young adults present themselves to the community dressed in prestigious adult clothing and plastic sunglasses, demonstrating 'exotic chic' and modernity.

A cloth's patterned designs can also signify changes in life status. In Mali, Bamana *bogolanfini* cloth, woven from cotton and painted with an iron-rich mud pigment, is used in female rituals at puberty, marriage, motherhood and death. (Figure 2.3) A piece of *bogolanfini* cloth presented to a girl by her female sponsor during the puberty excision ceremony calls for a special painted pattern. In this liminal period when the child is transformed into an adult marriageable woman, she wears this special *bogolanfini* cloth with a complex circular motif. The motif is believed to lock power into the cloth to protect the girl from sorcery and absorb her excess power (*nyama*) released when she bleeds from the excision operation (Brett-Smith 1982: 21). Patterned *bogolanfini* cloth is worn again during the ceremony marking a newly married woman's move to her husband's village, and on the day she gives birth to her first child. The final destination of the marriage *bogolanfini* cloth is as the woman's burial shroud (Aherne 1992: 8). The use of the woman's cloth as a shroud demonstrates the many overlapping mediating functions a single piece of cloth can have during its life history.

Mediation of Political Power

It is hard to imagine an African society where cloth in its many forms does not support leadership. By its very nature, cloth is a repository of wealth and meaning, used by leaders to signify their special status and to consolidate political alliances. In leadership contexts, whether cloth is worn, used to enhance the environment surrounding a leader, or given to others as a demonstration of wealth or solidarity, it conveys a message of empowerment.

There can never be too much cloth for an African leader. The treasury horde of cloth must be continually replenished, because cloth and clothing are one of the most common gifts presented by African rulers to individuals who have performed services. To ensure that cloth remains a controllable prestige good, the production of indigenous cloth associated with leadership was often controlled by rulers in chiefdoms and state societies. With the introduction of European trade goods, the use of textiles such as velvets, damasks and brocades was governed by sumptuary laws, restricting their

Figure 2.3. Bamana *bogolanfini* cloth painter, Nakunte, and neighbors discussing designs for cloth. A completed *bogolanfini* cloth is suspended from the line. Mali. Source: Tavy Aherne.

use to the ruling elite. Used in leadership contexts, these luxury cloths functioned to visually emphasize the leaders' political links forged with the West. At the same time indigenous cloth continued to be important to leaders, legitimizing the cultural continuity of office.

Indigenous cloth types and clothing are often used in the performance of sacred rituals of continuity and reaffirmation (Schneider 1987: 415). Bark-cloth, for example, was used almost everywhere in tropical Africa for everyday wear in the past but has outlived its general everyday utility. It became a symbol of continuity with the cultural past when worn by leaders during the colonial and independence periods. Among the Asante, by the 1920s, bark-cloth (*kyenkyen*) clothing had been abandoned by the general population in favor of factory trade cloth. However, the *Asantehene* (king) continues to wear barkcloth during the Odwira New Yam Festival, an annual ritual of renewal to honor the king's ancestors and ensure the continuity of the state. The wearing of this historically important textile of natural fiber mediates links with the natural world and the cultural past (McLeod 1981: 149).

Mediation of Supernatural Forces

Throughout Africa one can find small pieces of cloth in markets where ingredients for magical medicines are displayed. This special cloth is meant to be incorporated into charms, talismans and other types of medicines, as well as used in the construction of masquerade costumes. As a repository of supernatural power, cloth, with its qualities of containment and boundedness, is used as both a container and agent of spiritual empowerment. Hausa traders of northern Nigeria regularly purchase strips of caliphate cloth, a luxury strip-woven cloth, for resale to Koranic scholars as amulet covers.

In acts of contagious magic, cloth formerly worn by a person is thought to have absorbed the essence of the wearer. Zulu girls in South Africa wear the clothing of their absent lovers who work in the mines in a ceremony called *nomkhulbulwana*:

> The ones we are thinking of when we do this thing are the men who love us. We wish to think of them. . . . If we wear the dress of our lovers then *Nomkhulbulwana* sees that we want her to assist us in marrying them. (Berglund 1976: 68, cited in Jackson 1989: 207)

In southern Togo, a type of protective medicine figure carved from wood (*bociaw*) must be combined with cloth worn by the person who commissions it. Described as a kind of 'death-exchanging sculpture' (*kudiaw-bociaw*), it is used by individuals to trick malevolent forces and spirits by providing a human image that acts as a surrogate. The cloth, tied around the figure's neck or waist, is indicative of the sculpture's role in psychological projection (Blier 1995: 277).

> The cloth carries the odor of the person . . . As he already had worn the cloth and everyone saw the cloth on him, if he rips this cloth and puts a small piece of it on the sculpture, when misfortune sees this sculpture, it will think that it is this person. (Informant Ayido cited in Blier 1995: 277)

Cloth also plays an important role in dressing the spirit, making it visible. Masqueraders throughout sub-Saharan Africa are contained in costumes of cloth which not only conceal the human shapes who carry them, but layer their bodies with meaning, charging them with spiritual agency. (Figure 2.4)

> Dress creates spiritual beings; specific spirits require particular types of attire, which must be provided by those faithful to them. Clothes express the commitment of the living to the spirits and the harmony between them. Clothes give substance to these incorporeal beings – they 'extend the spirits' personae in space and time.' The garments themselves come to have potency (Hendrickson 1996a: 9).

In the African context, ancestors are common spiritual entities who appear encased in costumes of cloth. Among many peoples living along the Niger/ Benue river valleys in Nigeria, including the Yoruba, Nupe, Igbirra, Idoma, and Igbo, cloth is used to fabricate a spectacular ancestral masquerade. Burial shroud cloth is used to construct masquerades to honor the collective elder dead. Belonging to a 'tall ghost' masquerade genre, they are made with elongating mechanisms to manipulate the height of the costume (Kasfir 1985). *Ndako Gboya*, a Nupe 'tall ghost' masquerade, is the oldest, most powerful and widely distributed of all Nupe masquerades. The costume is regarded as sacred, with a spirit that must be invoked (Nadel 1954: 198). Appearing at funerals of *Ndako Gboya* cult members, the masquerader is reputed for its ability to find and punish witches and purify the community. The masquerade is constructed with a bamboo frame that supports a long tube of white, fringed, strip-woven cloth (more recently factory cloth) that allows the encased dancer to elongate and collapse the cloth tube with a stick, causing it to sway back and forth like an otherworldly apparition. (Figure 2.5) *Ndako Gboya* can see and move simultaneously in all directions while growing in height to around fifteen feet before suddenly collapsing. Representing the collective power of incarnate male ancestors, the *Ndako Gboya* masquerader appears 'to grow from the ground and is swallowed by the ground' (Nadel 1954: 198).

Figure 2.4. Dan masquerader wearing cloak of strip-woven country cloth and skirt of raffia, accompanied by male attendants, Liberia. Source: William Siegmann.

Figure 2.5. Nupe Ndako Gboya masquerader. Fringed costume is made of white strip-woven cloth, Bida, Nigeria. Source: Judith Perani.

Among the Mende of Sierra Leone and the Vai and Gola of Liberia, cloth is used to construct the costumes of the spirit entities controlled by the powerful men's Poro association, including the *Gbini, Nafali* and *Falui* masquerades. The *Falui* masquerader that identifies witches and sorcerers is dressed almost entirely in strip-woven country cloth, which is the source of its power. As with the above mentioned *Ndako Gboya* masquerader, the costume, made from cloths used to wrap a body prior to burial, possesses the power of the ancestors (Edwards 1992: 155). For highland peoples in the island nation of Madagascar off the East Coast of Africa, cloth mediates with the supernatural. Central to the creation of the ancestors, it plays a critical role in substantiating ancestral claims to authority. Indigenous silk cloth in particular provides a focal point in reburial ceremonies, where ancestors are periodically commemorated through a process of exhuming and rewrapping remains in new shrouds (Feeley-Harnik 1989: 74).

Finally, sacrifices and presentations of cloth to deities and to persons possessing supernatural powers are a common practice. Among the Yoruba, cloth is a suitable 'gift' to be left at the crossroads for a witch who is troubling a person, as well as an appropriate offering to a deity.

Mediation of Cultural Space

Cloth's ability to indicate boundedness is evident in its function to separate private and public space in the built environment and to emphasize ritual spaces. The cloth walls of tents of the nomadic Tuareg separate the inner cultural realm from that of nature. To dress the inanimate, to intentionally drape a wall (see Figure 3.2), erect a canopy, or cover the ground with cloth, sets that space apart from everyday space. The wedding bed, the funeral bed (Figure 2.1), the shrine and umbrellas of leadership are all examples where 'cloths of honor'[6] demarcate special space. Cloths of honor can also provide a backdrop for newly initiated individuals presented to the community. At the end of Mende puberty initiations, the new adults are displayed under canopies of prestige *kpoikpoi* country cloth held over them by parents and elders to emphasize their newly acquired status (Edwards 1992: 152).

Cloths of honor also function in purely religious contexts. Important shrines are 'dressed' with cloth. Ijebu Yoruba *itagbe* shag cloths (insignias of the powerful *Ogboni* society), or a photo of a high-ranked individual wearing *itagbe*, are hung behind shrine altars where they function as 'the visual equivalent of prayer' (Aronson 1992: 57). In some cases, the sacred objects of the altar may be concealed by a cloth. The Asante in Techiman-Bono State drape the oldest and most important ancestral brass-pan shrines with prestigeful *kente* cloth (Warren 1975: 18). In Nigerian Bini shrines dedicated to Olokun, 'the Lord of the Great Waters,' female *Imona* ('designers') selected by the deity decorate his space. Olokun demands attention through beauty in dance, song and elaborate shrine decorations (Ben-Amos 1980a: 46). One specialized group of shrine designers (*Itukpon*) drape the shrine with rich fabrics and hang red cloth whose 'threatening power' deflects evil and maintains ritual purity behind the main altar (Ben-Amos 1978: 52).

Mediation of Culture Change

Finally, it is impossible to consider the mediating functions of cloth in Africa without looking at the way in which cloth and dress enter into culture change. While culture change is a constant, the introduction of new forms of cloth and dress resulting from European intervention increased the options available for self and group expression. The introduction of cotton factory cloth and European-style garments changed consumption patterns and created competition for indigenous industries. The wearing of European-styled clothing became associated with a commitment to modernization and fashion. Government clerks and other members of the colonial bureaucracy, school children, and the educated elite all adopted European-styled clothing. Readily available imported cloth led to the waning and extinction of certain textile and clothing traditions. Where barkcloth clothing formerly was the norm, such as among the Amba people of Uganda, trade cloth and western clothing styles quickly took precedence to signal success in life in the changing society (Winter 1959: 27).

As the popularity of imported factory cloth grew, manufacturers in Europe developed patterns and designs to meet the tastes of the African market (Picton 1995a). By the 1970s, cloth began to be manufactured by factories in West and East Africa to meet local demands, with patterns that incorporated regional motifs, themes and languages. For almost a century and a half, *kanga*, a lightweight cotton cloth used as wrappers and head shawls, has been popular with Swahili-speaking women along the East African coast. Unlike the factory cloth of West Africa, printed with a repetitive design and sold as yardage, *kanga* is manufactured as standard-sized rectangles featuring decorative borders and a central motif. Although *kanga* cloths are designed by, and bought by men, women are the ultimate patrons, instilling meaning through use.

> Women . . . treasure their *kanga*. They are often given as gifts (in some regions the husband has to buy his wife four *kanga* every four months) and are usually kept in chests, some of them only to be worn on special occasions. Women might go out together wearing the same *kanga* in order to signal their friendship and *kanga* have also been used as a currency. At times of financial crisis they may be pawned

by the women, but only by women, since although *kanga* are paid for by men they constitute part of a woman's wealth. (Hilger 1995: 44)

The criteria used by women in selecting *kanga* cloth include quality, design aesthetics and the proverbs incorporated into the designs. A *kanga* cloth is a 'form of visual entertainment emphasizing social, religious or political issues' (Hilger 1995: 45). While popular designs recur, the proverbs are the real attraction for the consumer, covering a range of social concerns – 'Mothers' milk is sweet,' 'Hurrah to the car of the president,' or 'One cannot eat poison without experiencing bitterness' (Hilger 1995: 45). Factories are aware of the educational potential of *kanga* designs. Political parties commission cloth with partisan mottos and governments encourage development goals through mottos stressing health and mass education programs (Hilger 1995: 45).

The availability of new materials does not always mean the abandonment of indigenous styles of dress. Instead it may encourage innovative blends of the old with the new. In southern Africa, the Ndebele took advantage of new materials to develop a modern form of the woman's beaded wedding apron (*jocolo*) described earlier. In recent years beads have been sewn onto canvas instead of leather. Some women have even abandoned beading altogether, using plastic as a backing for patterns made from colored electrical tape, plastic, rickrack and lace. Thus, the plastic wedding apron can be viewed as a pragmatic adaption by women to a changed society:

The demands of modern life have impressed the value of time upon the minds of the Ndebele women. Those living close to cities can work in a home or factory, which enables them to purchase the basic necessities and possibly a few small luxuries as well. Those women no longer have either the time or the inclination to sit for weeks working on beaded garments. It is far easier to walk to town, buy the necessary plastic materials and put together the 'traditional' aprons in only a few hours (Priebatsch and Knight 1978: 25).

Another direction in which indigenous cloth and dress traditions can move is toward the African world of contemporary fashion and beyond. Bamana *bogolanfini* cloth, mentioned earlier for its significance in women's life cycles and to hunters, is an example. Today, new forms of this mud cloth, termed *bogolan*, have entered the sphere of contemporary "fine arts" in Bamako, Mali. It is sold in tourist markets and fashion boutiques for use in contemporary clothing and home furnishings (Rovine 1997). New forms of the indigenous cloth are being developed 'at a dizzying rate,' due to a new patronage from the modern elite of Bamako and the insatiable tourist and fine arts global market. The diversification of the market and the continual shifting mix of artists, market agents and consumers results in constant changes in the product (Rovine 1997: 41). Demand in the United States has added to this dynamic as *bogolan* was discovered by American fashion designers and interior decorators, to the extent that factory cloth replicas are now available.

In culture change, the introduction of new materials and forms of dress is seldom a matter of replacement of indigenous forms. Rather, it is a stimulus for acts of creative transformation integrating the old and the new. The importance of cloth and dress in mediating a wide range of social, economic, political and religious practices is clear; we turn now to the crucial role of African art patrons in activating these mediating functions for cloth, dress and artforms in other media.

Notes

1. See Picton and Mack (1979) for a more detailed and comprehensive description of African textiles.
2. Warp yarns run the length of a cloth, weft yarns run across the width of the cloth. 'Yarn' is preferred to 'thread' as a generic term for spun and plied fibers used in weaving (Picton and Mack 1979: 23, Joseph 1984: 149)
3. Warp floats are rare. A recent type of narrow-band warp float cloth introduced to Yoruba weavers from Senegal in the 1990s will be discussed in Chapter 8.
4. Anthropologist Victor Turner suggests that these colors are symbolically linked with body fluids and by-products 'whose emission, spilling, or production is associated with a heightening of emotion' (1967: 88–9).
5. This concept of arenas of value draws upon Bohannan's discussion of 'spheres of exchange' (1968) and Appadurai's discussion of 'regimes of value' (1986).
6. Stokstad uses the term 'cloth of honor' to refer to the practice of using textiles to define sacred space or the space surrounding a significant leader. Hanging a rich, highly decorated cloth behind an altar or throne calls attention to the 'exalted status of the space before it' (Stokstad 1995: 523, G4).

3

Art Patron Roles

In an art patronage system, producers, consumers and products are linked in dynamic interactions that continually recreate art traditions in response to patron demands. Three features of the patron-artist transaction are essential to understanding the mechanisms and processes of art production in Africa. These are the closeness of the bond between art patron and artist; the ethnic identity of the art patron and artist manifest in ingroup or outgroup patronage transactions; and, the circumstances and statuses that motivate individuals and groups to take on the role of art patrons.

Nature of the Transaction Between Art Patron and Artist

Two broad categories of art patrons can be distinguished on the basis of the bond between art patron and artist: commissioning patrons and consumer patrons.[1] A *commissioning patron* enters the artistic process during the preproduction period. Production does not begin until the art patron contacts the artist and expresses a need for a product. The commissioning patron initiates artistic production either directly or through a commissioning agent, such as a king's messenger or trader. Preproduction understandings between patron and artist define the nature of the artistic act by setting parameters of acceptable style, form and production behaviors. Commissioning patrons have the greatest opportunity to influence the appearance and meaning of the final art product, as well as to introduce innovation. Through complete sponsorship of artists or by providing payment, commissioning patrons can encourage artists to exploit their own creative potential and explore the creative limits of the art tradition. Moreover, the personalized nature of transactions between commissioning art patrons and artists causes artists to monitor the quality of the art product. An artist's concern with maintaining a high qualitative standard appears to be directly related to assuring a patron's satisfaction.

In contrast, a *consumer art patron* enters the scene in the postproduction period as a customer for the artist's products. The relationship between consumer art patron and artist is less complex than for a commissioning patron and artist. The patron who purchases for personal use is a terminal consumer, buying stockpiled products either from the artist or from traders in the marketplace. Traders and market agents function as intermediate consumer patrons, purchasing for terminal consumer patrons. In producing for consumer patrons, the artist views the art product primarily as a commodity resulting in more standardized production. In such cases, the artist is mainly interested in meeting the minimal qualitative requirements necessary for the product to sell.

Ethnic Identity of Art Patron and Artist

With *ingroup art patronage* both patron and artist belong to the same ethnic group and are familiar with the group's art traditions, as well as with the nomenclature system for the different types of art products. In the following examples of ingroup patronage, a commissioning patron and artist engage in contractual transactions. When patron and artist share the same expectations concerning the desired outcome of a verbal contract, there is no need for prior payment. On completion, the product is turned over to the patron at which time the artist is rewarded. In Liberia, Zlan, a Dan woodcarver, recalled a commission from a wealthy patron, typical of verbal contracts between ingroup patrons and artists in African village-based societies.

> I went to a place called Deu, there lived a rich man named Bu; he had called me. 'You must carve for me a woman and a man, and four big rice bowls for my women.' I made him even ten! In addition a stool . . . Bu gave me a big cow, and slaughtered a second in my honor. (Himmelheber 1960: 174, cited in B. Johnson 1986: 24)

While this contract indicates only the type and number of desired objects, such ingroup verbal transactions can specify details of size, shape, material and iconography. For example, when a Yoruba commissions an *ibeji* statue to commemorate a deceased twin child, it is understood that the carver will work within the accepted parameters of his substyle while executing the figure's posture and sexual features. The patron may specify details of headdress, facial marks and body decoration, thus personalizing the commission.

Architecture may require a more detailed verbal contract such as that recorded for a Hausa builder during the early colonial period (Taylor and Webb 1932: 169–91).

Tanko said he wanted a good square compound with four huts, a mud-roofed house, a square house and an entrance-hut; the door of the house to face south or west. Audu said he agreed . . . We will talk it over and mark out the house exactly as you have explained it to me . . . Tanko said to Audu: Twelve shillings and sixpence for each hut. Tanko said No. I will pay eleven shillings, but only when the building has been completely finished. Audu agreed. (Taylor and Webb 1932: 169)

Details of facade decoration were left up to the builder who was familiar with the aspirations, achievements and affluence of the commissioning patron. Audu used the money that Tanko was willing to spend on each building as a gauge to determine the degree of elaboration for the facade design.

When ingroup patron-artist transactions involve religious needs, aspects of the supernatural enter into the demands to be met by the artist. Among the Anang Ibibio people of Nigeria, artists are imbued with supernatural powers which they are expected to activate when carrying out commissions. Monetary payment is expected and based on the type and quality of the artwork and the reputation of the artist. In transactions involving masks for the *Ekpuk* ancestral association, the carver is both artist and religious specialist and must please a collective of patrons. He may live in the compound of the association's head for several weeks to produce masks for members, but more often members come individually to him to place orders. For some types of masks, the patron must present a fowl prior to production to be sacrificed to the carver's guardian spirit. The carver may listen to the patrons' description of the desired features for the mask in the preproduction phase, or copy an old mask brought by patrons which functions as a prototype and a kind of concrete contract. Generally, older *Ekpuk* patrons are conservative while younger patrons may change their mask types each year. If the young man suffers a mishap when dancing his mask, he may doubt the supernatural powers of the maker and go to another carver and request a different mask form. Conversely, if he has experienced good fortune, he regards his old mask as auspicious, requesting that the old mask be copied when a replacement is needed (Messenger 1973).

Outgroup art patronage occurs when the patron and artist belong to different ethnic groups. Common cultural understandings cannot be assumed, so that when an outgroup commissioning patron enters into negotiation with an artist prior to production, there may be a need for a detailed exchange of information concerning the attributes of an art object. Alternatively, when artists produce and stockpile market commodities for outgroup consumer patrons, the artists' often faulty perceptions of what patrons want may affect the artforms. Yet, outgroup patronage has important implications for change processes in art traditions. In Rene Bravmann's 1973 study of art tradition mobility in Africa, he argued that the phenomena of 'open frontiers' between ethnic groups be recognized as a facilitator of change. Outgroup patronage across porous cultural boundaries triggers artistic change, as seen in an example from central Nigeria in which male Fulani pastoralists asked Nupe cloth sellers in the Bida market whether a black and red cloth (*maji*) could be replicated and modified. While Nupe women weavers living one hundred miles east of Bida had been producing *maji* for Fulani pastoralists, this cloth was not part of the repertoire of the Bida weavers. Communicating through intermediary market cloth sellers, Fulani pastoralist consumer-patrons requested that the *maji* cloth be made wider and tailored into a large three-panel cloth for use as a shoulder cape. Not only did Bida weavers respond positively to the request, but they incorporated the *maji* prototype into their regular repertoire, creatively interpreting it by adding an array of colorful weft-float patterns. Additionally, they called the new style 'Fulani cloth' after their new outgroup patronage market.

When outgroup patronage occurs over a long period of time, it can have significant impact on an art tradition. An Igbo artist, Ogwogwo, in south-eastern Nigeria expanded his repertoire of Igbo mask types after regularly carving masks for a neighboring Idoma masquerade association based on the Idoma prototypes (Nicklin and Salmons 1984: 42). Outgroup patrons also may alter or transform the original meaning of art products they purchase. In Ghana, Degha consumer patrons purchased stockpiled *akuaba* 'fertility' statues from Asante woodcarvers and integrated them into their own religious system. They changed the name to *kayere*, using the figures as shrine guardians and surrogates for deceased twins. Later, Degha carvers began to copy the Asante statues, introducing a greater degree of naturalism (Bravmann 1973: 17). Further examples of outgroup patronage associated with foreign patrons are discussed later in this chapter.

Art Patron Roles

The motivations that move an individual or group to become an art patron are closely tied to social roles associated with individual or collective social needs, so that each act of art patronage is embedded in a dominant social role that the patron acts out during transactions. We distinguish seven categories of patron roles:[2]

Figure 3.1. Bandi man wearing *supuhupu* cloth gown, Bolahun, Liberia. Source: Judith Perani

1. Self-motivated individuals influenced by their social and psychological needs related to the expression of self, the desire for social prestige, and the forging of social or spiritual bonds,
2. Kin group members motivated by the collective interests of family and larger kinship group,
3. Non-kin collectives such as age groups and voluntary associations motivated by common interests related to group membership,
4. Political and social elites motivated by the desire to enhance prestige and, in the case of leaders, reinforce political authority and position through public display,
5. Religiously-motivated individuals and groups (worshippers and practitioners) inspired by the desire to contact and please the spirit world and manipulate supernatural powers,
6. Traders motivated by economic speculation and the profit motive, and
7. Foreigners (Western expatriates and tourists) motivated by a desire to own 'African Art' or profit from it.

Frequently the different art patron roles overlap. A single individual may act out more than one art patron role simultaneously. When this happens, the boundaries between role categories become blurred. Self-motivated individuals and leaders, for instance, are both interested in expressing prestige and wealth. The individual's interest in conspicuous consumption is intimately tied to personal status, whereas a political leader's concern with prestige symbolizes the larger political entity he represents. Also, a self-motivated patron may act on the advice of a religious functionary, who interprets a spirit's desires, thus affecting the commission. In some cases, where self-motivation activates the patronage act, the artist and patron are one. The Isoko people of southeastern Nigeria, for example, do not clearly distinguish between the roles of artist, patron and religious functionary. An art object is created by the person who uses it in an introspective transaction, a phenomenon Peek describes as 'artist as audience' (1980: 60).

Although patron role behaviors often overlap, it is useful to look at how the salient features of role types influence patron-artist interactions, art production processes and art products themselves.

Self-motivated Individuals

Throughout life men and women function as self-motivated art patrons, prompted by daily needs, demands of domestic existence, social obligations and self gratification. 'Every person, whether an artist or not, makes continuous choices. Everyone is also an art patron and critic – sometimes only in personal decoration, often in other contexts' (Cole and Aniakor 1984: 24). In overreaching roles such as family member, suitor, and socially prominent person, individuals carry out patronage transactions.

A single artform takes on different meanings according to patron needs. Asante family members from all social strata of society, commission decorated wooden combs used by women as an indication of prestige (Antiri 1974; Cole and Ross 1977). The most elaborate combs are requested by men as gifts for women (Cole and Ross 1977: 51). The presentation of such a comb often commemorates a special event, such as a wedding or birth. The motif carved on a comb's handle, specified by the male patron, can reflect a special spousal relationship. In a royal context, Asante Queen Mothers commission palace carvers to carve combs for themselves, specifying design, size, shape and motifs symbolic of their matrilineage (Antiri 1974: 32).

In some cases of religious patronage, the self-interest of the patron results in art products imbued with the motivations, desires and personality traits of the person, as seen in the following account of the making and use of a Yoruba Egungun ancestral masquerader. Olugbeji, a Muslim Yoruba from the town of Ilaro, who had a reputation for trouble-making was burdened with misfortune and was told he must honor his mother's lineage with an Egungun masquerade to allay his problems. Olugbeji consulted with Ilaro Egungun association elders about his intentions and reasons for wanting a masquerade. Given permission, Olugbeji decided on the *Egun eleere* mask type that carries a whip because of its noise-making reputation. The name he chose, *Alapansapa*, was copied from a famous Ibadan masquerader known for its mischievous, unpredictable behavior. Olugbeji then went to a wood-carver where he selected a crest mask featuring a female coiffure from a group of stockpiled masks. While, at first the masculine identity and personality of the masquerade seemed at odds with the female headdress, this visual paradox is better understood in light of Olugbeji's motivations:

> The patron desired a masquerade that would enhance his reputation, reflect his personality, and honor certain women, the elderly woman who gave him advice as well as his mother. The solution was a masquerader named *Alapansapa* with a carved headdress and whips . . . evoking its owner's personality and reputation as a somewhat troublesome individual. At the same time Olugbeji's choice of headdress honors women. (Drewal 1984: 96–7).

Leaders also indulge in self-patronage. In the powerful Kuba kingdom of Democratic Republic of Congo, innovation in the arts is prized; kings, carvers and embroiderers gain social esteem by introducing new artforms or decorative motifs. Each Kuba king is expected to invent a pattern for embellishing his royal drum. If the pattern becomes popular, it may be adapted to other media, such as cut-pile raffia cloth. One Kuba king, in the 1920s, was intrigued by the tire tread patterns made on the sand by a missionary's motor bike; after he had it copied, the pattern (named after the king) entered the repertoire of Kuba woodcarvers and textile artists (Vansina 1978, cited in Mack 1980: 163).

Artists themselves also indulge in self-patronage, producing artforms for self use without the encouragement of a commission. Twins Seven-Seven, a contemporary Yoruba actor, author and painter, is a product of a changing cultural milieu where individuality is rewarded. In Oshogbo, Nigeria, an art movement oriented towards an international audience emerged in the 1960s, a time when Twins reinvented himself in a series of introspective transactions of self-motivated patronage by creating a flamboyant personalized form of dress.

> Seven-Seven appeared one night at a dance held at the Mbari Mbayo Club. His appearance fascinated us at once: a blouse of rather bright Nigerian cloth which had 'Seven-Seven' embroidered across the back, narrow trousers with pink buttons sewn along the seams, zigzag edges cut into sleeves and trousers, pointed Cuban-heel shoes and an embroidered, tasseled cap. Even in a colourful town like Oshogbo he caused a minor sensation. (Beier 1968, cited in Mount 1973: 148)

Kin Group Members

Art helps to strengthen kin group relationships and alliances between families. Among the Lele of Democratic Republic of Congo, institutionalized or spontaneous gifts of cloth function to 'smooth all social relations' (Douglas 1967a: 107–1). Within the kin group, the exchange of raffia cloth is thought to reduce tensions, acting as a peace-offering when there is conflict. There are occasions when presentations of cloth are expected and formalized, such as the gift exchanges between two kin groups prior to a marriage between two of their members.[3] In an extension of kinship ties for purposes of alliance, Lele villages give raffia cloth as tribute to their clan chief who then makes one of his daughters available as a communal wife to the local age-sets, so that 'the whole village regards itself as her legal husband and as son-in-law to the chief' (Douglas 1962: 229).

Marriage transactions of dowry and bridewealth are particularly important in generating demands for specific types of art products. Among the Nupe of central Nigeria, it is customary for a man to present a wooden stool, richly incised with geometric patterns inspired by Arabic script and designs, to his wife upon marriage for use in domestic and marketing activities. Generally, a man chooses from stockpiled stools in a workshop, but if a personalized stool with more elaborate designs is desired, he special orders it from a woodcarver. While belonging to his wife, the stool's size and degree of elaboration reflect the husband's prestige.

Non-kin Corporate Groups

Institutionalized age grade systems and voluntary organizations are types of collective groups that act corporately as art patrons. In age grade systems, individuals pass through a hierarchy of stages which are progressively more senior. The rites marking passage from one age grade to another, along with the social responsibilities attached to each stage, stimulate members to act as art patrons. Among the north-central Igbo, youthful age group members commission a range of lively 'locust spirit' masks for their masqueraders who invade villages during dry season festivals, entertaining villagers with playful, athletic and acrobatic dancing (Cole and Aniakor 1984: 118). A sense of competition exists among age grade youths during the commissioning process, leading to a proliferation of mask types and artistic innovation (Cole and Aniakor 1984: 118). Members of Fante *Asoafo* military societies are active patrons of the arts that serve to aggrandize their group. Each *Asoafo* has its own name, number and emblems which are displayed in costumes, public shrines and flags. 'Violation of the artistic prerogatives of one company by another is considered an act of aggression,' causing government legislation to enforce artistic exclusivity (Ross 1979: 3). A typical four by six foot flag is decorated with appliquéd pictorial motifs referring to the association's past history and power (Ross 1979: 15). New flags are created when an *Asafo* captain is installed. The new officer must commission and pay for the flag, which then belongs to the association (Ross 1979: 9).

Political Leaders   The role of leader as art patron in Africa's centralized states and smaller chiefdoms is well-documented.

> What is clear for leaders in all African societies – is that they are actively engaged in creating culture. Leaders cause art to be made, often dictating specific form and iconography. In conjunction with artists, chiefs and other patrons leaders invent art. Then in commanding its use, they have a strong hand in molding the events and the people for whom they are responsible. (Cole 1989: 37)

Kings, emirs, regional chiefs, advisors, court officials and retainers who serve and support political structures are among the most important art patrons in Africa. Through their commissions of important leadership arts, such as dress and regalia using complex techniques and elaborate iconography, they directly impact art traditions.

... leaders for their part have an extraordinary capacity to call art forms into existence, to ramify their meaning, and to cause them to change. In these respects, no one else in African societies – including artists – approach their capacities. (Fraser and Cole 1972: 325)

Leadership regalia projects a grand, elevated, prestige-laden image of the political persona to the community, stimulating patriotism and loyalty to the office. Regalia is usually made of highly valued materials exclusively reserved for leadership contexts. In addition, leaders tend to be surrounded by works of art which define space and indicate wealth.

Each act of art patronage initiated by a leader is embedded in the dominant social role of ruler. According to Mr K. Okrah, state linguist for Jerry Rawlings, President of Ghana,

> The term 'patron' is not easily applicable to a powerful king or chief. When an Asante king or chief requests an item, such as a piece of special cloth, the request is made through a special messenger whose main responsibility is the acquisition and maintenance of cloth. This messenger's title is *ntomahene* (chief of cloth); his role as messenger to the chief and cloth custodian are integrated into the political and social hierarchy. The role of the leader acting as an art patron is not a separate thing. (Okrah 1997)

The leader is regarded as the custodian of state regalia stored in a palace treasury, along with a reserve of valuables for gift-giving occasions such as the appointment of titled officials to court positions. During installation ceremonies, it is common for leaders to present special regalia of office which visually define role, status and obligation of the new official in the court hierarchy. A leader's own installation ceremony and other political rituals generate special occasions requiring commissions of items of leadership art. For example, in the Kuba Bushong Kingdom, a king was required to commission a wooden *ndop* figure to serve as his spiritual double after his accession to the throne. The *ndop* depicted the king in a cross-legged posture seated on a throne wearing distinctive regalia including hat, arm-rings, plaited belt and ceremonial cloth. Of particular significance in the carving was the *ibol*, a unique ceremonial object placed in front of the king to identify him and his reign. The form of the *ibol* was determined by each king during the commissioning process (Vansina 1972: 41–53).

Although all types of patron-artist transactions can be found in African state societies, cliental transactions, in which the king sponsors an artist during the production period, are the most common. These transactions are characterized by a power differential weighted in favor of the patron. Transactions between leaders and artists tend to be highly structured, rigidly programmed proceedings allowing for little variation in a sequence of events, with a set of rules for procedure and behavior. This, however, does not mean that the artist is denied artistic freedom in cliental transactions. For example, in 1976 Asantehene Opoku Ware II (king of the Asante), sent a court messenger to Osei Bonsu, the king's chief carver, requesting a linguist staff with an unusual motif. The king left the decision for the staff's design to the carver. Thus, the ingroup verbal exchange between the king's messenger and the artist was brief because a common understanding existed between patron and artist about the linguist staff genre. The expectation was that the staff would be covered with gold leaf and be of the finest quality. The artist chose the motif of 'circular rainbow', symbolizing the leader's ability to protect his people. The motif already existed in stool iconography but was unknown on linguist staffs. The king's contribution to the transaction was the activation and sponsorship of production. In turn, the artist tapped his creative potential, innovating a linguist staff design by borrowing an existing leadership motif from a different art genre and incorporating it into the staff's finial (Ross 1984: 38).

Another example of a direct cliental transaction between a leader and artist comes from the Benin kingdom in Nigeria. When the *Oba* (king) needed an item of regalia, he sent a messenger to summon the chief of his wood and ivory carving guild (*Igbesamwan*) who lived in a special ward of the capital city to discuss the commission.

> The carvers felt their king was their raison d'etre. They existed solely to serve him and they relied on him not only for their economic needs but also for their social standing, since any respect that they had within the social system came from their being servants of the *oba*. (Ben-Amos 1975: 178)

When a royal commission was received, the entire guild decided which of their members would go to the palace daily to carve the commissioned items. Before the king's order was carried out, special offerings of wine and kola nuts were made to the guild's protective deity to guarantee success. Elders of the guild, too old to carve, served as the final critics of the completed work, ensuring a high standard of quality (Ben Amos 1975: 177). The artists who made carvings for the *Oba* were rewarded through an established system of recompense. Each carved product had a set price; for instance, a carved rattle staff (*ukhurhe*) was rewarded with a goat, kola nuts and cowrie shells. In the event that the *Oba* was particularly satisfied with the staffs, he presented the head carver with a wife (Ben-Amos 1975: 175).

Leaders are regarded as the conservators of the state's art traditions. Through their sponsorship of art production, they assure a high standard of quality for the items produced. The control leaders have over production and use of leadership arts generally has led to a continuity of form in royal art. While leaders tend to be conservative in their taste preferences, there are examples where the opposite is true, and leaders elect to sponsor innovation in art production and through their patronage expand the boundaries of an art tradition. The Asante *kente* strip-cloth tradition in Ghana was kept dynamic through royal patronage. *Kente* cloth weavers were expected to continually produce new patterns for the *Asantehene* (king). According to R.S. Rattray, an English colonial administrator in 1920s Ghana, the Asante king

> appeared to hold the 'copyright' on all new *kente* designs, and these he would either reserve for himself or allocate them to great men or women in the kingdom; these designs then became their 'tartan' (Rattray 1927: 235).

With the royal expectation that new designs would constantly become available, weavers experimented with the infinite numbers of patterns possible in strip weaving. With the king as patron, *kente* weavers were stimulated to do their finest and most original work, keeping the prestige cloth tradition dynamic while maintaining high quality. Innovation was generally encouraged, but certain patterns in the repertoire had to be reproduced exactly. One such cloth, *Amanahyiamu* ('the nation has met together'), was always worn by the Asantehene during the Odwira, an annual renewal ritual ensuring the state's continuity (McLeod 1981: 156). Royal patronage could also be the impetus for the rise of a whole new tradition. The early twentieth-century Benin king, Oba Eweka (1914–1933), found the repertoire of the traditional *Igbesamwan* carving guild to be too limited. He, therefore, extended his patronage to support a modern group of woodcarvers, *Omada*, made up of his palace pages who were willing to experiment with new forms. He encouraged them to copy ancient bronze sculpture in ebony wood. To this end, the *Oba* sponsored a carving school in the palace, encouraging a new form of Benin woodcarving that appeals primarily to outgroup foreign patronage (Ben-Amos 1975).

Economic and Social Elites Men and women of importance, inspired by a desire to enhance personal prestige, often act out art patron roles. Individuals who have established their elite affiliation by acquiring a formal status, such as title-holder or elder, or simply by gaining wealth, constitute an active group of self-motivated patrons who encourage the production of high quality art products. Religious demands often combine with these acts of patronage, as art products commissioned to fulfill religious purposes often have secondary functions of expressing patrons' status and prestige. For example, after an Okpella woman of central Nigeria has taken title, she is expected to commission a commemorative 'dead-mother' mask for herself and accompany it during the Olimi festival performance. During the commissioning trans-action, the woman specifies iconographic motifs to be incorporated into the mask's superstructure, including images of children, pythons and accoutre-ments of wealth, all of which symbolize the legitimate authority of a high status Okpella woman (Borgatti 1979).

There are numerous instances in Africa where wealthy individuals commis-sion and purchase art products expressly to show secular wealth and prestige through conspicuous consumption. Cloth and clothing, combs, pipes, staffs, containers, spoons, musical instruments, weapons and horse trappings are examples of utilitarian objects which can serve a prestige function. The ownership of embellished and decorated utilitarian objects suggests 'a hierarchy that situates those that have them in a higher social and economic position than those who have equally useful but unembellished objects' (Cole 1989: 128). For example, elaborately carved anthropomorphic drinking cups, commissioned by Kuba and Kete male elders of Democratic Republic of Congo who request particular symbols to represent them, convey the owner's prestige.

Architecture is a particularly strong marker of prestige and wealth. In the early colonial period in northern Nigeria, a class of nouveau-riche Hausa traders and merchants emerged in response to the Kano groundnut boom which brought surplus wealth to the economy. These merchants encouraged the development of a distinctive Hausa vaulted-dome architectural style between 1920 to 1940. At this time the best Kano builders, no longer restricted to working only for royalty, were free to work for these wealthy merchants. Some of the houses commissioned by merchants during this period emulated the royal palace in size and complexity of decoration. For instance, the boldly patterned, brightly colored, coffered domes of Kano palace reception chambers, designed by the early twentieth-century builder Bala Gwani, were the inspiration for decorating the entrance hall of a wealthy Kano trader, Alhaji Ado (Moughtin 1985: 139–45). In Zaria Emirate, builders excelled in the execution of embossed facades with western-styled motifs, such as bicycles and airplanes, that appealed to their wealthy patrons. In the 1940s, one builder innovated a 'horror vacuui' embossed style of exterior and interior decoration, combining Koranic designs with Western represent-ational motifs for houses belonging to Zaria traders. The relationship between a Zaria master builder and a wealthy patron, Alhaji Makudawa, from the city of Katsina in the 1940s, is reminiscent of the kind of full sponsorship wealthy art patrons often provided for Western artists in the Italian Renaissance period. Alhaji Makudawa offered the builder a high salary, providing him with daily meals and kola nuts (Aradeon 1987: l8). The result was one of the most prestigious dwellings in Katsina, featuring a reception chamber decorated with a complex vault system and elaborate embossed designs.

The exchange of money as a promotor of artistic creativity is common in transactions marking the patronage practices of contemporary political and business elites. In the early 1980s, the authors observed male metalsmiths and female metal decorators in Kura, Nigeria carry out commissions for personalized ornamental aluminum spoons for wealthy Hausa politicians. These spoons were incised with political party labels and/or the names of individual politicians. They sold for a significantly higher price than the usual stockpiled market spoons. Financial encouragement motivated the male smiths to use more aluminum for widening and thickening the spoon's handle, providing a larger decorative field. Two popular motifs used on the handle were the *kobo*, the smallest denomination Nigerian coin, an indicator of accumulated wealth, and the key, a symbol of a popular political party. The higher price paid for these commissioned spoons allowed the aluminum artists to apply their skill in creating more aesthetically elaborated art objects (Wolff 1986).

In the contemporary context, wealthy educated elites on occasion become art patrons in the Western sense, that is, they collect 'art.' Very often their focus is on their own disappearing cultural heritage. An example is Chief Edo-Osagie, a successful Nigerian businessman and member of a prominent chiefly family of Benin, recognized as 'a collector of works of art' (Offonry 1987). Edo-Osagie's huge house in Benin City, described as a 'living museum,' reflects his particular interest and taste. Brass figures, carved ivory tusks and ebony carvings commissioned from a carving cooperative in Benin City are displayed in a museum-like ambience (Offonry 1987: 43–50).

Religiously-motivated Individuals and Groups

The production of ritual art often involves calling upon supernatural forces for inspiration to produce masks or figures which become receptacles for extraordinary powers. In this potentially dangerous activity, the contract between patron and artist is both an economic agreement and a pledge of ritual cooperation, often involving additional religious specialists. In some societies, the roles of ritual specialist and artist are linked. The blacksmiths of the Bamana of Mali, for example, who carve wooden masks for the Komo Association, also manipulate the power-laden medicinal materials that cover the masks. A member of the blacksmith caste also performs the Komo mask during secret Komo ceremonies (McNaughton 1979).

Compared to other types of patron-artist transactions, the interaction characterizing ritual patronage tends to be straightforward. Knowledge of prototypes and the range of allowable innovation is shared by artist and patron. Most commonly commissioning patrons specify only the type of art product. 'The patron seems to make few stipulations outside stating the type of object he needs; there is little aesthetic, stylistic, or symbolic input' (Ben-Amos 1980b: 56). In most cases, the understanding is that in such commissions the artist is both fabricator and religious specialist. Philip Peek's observations about the interactions between Isoko patrons and artists have broad applicability to other regions of Africa:

> The Isoko artist and audience/patron interaction is informal, with control of the product primarily in the artists' hands . . . the artist makes all decisions concerning the execution of the commissioned work, whose preparation often involves special medicines and powers . . . Function seems to minimize artist-audience interaction. Criteria are established by tradition and religious function, with the artist free to create within these bounds but without significant input from the patron . . . Supernatural sanctions are far more serious than mere mortal response to an artistic performance. (Peek 1980: 58–9)

A religious patron must please not only self and community, but also the spirit world. Thus, the resulting art products are often subject to ritual process before, during and after the creative act. In such a situation, innovation may be introduced, but generally a premium is not placed on novelty. Instead, because the emphasis is on art products functioning correctly in ritual contexts, it is more common for patrons to encourage artists to work from well-accepted indigenous prototypes. Both art patron and artist have a stake in seeing that the finished art product meets ritual and social expectations.

Individual Religious Practitioners Individual religious practitioners and representatives of religious cults and masquerade associations commission ritual items to control and honor supernatural entities. Priests, diviners, and masqueraders use distinctive paraphernalia and costume to support their religious roles, as they function as intermediaries between the spirit world and the corporate group or individual worshipper. As art patrons, religious specialists must balance the demands of the sacred and social world to please both spirits and humans.

> In Africa . . . by far the most important group of cultural spokespersons who influence the shaping and the explication of art are the geomancers [diviners], who, in their many-sided roles as seers, consultants, therapists, medical practitioners, religious interpreters and philosophers, act as conduits and intermediaries

between the sacred and social realms, revealing the wishes of deities and spirits to members of the society. Geomancers, accordingly are often actively involved in the process of art creation. Frequently, it is they who indicate when a work should be commissioned, what formal qualities it should have, and where it should be placed. (Blier 1988: 80)

African diviners frequently interpret and communicate the requests of supernatural entities to human beings. They are instrumental in advising select members of the living community to assume the role of art patron and commission an art product for a supernatural entity. Among the Baule people of Côte d'Ivoire, nature spirits and spirit spouses may be identified by a diviner as the source of an individual's misfortunes. The spirit spouse may appear in the person's dreams, demanding that a figurative sculpture be carved to honor and placate it. Communicating with the living through a diviner, the spirit then indicates which wood should be used and specifies details of scarification, coiffure, age and posture (Vogel 1980: 73).

In some cultures, illness or infertility is a signal that a spirit desires to be appeased with an act of art patronage. Among the Chokwe of Democratic Republic of Congo, if a man who has inherited a *pwo* dance mask falls ill, a diviner may determine that the *pwo*, a female ancestor, is causing the sickness. The diviner orders the man to reactivate his mask or have a new one carved (Bastin 1984: 92). Working privately in the bush and using a beautiful woman as a model, the Chokwe carver then proceeds to make the mask.

Among the Frafra of northern Ghana, brass bangles may be commissioned from a brassworker upon the advice of a diviner. In the latter situation they are regarded as auspicious in averting misfortune and providing protection from potentially harmful bush spirits (Smith 1982: 40). In northwestern Liberia, the production of a special Bandi cloth (*supuhupu*) is overseen by a diviner. A person seeking spiritual protection consults a diviner who orders the person to 'make a sacrifice consisting of a mixture of different elements,' such as a cloth combining different patterns of strip cloth. *Supuhupu* cloth, constructed from several types of country cloth strips, including strips tie-dyed with indigo and strips stained a brownish-grey color by the steam from a blacksmith's forge, is the ultimate sacrifice cloth because the individual must order and buy cloth which must not be used for any other purpose than that indicated by the diviner. When tailored into a woman's wrapper or man's gown, *supuhupu* cloth is believed to provide spiritual protection for the wearer (Perani and O'Connell 1974).

Corporate Religious Groups Male and female members of a religious association can act as corporate art patrons when they commission art products to meet the collective needs of the group. The same members, however, may operate as self-motivated art patrons, commissioning art products, such as masks, identified with them as individuals. Introduced into public displays associated with the group, art products enhance the prestige and power of both individuals and the larger group. A type of Yoruba ancestral masquerade, *Egun erin* ('elephant ancestor'), is locally known as the 'rich man's Egungun' due to the aesthetic quality and cost of the costume's manufacture. When a man commissions such a masquerader to honor an ancestor, the masquerade is admired by the entire community when it performs in annual ancestor festivals. The man's personal prestige as well as that of his lineage group is enhanced. Sometimes an individual requests an innovation that becomes popular and is eventually incorporated into the tradition. This happened when an Egungun cult member requested that his *erin* mask be carved with large upright ears rather than the usual smaller ones. When his mask received a favorable audience response, other cult members began to order similar masks from the Adugbologe woodcarving family of Abeokuta, thus triggering an innovation in the masking tradition (Wolff 1981). (Figure 3.2)

In an example of outgroup ritual patronage from southeastern Nigeria, members of the Ekpe men's association of the Aro Igbo people commission special stitch-dyed *ukara* cloth for initiation and funerary ceremonies, from neighboring Idoma-related people residing in northern Igbo country. Only men belonging to the highest Ekpe grade are entitled to wear *ukara* wrappers decorated with geometric, figurative and ideographic power symbols. (Figure 3.3) Ekpe members can request specific designs for the *ukara* cloth and may personalize the cloth further by asking that their names or mottos be included in designs. Aro Igbo traders play a mediating role by functioning as contractors in the production of the cloth, thereby illustrating an overlapping relationship between ritual art patrons and trader art patrons. The traders purchase factory cloth from the market, give it to tailors who cut it to required lengths, and then communicate the specific designs desired by Igbo Ekpe patrons to the Idoma cloth designers and dyers. The Aro traders retain control of the entire *ukara* production process due to the great distance between the producers and terminal consumers (Bentor 1995).

The patron-artist transactions between Gola male artists and female Sande association officials in southwestern Liberia offer another example of corporate patronage (d'Azevedo 1973a). All women of the area are initiated into the Sande secret association which carries out political and social control functions through powerful spirit entities given concrete form by masquerades. When a mask symbolizing female authority is to be carved, Sande officials seek out a carver of great repute to enhance the association's prestige. Carvers can be approached directly by Sande officials, but more often an elder male

Figure 3.2. Yoruba *erin* Egungun masquerader, Abeokuta, Nigeria. Source: Norma Wolff.

Figure 3.3. Igbo Ekpe members wearing *ukara* cloth, accompanying a masquerader in an Ekpe funeral celebration, Nigeria. Source: Eli Bentor.

Poro secret society member or village chief functions as an intermediary in the commissioning process. The transaction begins when the women commission a mask from the male carver who then becomes privy to knowledge held secret by the Sande association (1973a: 145–7). Male access to female secrets has the potential to transform the patron-artist transaction into a gender conflict. Upon approaching the woodcarver, the Sande representative presents small gifts of money and food; formerly, large sums of money and a slave were given. During the production period the artist is often totally supported by the Sande patrons. Yet, the patron-artist transaction is seen as a struggle. Sande members visit the carver and attempt to direct his work by insisting on coiffure design, the form of neck rings, and other iconographic motifs such as horns, fish and snake scales. The carver may resist patron directives, and in extreme cases, destroy an unfinished work due to continuous patron criticism. Tension between carver and Sande officials may persist throughout the production period and sometimes even after the mask has been performed. In the end, the Sande patrons and woodcarver agree on permissible innovations and refinements of existing models, for fear that a spirit will refuse to inhabit a mask that is iconographically incorrect.

Private Worshippers The need for private worship provides another important impetus for art commissions. These acts of art patronage are to an extent self-motivated but often result in art products used by the larger community. A wide variety of art forms are used in private ancestral commemoration. One example is the Fon *asen* metal staff tradition from the Republic of Benin. An *asen*, made from brass or wrought iron, is a figurative tableau supported by a round platform attached to a thin metal post planted in the earth. All strata of Fon society, including the royal family, use *asen* in ancestral worship rituals. The material, degree of elaboration and complexity of design are determined by commissioning patrons and reflect individual wealth and prestige. In requesting an *asen* to commemorate a deceased parent or sibling, a patron may select specific motifs or simply describe the life of the deceased to the artist. An unusual feature on some *asen* is the inclusion of a portrait representation of the standing or kneeling patron. The *asen*, in this case, functions not only as a memorial to the deceased, but as a visual reminder of the patron's generosity to the family (Bay 1985).

The public display of supernatural power is also a motivator for individual art patronage. Among the Mande-speaking people of Mali, when hunter association members appear publicly, their special shirts, covered with attached power medicines (amulets and charms), identify them as men of power (McNaughton 1982). The construction of a hunter's shirt provides an example of a series of introspective transactions extending over the life history of the art product. The shirts begin as simple handwoven cotton garments, sometimes made from mud-dyed *bogolanfini* (see Chapter 2). The hunter continues to add amulets and natural objects, such as horns, fur and tusks from the animals he hunts, to the shirt so that the garment itself projects supernatural power (*nyama*) to protect the hunter in the bush and display his status in public contexts. The young hunter starts out with only a few amulets designed to harness supernatural energies for protection and to enable success in the hunt. While many hunters' shirts are not altered significantly, over time those belonging to the category of 'great hunters,' who possess extensive knowledge of flora and fauna, are totally covered with an accumulation of amulets and animal parts (McNaughton 1982). The wearing of such a shirt is a clear expression of indigenous 'power dressing'.

In Sierra Leone, contemporary politicians may commission 'country cloth' (cotton handwoven strip cloth) treated with medicines for garments that protect the wearer from the bad medicines of rivals and personal danger. When cloth is destined for protective purposes, the patron takes the yarn to the weaver, giving special instructions such as 'Do not use imported thread, because I want to take it to someone who will make it powerful for me' (Edwards 1992: 156–7). In a similar context, Kono politicians in northern Sierra Leone may wear shirts that ward off bullets or sorcery challenges (Hardin 1993: 140–1), thus identifying the wearer as one who strives for individual power.

Spirits Supernatural force is never far away in acts of ritual patronage and process. In fact, in many cases a supernatural entity can be regarded as the source of art patronage, with the religious functionaries and groups acting as intermediary patrons. According to Ben-Amos,

> the gods and ancestors are in many cases the ultimate patrons, with much more clout than any chief or emir. They commission artworks, mainly through dreams and divination. They often stipulate the exact forms these works will take, and they punish severely those who do not comply. (1980b: 57)

Among the Dan-We people of southeastern Liberia and western Côte d'Ivoire, masks are commissioned after a forest spirit appears in a person's dreams, asking for a mask to be made that allows the spirit to enter into the human community (Fischer 1978: 18–19). (see Figure 2.4) In effect, Dan-We masks result from a tripartite contract between the spirit who dictates the form of the mask, the person who interprets the spirit's order through the dream process and the artist who carves the mask (Siegmann and Schmidt 1977: 2). In another example from southeastern Nigeria, an Ibibio cult member became a priest when *Mammy wata* (a water spirit) urged her to have a carving made and a shrine erected (Salmons 1977: 11). During the commissioning process the *Mammy wata* worshipper gave the carver specific instructions about materials, iconographic theme and deadline for completion. Representing the needs of the spirit, she demanded that the carving depict a woman standing in a canoe with six paddles and be painted with natural pigments. After the necessary sacrifices to the *Mammy wata* spirit, the worshipper danced publically with the carving on her head, displaying her newly acquired priestess position in the *Mammy wata* cult.

In contexts where persons go into trance, religious practitioners may guide those possessed by spirits towards art patronage appropriate to pleasing the supernatural entities. In the rituals of Bori, an indigenous spirit-possession cult found among Hausa in northern Nigeria and Niger, cloth is an important religious mediator with the spirit realm. By wearing garments made from a particular type of cloth, Bori devotees attracted spirits to possess them (Onwuejeogwu 1971: 286). Caliphate cloth, for example, is viewed as a repository of spiritual power; this belief may predate its nineteenth-century adoption for Muslim-styled dress by the Fulani-Hausa political elite (to be discussed in Part II). Hausa healers advise Bori cult members to buy cloth strips for distribution to disabled people, an act of gift-giving that protects the Bori members from becoming possessed by threatening malevolent spirits. Healers also may advise Bori devotees to purchase cloth wrappers and gowns to clothe the spirits. (Figure 3.4) As patrons of cloth, Bori devotees develop a relationship with the supernatural by providing attire for the spirits. 'Clothes give substance to these incorporeal beings . . . They extend the spirits' personae in space and time. The garments have potency.' (Hendrickson 1996a: 9) Among the Mauri Bori worshippers of Niger, 'clothes concretize the conversation between humans and spirits by literally providing the connecting threads through which they can relate to each other' (Masquelier 1996: 74). The special clothing offers a devotee a benevolent spirit's protection. In the case of possession by a malevolent spirit, the destruction or giving away of the spirit's clothing releases the cult member from further possession. Caliphate cloth, therefore, as used by the Bori cult, was believed to have the power to control the spiritual realm.

Finally, direct transactions between artists and spirits must be noted. Innovations are sometimes credited to spiritual influence through visions and dreams without the input of a commissioning human patron. According to Benin woodcarver David Omoregie:

The spirit of the ancestors works in me, directing me. When I sleep, I see things I have never done before . . . Sometimes I wake up at two in the morning, take

Figure 3.4. Hausa *bori* shrine draped with *saki* cloth. *Bori* worshipper in front of shrine is wearing a leather apron, Tamroro, Niger. Source: Alice Burmeister.

medicine, and draw out a design from my dream. If I have a big order, I will do it step by step and every night the ancestors will teach me step by step. (Ben-Amos 1980b: 57)

Traders

When the primary emphasis is placed on the economic dimension of an art product, the role of the trader, functioning as an intermediate patron between artist and terminal consumer, becomes particularly important (Perani and Wolff 1996b: 251). Traders engage in marketplace transactions, where art product values are determined in contexts removed from the production site. Operating as an intermediary in a complex network of supply and demand, a trader expresses the needs and demands of the terminal consumer patron to producing artists. The terminal consumer plays a critical role in influencing the dynamics of continuity and change in art production in the context of a marketplace system. As a patron type, traders differ from leaders and religious functionaries because they treat art products primarily as economic commodities to be exchanged for cash or other valuable goods. Compared to leader patronage practices, the power differential in the trader patron-artist transaction is more balanced as both parties are mainly motivated by the impetus of profit. Similar to leaders, however, the purchases of traders can have a strong impact on the quantity, quality and distribution of art products (Perani and Wolff 1996b: 251).

Traders also act as agents of diffusion, carrying art products over wide geographical areas. Often they may stimulate local demand for non-indigenous art products produced in other regions of Africa. In Ghana, for instance, Asante traders purchase stockpiled items of royal regalia, including state umbrellas, gold pieces and woodcarvings from Asante artists for resale to outgroup Gonja chiefs in northern Ghana. When a higher quality regalia item is desired, Gonja traders act as intermediaries and travel to Kumasi to directly order regalia from Asante artists (Bravmann 1972: 158). Sometimes, traders encourage local artists to copy a foreign tradition, evident in the proliferation of western forms such as salad bowls and forks, toothpicks, 'madonnas' and ash trays offered by the purveyors of tourist arts. Knowledge of new markets tapped by traders also encourages artists to relocate to new regions in order to work as itinerants, taking advantage of the new sources of demand. For example, in the late twentieth century, some Ewe *kente* weavers from Ghana moved to Senegal and then to Nigeria as new markets for their products opened (see Chapter 8).

Traders moving between ethnic groups in southern Nigeria created a complex network of trade, cloth production and consumption for the Ijebu-

Ode Yoruba, the Akwete Igbo and the Kalabari Ijo peoples (Aronson 1980). The Igbo and Kalabari Ijo people have a long history of trade exchange carried out through the creeks of the Niger Delta. One commodity was a type of elaborate weft-float cloth woven by southern Yoruba Ijebu-Ode women and traded east to the Ijo, who used the cloths for dress at special occasion ceremonies. When this trade was disrupted in the nineteenth century, Kalabari Ijo turned to women weavers in the Igbo town of Akwete, requesting them to reproduce cloths with designs similar to those found on the Yoruba Ijebu-Ode prototypes. The Ijo attraction to Igbo cloth was tied to 'a long-standing . . . passion for many varieties of cloth introduced to them through trade' (Aronson 1980: 63). (see Figure 2.1) It was common for the Kalabari Ijo to give cloths, which they had received from trade, to Akwete Igbo women traders who dealt directly with Akwete women weavers, commissioning cloths with specific colors and designs from the prototypes. Another type of cloth, brought for copying to the Akwete weavers from the Ijo region, was imported plaid Indian madras with embroidered motifs, known as 'George cloth'. (see Figure 2.1) The local weavers integrated the styles and designs of George cloth to produce a distinctive Akwete cloth. The introduction of George cloth into the repertoire of Akwete weavers demonstrates 'how the demands of one group can influence the arts of another' (Aronson 1980: 66). The Akwete tradition also shows the part traders play in diffusing cloth types and designs to influence the development of existing art traditions. The replication of Ijebu-Ode patterns by Akwete Igbo weavers brought about a creative transformation of that tradition, a kind of design revolution.

While traders are often itinerant within local or long-distance trade routes, many buy and stockpile goods for resale in sited marketplaces where buyers and sellers congregate. The commodities sold in such markets are usually confined to utilitarian and domestic art products. The market agents or vendors provide a service to their customers by making art products available on a year-round basis. Particularly in the rural areas, art production waxes and wanes according to the season, when done by farmers who see it as a supplementary economic activity. Although production of pottery tends to be a dry season activity in tropical regions of Africa, market traders accumulate sufficient surpluses to keep their customers happy year-round.

The market vendor, whether buying from an intermediary trader or producers, does not tend to be a source of innovation. Instead, the goal of purchasing products is to ensure a quick turnover in goods known to be popular with their customers. Market traders seldom ask for innovations, although they can pass on the desires of specific customers. Generally, both artists and terminal consumer patrons are comfortable working through an intermediary in this system of marketing.

Because the Hausa of northern Nigeria are among the most ubiquitous of West African traders, some generalizations about the role and practices of Hausa traders in Kano State illustrate the complexity of the trader art patron role in stimulating art production, as well as set the stage for the discussion of Hausa trade practices presented in Chapters 6 and 7. Economically, the most important type of patron to Hausa artists is the trader who buys for resale to terminal consumers or other traders and have face-to-face contact with the producers. The terminal consumer patrons, whose decisions to buy or not buy feed back to affect future production make up a diverse group, including rural and urban Hausa commoners, the Hausa-Fulani nobility and royalty, Nigerian educated elite, expatriates and tourists of many nationalities, and the nomadic Bororo Fulani and Tuareg peoples of the region. Their tastes and desires are transmitted to artists almost entirely through the channel of traders. One reason is the problem of logistics for the terminal consumer patrons. Although art products are readily available in the markets and shops, obtaining them directly from artists is not convenient. Art products tend to be produced as home enterprises in Kano City as well as in the rural towns and villages of Kano State. Even today reaching the rural workshops where weaving, calabash decorating and leather tanning are done, for example, may necessitate the use of special vehicles to travel the unpaved roads of the area as well as long walks. Within the city walls of Kano, for one not familiar with the area, finding a working artist means hiring a local guide, so that transport and service costs add to the price of bargaining directly with artists. Therefore, for the terminal consumer patrons of Hausa art products who shop in the central market of Kano City, in the periodic markets in the surrounding countryside, or in the tourist shops associated with the city hotels, where goods are stockpiled, traders provide a convenient and time-saving way to obtain art products.

Producers perceive an economic advantage to dealing directly with the traders. A permanent relationship is normally established between an individual artist or home enterprise and specific traders. The traders or market agents may regularly visit workshops to commission or buy goods, or may be contacted by artists who come to their market stalls. A lasting relationship is based on mutual trust, allowing for flexibility in payment. The artist leaves the products with the trader on consignment or may be paid on the spot, depending upon the financial fortune of either at the time. The trader-patron supports the artist, with whom he has established a relationship, by ordering ahead or buying all stockpiled products. Picking and choosing only the best of stockpiled goods, as is often the case with Western customers, is not usually done. Artists, therefore are guaranteed an immediate reward for their time and effort. In some cases where the raw materials for manufacture are costly, a wealthy trader subsidizes production by furnishing the artist with the necessary materials needed for manufacture.

Foreigners

As outgroup patrons, 'Europeans' (travelers, expatriates and tourists from Western Europe and the USA) always instil new meanings into African art. In the process referred to by Jacques Maquet as 'art by metamorphosis,' the trajectory of an artwork's life history becomes diverted to a Western context of display and aesthetic appreciation (1986: 17–22).

The European desire for African art has a long history. African art has flowed out of the continent as items of trade and travelers' 'curiosities' for centuries. As early as the seventh century, Muslim caliphs of the Middle East were importing copper flasks from Lamu, an island off the Kenya coast. In this ancient trading port where Arab traders came for slaves, gold, ivory and spice, skilled Swahili artist-slaves produced for both local and export demands (Ghaidan 1971: 56).

In West Africa, the best known example of early foreign patronage is the sixteenth-century tradition of elaborately carved ivory trumpets and vessels made by coastal Sherbro ivory carvers in Sierra Leone for Portuguese sailors and merchants. The Portuguese patrons commissioned a variety of technically accomplished European forms such as saltcellars and pedestal serving bowls decorated with European motifs, such as hunting scenes, but carved in an 'African style.' In some cases, the Portuguese patrons appeared to have requested a variation of an African form, such as modifying indigenous trumpets into hunting horns decorated with the royal and personal arms of Portugal and its noble families. The commissioning patrons must have shown European narrative prints to Sherbro ivory artists, asking that the scenes be carved in bas-relief. It is speculated that the exacting demands of European commissioning patrons may have led to relocation of the artists to Europe, where they made carved ivory gifts used for exchange among European elite (Fagg 1981).

As the European presence in Africa grew during the nineteenth century, resident colonial officials, traders and missionaries regarded African art as mementos and souvenirs.[4] The initial impact of Western patronage on African art traditions, however, was limited, as these expatriate foreigners acted as marketplace patrons, selecting what appealed to them. For some European patrons, the choice was made for them when presented with gifts by local leaders. By the late nineteenth century, resident European and American expatriates and visitors were more active in commissioning local African artists, introducing new directions into indigenous art based on aesthetic expectations tied to Western traditions. Sculpture, in particular, became a focus of contractual transactions between outgroup European commissioning consumers and African artists. The European patrons' desires to have mementos of their experience in Africa that were 'readable,' making them suitable gifts for the people 'back home,' influenced the commissioning process and the artists' perception of the market. It is in these early transactions that we see the emergence of 'tourist art,' which has the characteristics of pidgin language with a 'minimal system which must make meanings as accessible as possible across visual boundary lines' (Ben-Amos 1977: 129).

An outgroup patronage demand for naturalistic sculpture depicting life in Africa appeared in the early colonial period and remains to this day throughout the continent. Requests for personalized art products were also common, as seen in the ivory tusks carved by the Loanga at the mouth of the Congo River during the nineteenth century. These tusks, carved in bas-relief in a continuous narrative scene spiraling from the bottom to the tip of the tusk, are examples of early tourist art. The iconography, depicting scenes of daily life along with portrayals of Europeans, was shaped by the taste and demand of foreign patrons. A personalized carved tusk in the collection of the Cincinnati Art Museum was commissioned from a Loanga artist by an agent for a British trading company. The elaborately carved tusk was inscribed with a personalized band reading 'Souvenir of Africa 1885 to 1888. Presented to Henry Brockman [Steckelmann's uncle] by Carl Steckelmann' (Mount 1980: 41).

In some cases the contractual transactions of European patrons have a lasting effect on art traditions when their innovative suggestions are integrated into the indigenous tradition. A northern Nigerian example from the early twentieth century highlights the kind of impact that British colonial officers as patrons had on indigenous architecture. Colonial rule and the stationing of British personnel in the province of Northern Nigeria generated changes in indigenous architectural design as the expatriate life style created new spatial requirements. Colonial administrators commissioned professional Hausa builders to design 'modern' mud structures for use as administrative offices, law courts and private residences, using the vaulted dome style and flat mud roofs well suited for the dry hot climate, but with interior layouts suitable to European needs. In Kano City, colonial buildings built between 1900 and 1910 still stand today as official government buildings.[5]

In the 1990s it is common to find lively workshops of artists producing products for the Western market, sold locally or destined for the export market. Working primarily for Western outgroup patrons, artists are motivated by financial gain and draw increasingly away from their tradition. In Nigeria, Nupe brass workers, who worked only for rulers and wealthy individuals in the past, have incorporated decorated ashtrays, serving trays, chalices and wine glasses into their repertoires in response to twentieth-century tourist patronage. Asante woodcarvers, who produce *akuaba* 'fertility dolls' in their thousands for export to Europe and America, experiment with expanding their repertoires to include *akuaba* candlesticks, napkin holders and salad forks to serve a global market. In East Africa, Kamba carvers produce stereotyped animal figures over and over again because of their popularity with tourists and market agents who buy for export. In all of these industries as indigenous function is lost, forms change, and artistic individuality declines unless the market demands new types of commodities.

Innovations tend to occur primarily in the context of face-to-face contractual transactions with outgroup foreign patrons. For example, Isoko woodcarvers in Nigeria have increased their rate of innovation as a result of their contact with foreign patrons.

> Modern carvers seem to respond much more directly to customers' requests. Their subject matter varies tremendously, from monumental ashtrays and busts to unique representational pieces. Not only do they produce objects that are nontraditional in subject, but they also avidly strive for realism. One carver, who normally worked from photographs, . . . boasted, 'I can carve anything. If you show me a photo, I could reproduce it.' (Peek 1980: 58–9)

Commodification, with the standardization of artforms is common, at the same time that innovation is encouraged.

> Innovation, after all, is fundamental to a genre that depends upon its novelty for acceptance by a foreign patron . . . a spiraling off into new forms would have been much more difficult in the precolonial past. But the radically different situation introduced by foreign patronage opened the way for invention. (Kasfir 1992: 48)

When artists interact with trader and market agent intermediaries who deal in 'tourist art,' they are in a more vulnerable position than when working directly with the ultimate patrons. Working for an impersonal Western patronage and dependent upon a fickle market, the artist's understanding of the taste of the ultimate consumer is based on information passed on to them through these intermediary patrons. This can lead to the emergence of 'Afrokitsch' which combines stylistic characteristics of the indigenous African arts with new 'modern' forms (Costentino 1991). Examples include a Yoruba wooden ballpoint pen carved in the form of a human figure (Costentino 1991: 241) or an Ifa divination bowl with grooves on the rim, transforming it into an ashtray. Artists who work only through entrepreneurial traders have vague notions of what their ultimate patrons crave. For example, young Songye village men in Democratic Republic of Congo, who made raffia baskets for urban Europeans in the 1960s, had no direct contact with their consumers. Yet, they seldom used blue-dyed raffia because 'Europeans don't like blue,' and they made trays with six or eight rings to hold drinking glasses because 'when Europeans get together there are always six or eight of them' (Merriam 1968: 16).

   For certain foreign patrons, 'authenticity' becomes important. Authenticity tends to be in the mind of the beholder and often is not a true reflection of indigenous styles and aesthetics. Art showing evidence of modernity is often rejected by patrons seeking their idea of authentic. For example, until quite recently Western patrons showed little interest in woodcarvings depicting Europeans or Africans wearing Western dress. As described earlier, Baule carvers are commissioned by indigenous patrons to make figures of spirit spouses. Beginning in the colonial period these figures, often depicted in Western dress, were

> neither a replica of a European nor the expression of a wish for a European other-world lover, but rather a desire that the Baule other-world lover exhibit those signs of success or status that characterize a White-oriented or -dominated world. (Ravenhill 1980, cited in Steiner 1994: 148).[6]

These *colon* figures held little interest for Western collectors of African art.

> In 1945 . . . *colon* statues had no value whatsoever in the art market. In the region of Bouake, where there were many such carvings, we called them 'painted wood' and would give them as gifts to customers who purchased large quantities of other merchandise . . . But some clients even refused to take them for free. (Werewere-Liking 1987, cited in Steiner 1994: 148)

Only in the late 1980s did colonial figures gain popularity among Western collectors, causing tourist replicas to proliferate.[7]

   Different understandings of authenticity also play a role in the contemporary consumption of exported African art. American consumers of African art range from art collectors who measure authenticity in terms of whether a piece of art has been used in ritual context at its place of origin, to those who value the utilitarian aspects of an Asante brass bottle opener with a handle in the shape of a fertility figure.

   When artists work directly with their ultimate patrons, they can more successfully gauge consumer demand and thus continually adjust their repertoires. In an interesting case reported by Jeanne Cannizzo (1983), a Mandinka textile artist, Senesse Tarawallie, developed two forms of tie-dye *gara* cloth in response to two different patron groups in his town of Bo, Sierra Leone. In the mid-1970s, Senesse was producing what he called 'African Man *gara*' for local indigenous consumption and 'Peace Corps *gara*' for the expatriate market.[8] African Man *gara* was used for wrappers and tailored clothing worn by local women, men and children. Peace Corps *gara* was purchased by expatriates for wall-hangings, gifts and souvenirs, and only occasionally for clothing (Cannizzo 1983: 62). The two types of tie-dyed *gara* were skilfully made with similar techniques but differed in colors and designs. While local patrons liked bright colors made from imported dyes, expatriates preferred the darker more subtle hues of indigenous dyes. The divergent tastes of these two patron groups was recognized by Senesse as he altered his work to please 'the assumed European aesthetic.'

> Only rarely are the [Peace Corps *gara*] pieces anything other than dichromatic . . . the design inventory is reduced and the designs themselves are simplified . . . Senesse is also careful to ensure that no seam or stitching shows, which sometimes occurs when smaller pieces are joined to produce a *lappa* length; his expatriate customers check for this 'fault.' The artist feels that while considerations such as design placement and the pre-dyed condition of the fabric are important to these buyers, unlike his African customers they are unconcerned with the underlying damask patterns and the lustrous patina of the finished product. (Cannizzo 1983: 62)

Unlike indigenous patrons who bought stockpiled cloths, expatriates sought face-to-face transactions in which Senesse readily accepted commissions for particular designs or colors and for items such as bedspreads (Cannizzo 1983: 62). While Senesse was ready to innovate for his expatriate customers, receiving higher prices for Peace Corps *gara*, he was most proud of his African Man *gara*, deriving his greatest sense of aesthetic satisfaction from their manufacture. He complained that Peace Corps *gara* was artistically uninteresting and judged these cloths 'primarily on their ability to sell and to merit European acclaim' (Cannizzo 1983: 62). Another aspect of foreign patronage is brought out in the above *gara* example. Cannizzo, who documented Senesse's work, became what Dele Jegede (1984) has labeled an 'advisor-participant-consumer' patron. Such patrons, usually American or European, take an active role in mentoring indigenous artists, encouraging them to develop new products for foreign patrons. In this case, Cannizzo, a Peace Corp volunteer at the time, commissioned Senesse to use natural dyes (kola and indigo) rather than the imported dyes to create the prototype of Peace Corps *gara* which she dubbed 'Anthropologist *gara*' (Cannizzo 1983: 62–4).

From the examples provided here, it is clear that art patronage is incorporated into a wide variety of social roles associated with every aspect of individual and group life. Among these, leaders are particularly instrumental in stimulating art production. The primacy of the leader as art patron in state societies is given fuller consideration in Chapter 4.

Notes

1. The concepts of 'commissioning patron' and 'consumer patron' were first articulated in a 1978 ASA panel co-sponsored by the authors on Art Patronage in Africa and expanded upon in essays by the authors in *The Dictionary of Art* (Perani and Wolff 1996a, 1996b).

2. This typology of patron roles is based on observations from our fieldwork and on our examination of the African art literature.

3. Among the Lele, cloth also plays an important role in exchanges involving changes in social status, payment for services, fines for inappropriate behavior and tribute. Entrance into cults, age-sets and statuses also involves cloth 'dues'. Services of religious specialists such as diviners and healers are paid for by set amounts of cloth (Douglas 1967a: 107–8).

4. An interesting account of the collector proclivities of British expatriates during this period is found in Cannizzo (1989).

5. These buildings include Gidan Dan Hausa (today, the official residence of one of Kano's titled officials), Gidan Makama (today the Kano Museum) and Gidan Beminster (used for Kano State cultural organizations).

6. See Ravenhill (1996) for an extended discussion of the relationship of fashion in dress to the images of Baule otherworld mates.

7. Steiner suggests that the expansion of the market for colonial figures may be tied to an increased interest in American folk art because of the stylistic similarities between the two traditions (Steiner 1994: 191).

8. The expatriate market was not confined to Peace Corps Volunteers. It also included members of other voluntary development agencies, missionaries and contract workers on international projects (Cannizzo 1983: 62).

4

Leadership Arts in State Societies

In Africa, state-organized indigenous societies are characterized by rich and varied art traditions supported by a specialized division of labor. Leadership is manifested in kings, chiefs and emirs, along with a wealthy elite disting-uished by access to privileges bestowed by the head of state. Like the supreme ruler, members of the elite group are important patrons of the arts, visibly displaying their rank and wealth. The leader usually controls all or most of the land and the power of office is further enhanced through the leader's access to legitimized force. Added to this is the 'divine nature' of many African leaders who were ranked as only slightly below the deities. It is this investiture of several different types of empowerment in a single political role that makes understandable why leaders have such an impact on art production through their 'ability to commission, control, and distribute works of art, and to inform them with meaning'(Fraser and Cole 1972: 295).

Three kinds of commodities – prestige or luxury goods controlled by the elite, market-driven goods, and military gear – support the state and help maintain inequities in rank (Costin 1993: 3). Cloth, as a moveable good, plays a role in transactions typical of each kind of commodity. Luxury goods are particularly important in state systems to negotiate and signify power relations. As indicators of both wealth and power, such goods set the elite apart and tend to be subject to sumptuary laws. Cloth as a prestige good is worn by the elite, distributed to a favored few, and stored or traded as wealth. The production of market-driven goods that generate revenue is often controlled by the political elite. The surplus wealth generated from trade was an important precondition for state development in West Africa, where a specialized division of labor with artist groups who produced various types of goods for the state sprang up. Cloth as an economic good provided opportunities for the elite to add to their wealth and power through control of production and trade. Cloth was also used in the production of military gear. Specially trained workers produced weapons and gear of war used by the states' armies. Quilted attire of heavy cotton cloth was commonly manufactured as armor for Muslim warriors and horses in the Western and Eastern Sudan (Spring 1993: 35–9).

The Spiritual Dimensions of State Leadership

In both Muslim and non-Muslim West African states, secular and spiritual power interface in the personage of the king. Often, secular power is strengthened by spiritual power. In the indigenous non-Muslim West African kingdoms of Asante, Yoruba, Benin and Fon the office of divine ruler was spiritually sanctioned, and leadership regalia was imbued with sacred power. Among the Fon in the Republic of Benin, special symbols associated with the reigns of different kings had a sacred dimension. Fon diviners played a critical role in communicating to the kings the special symbols to spiritually sanction their reigns. Kings selected from these symbols when commissioning items of leadership regalia. For example, the motifs found in leadership regalia of the nineteenth-century Fon king, Glele, including the lion, hornbill bird, ram and special swords, derive from his personal divination signs (Blier 1990). Because of Glele's close divinatory association with lions, they appear in numerous artworks linked to his reign, including appliqué decorations on royal hammocks and umbrellas and life-sized wooden figures representing a lion-man, referring to the divinatory saying, 'No animal displays its anger like the lion' (Blier 1990: 52).

It was not uncommon for indigenous states to draw on the powers of Islam through dress traditions. A nineteenth-century European visitor to Ghana, Joseph Dupuis, observed that for a ritual of ancestral worship, the Asante king was dressed in a large white cotton cloth, covered with Arabic writing thought to empower the king (Gilfoy 1987: 37–8). The Asante also incorporated northern Ghanaian *batakari* war smocks covered with protective amulets containing Islamic script into the enstoolment ceremonies of their king to emphasize his military prowess. According to M.D. McLeod:

> The Asante use of these garments can only be understood in the context of their ideas about mystical power. Power for special purposes . . . is always sought from areas and peoples on the very edges of the Asante world . . . The savannah peoples, physically, socially and linguistically different from the Asante, were believed to have access to powers unknown in the forest zone and the Asante use of protective *batakari* is an example of this belief. (1981: 147–8)

Accumulation and Gift-giving of Prestige Goods

State leaders activate and control the processes of production and distribution, not only for unique commissioned examples of regalia but also for luxury goods, including cloth. Luxury goods and items of regalia, accumulated and stored in a treasury, are a demonstration of wealth, functioning as a resource available for use in public demonstrations of political and religious power and for distribution to deserving individuals in order to cement social relationships. In 1990, during a visit to Bida, the authors were shown a portion of the state's collection of embroidered caliphate cloth gowns stored in the palace treasury. In the following days some of these gowns were worn by palace officials during a state festival. (see Figure 6.1) Among the Kuba people of Democratic Republic of Congo, a surplus of embroidered raffia cloth separates the elite from the commoner (Vansina 1978: 185). Items from the king's treasury, including textiles of many types, were displayed and distributed to followers because 'prestige goods had to be flaunted, for they were the indicator of political success' (Vansina 1978: 186).

Due to the political weight carried by leadership arts that visually enhance the political presence, such goods take on the status of inalienable possessions, removed from the exchange system of the marketplace to circulate in a limited, but well-defined, social field. They are imbued with 'the intrinsic and ineffable identities of their owners and are not easily given away or sold' (Weiner 1992: 6). When used to empower individuals and the spaces they occupy, leadership cloth, garments and regalia, in particular, function as inalienable possessions. While they may be the result of a specific trans-action between a leader or his agent and an artist, they are not owned by the patron but by the state, and passed on from one office holder to the next. They are stored in the palace treasury under the care of a specified official who ensures their safety and proper use during state ceremonies. When a leader draws upon these inalienable possessions and puts on the robes of office, his body is transformed from its natural form to the 'body politic,' conferring the authority of the past to the present incumbent (Weiner 1992: 37).

In 1819 Thomas Edward Bowdich, a British visitor to Ghana, observed how the Asante king dressed his court officials in state garments to conduct business. The king 'enriches the splendour of his suite and attire as much as possible, sometimes provides it entirely, but it is all surrendered on the return ... and forms a sort of public state wardrobe' (Bowdich 1966: 247). It is also expected that through their roles as art patrons, leaders will replenish the palace treasury during their reign. Prior to an enstoolment ceremony, an

Asante king adds to the state treasury one or more items particularly identified with himself, such as cloths, rings and sandals (Cole and Ross 1977: 23).

A treasury horde of cloth and clothing had to be continually replenished as cloth and garments are among the most common gifts presented by African rulers to individuals who have performed service. For centuries African leaders have also presented valuable gifts of cloth to foreign visitors as a token of international diplomacy. In 1820, Joseph Dupuis, as a visitor to the Asante court, reported a gift of two handwoven camel hair blankets (*khasa*) (Gilfoy 1987: 108). Similarly, in 1862, a Hausa-Fulani 'robe of honor,' now in the Museum of Mankind in London, was presented by the Fon King to a British Senior Officer (Kriger 1988: 57), and in recognition of political alliance a *kente* cloth was presented by the Asante king to the British Princess Mary on her marriage in the early twentieth century (Rattray 1927: 237).

The distribution of gifts from state treasuries not only offers a mechanism for leaders to enhance their power, prestige and wealth through display and forge social alliances through gift-giving, but may well have played a role in the political and historical processes of state formation. Bravmann documented how gifts of regalia were distributed by the Asante to those they subjugated in the early eighteenth century in an attempt to meld together the disparate territories they controlled (Bravmann 1972). Speaking of the Cameroon Bamun kingdom, Geary saw the reverse of these integrative processes at work. In an area of many small kingdoms where there was a specialization of polities in particular art products, the Bamun kingdom's power and dominance was 'articulated in the visual domain, which the . . . court masterfully manipulated' (1993: 88). Not only did they appropriate the regalia and contents of the treasuries of subjugated leaders, but they also resettled artists of the conquered groups to their court (1993: 88).

As agents of the state, leaders commission and buy commodities and regalia for their palace treasuries, accruing gifts to meet diplomatic and protocol requirements in order to secure and cement political alliances within their court and beyond. The importance of items of dress associated with a political alliance does not fade with age. During the course of its life history, a single Nupe embroidered handwoven gown may be passed down to several owners through gifting. Despite indications of wear, the sequential ownership of the gown over many years contributed to an enhanced social patina and esteem as it acquires new layers of political and social meaning. Rather than passively reflecting processes of political obligation and linkage, items of dress and regalia become active agents of leadership, generating political power necessary for the overall effectiveness of leadership.

Tribute from subjects to a leader is also a kind of gifting, a way that leaders maintain their treasuries. Gifts associated with requests for help from individuals and groups is another way gifts move up the social ranks. In the less centralized Kono chiefdoms of Sierra Leone, a fine gown made from handwoven cloth is an important prerogative of chiefly office. An indication of a chief's power is evidenced by the fact that many cloths worn by chiefs are gifts from petitioners (Hardin 1993: 259). Kono gift exchanges, from the top down and from the bottom up, validate the intentions of the givers – cloth presented to a chief as tribute is a tangible recognition by individuals or groups of the chief's authority. When exchange transactions, up or down, involve significant differences in status and wealth between the giver and receiver, they can lead to long-standing patron-client relationships.

Organization of Court Artists

Due to the controlling nature and high demand associated with royal art patronage, many artists in state societies work as full-time specialists to serve the needs of the state. Leaders have the power to attract and coerce artists to the palace, where production can be controlled. Once attached to the state, commissions were embedded in cliental transactions where patron and artist were involved in binding life-time bonds in which the patron provided security, subsistence and sometimes prestige. The client artist in exchange offered services and loyalty. Artists who settled in or near the palace were often freeborn individuals who moved to take advantage of greater patronage opportunities. Sometimes, however, they were captured slaves from other ethnic groups.

The resettlement of artists from diverse ethnic backgrounds created a melting pot of different art traditions and styles in a single production center. This partly accounts for the widespread regional distribution of certain types of regalia, such as the embroidered gowns made of prestige strip-woven caliphate cloth in the Sokoto Caliphate (discussed in Chapter 6) or the carved wooden stools, masks and pipes from Cameroon Grassfields kingdoms. The nineteenth-century Bamun court of King Mbuembue, for example, incorporated slave artists from diverse geographical regions (Geary 1993: 34). Like gift exchanges to mark alliances, the resettlement of artists of subjugated peoples was a political strategy to integrate diverse groups into the state.

> . . . the Nguot, accomplished carvers and brass casters, formulated the typical Bamun court style. The Megnon were bead embroiderers, covering the wooden sculpture of the carvers with intricate beadwork in colorful designs . . . The appropriation and integration of the artists, their production of the most outstanding objects being used and displayed at the Bamun court, point to art as enacting ties between the numerous groups that make up Bamun. (Geary 1993: 88)

The turn-of-the-century Bamun king, Fon Njoya, is remembered for his innovative patronage of the arts. Partly as a result of trade contact with Muslim emirates of northern Nigeria, Njoya wished to transform his court into one with a Muslim style. Towards this end, he relocated Hausa weavers, dyers and leatherworkers to his palace at Foumban to produce items of leadership dress and regalia. Between 1908 and 1912 King Njoya was photographed several times dressed in a Muslim gown ensemble (Geary 1988). The ability of leaders to attract or command the services of widely distributed artists and resettle them in a single production center contributed to the mobility of art styles.

Artists attached to the state were well organized to carry out their assignments. Those connected to the Asante, Fon and Benin palaces were organized in hereditary kin-based work groups or cooperative guilds[1] that specialized in different technologies and materials. Artist guilds, headed by chiefs who mediate between court requests and artists, maximize production efficiency and provide a control mechanism over production and distribution. It was common in indigenous kingdoms for state leaders to provide complete sponsorship for court artists, offering shelter, board and financial support. In return, artists were expected to work exclusively for the leader. In the Benin kingdom the Oba established forty to fifty specialized guilds in special city wards located near the palace, where special cloths, leather fans and sculpture in brass, ivory and wood were produced. Regarded as 'servants of the Oba,' it was said that 'smiths and woodcarvers will never suffer from poverty' (Ben-Amos 1980a: 9–10). The Yoruba Alafin (king) of the Oyo Empire in Nigeria also settled artists in special wards of the capital to produce regalia for the court. Leatherworkers in particular played an important role. The lineage of royal leatherworkers, *isona*, was responsible for making leather slippers, pouffes, fans and saddles with needle embroidery and appliqué work, along with beaded staffs, beaded shoes and the bead-covered and cowrie-covered crowns for the Alafin (Kalihu 1991: 106).

> . . . the relationship between the *isona* and the Alafin is based on obedience and duty-bearing responsibility, which are expected of the *isona* in return for the protection and patronage given them by the Alafin. In return for these services, they are now rewarded with money and gifts. (Kalihu 1991: 107)

In addition, one of the Alafin's wives, a member of the leatherworking lineage, was responsible for the Alafin's wardrobe, selecting his clothes for different occasions.

Palaces and State-sponsored Building Programs

The importance of place (see Chapter 1) as a cultural arena is seen in centralized societies where the leader's palace and its environs are the locus of the political, economic and religious activities of the state. The residence of the leader is architecturally elaborated to stress his exalted position. The centrally-positioned palace houses his family, court, state shrines, and treasure storehouse. It is a special physical and social space that provides a setting for the sociocultural contexts in which leadership arts are used and receive full cultural meaning.

> Palace architecture physically and metaphorically separates the leader from those he rules. Important leaders in Africa invariably seem to have the most elaborate compounds and often added decorative features ... architecture tends to create isolating spatial envelopes for leaders that, like elevating devices, separate them conceptually from the mundane, everyday world. (Fraser and Cole 1972: 308)

The Yoruba palace at Gbongan has been described as a kind of material manifestation of the *oba* (king) and his royal office. As a symbol of the town's total identity, the palace is the focus of Gbongan history. It is an aesthetic focus particularly as a background for the verbal and kinetic arts through which the past is recreated (K. Barber, in Babayemi 1994: 148).

Functioning as a stage for the unfolding of court rituals and state festivals, a palace situates a leader's political authority. Within the palace grounds, wherever the leader goes the space around him is transformed, magnifying his grandeur. When British explorer Richard Lander visited the Yoruba palace of the Alafin, the king of the Oyo Empire, in the early 1800s:

> His Majesty was seated under the verandah, with two umbrellas spread over him and surrounded by above four hundred of his wives with many of his caboceers and other great men. (Allison 1956: 20)

Cloth can play a vital role in defining the special space of the ruler. When a new Alafin is installed he dons the robes of office, and enters 'a tent of beautiful cloths' located in front of the palace. When he emerges, these 'cloths of honor' taken from the tent are used as a moving canopy, in order to emphasize his pivotal role in society (Johnson 1921: 44). In the Cameroon Grassfields kingdoms special stitch-dyed indigo *ndop* cloths are used in the palace as demarcators and backdrops to enlarge and define the leader's space.

In some areas, architectural specialist groups arose to meet the needs of the political elite. An examination of Hausa state sponsored building programs in Kano, Nigeria illustrates how such a group evolved. The Hausa building guild emerged in the early nineteenth century under the leadership of a master builder, Babban Gwani. All Hausa builders holding the position of guild chief, *Sarkin Gini*, are descendants of Babban Gwani. The period 1820 to 1860 was one of tremendous boom in the Hausa building industry when members of the Hausa-Fulani political elite commissioned Babban Gwani to erect many important state buildings.[2] The wealth and slave labor resulting from Hausa wars provided the necessary resources for the building program (Saad 1985: 4). During that time, Babban Gwani designed and built the famous mosque in Zaria for Emir Abdulakarim. The mosque, which incorporated complex vaulted dome configurations, has since served as a source of inspiration for many Hausa builders (Moughtin 1985). It was customary for each new Hausa emir to commission the chief of builders to erect a new edifice or an addition to the palace. Consequently, a number of vaulted, domed public reception halls were built for Hausa-Fulani leaders, such as the complex embossed ceiling designs found in the reception rooms of the Kano palace, designed by Bala Gwani for Emir Abdullahi Bayero (1926–1952). To this day, the palace in Kano contextualizes the ostentatious dress displays associated with state-sponsored festivals. The palace gateway frames the leader and his entourage as they emerge from the privacy of the palace into the public arena. For a moment, the gateway focuses attention on the leader, intensifying his image as an icon of state power.

Embellishment additions to a palace are also evidence of art patronage and artistic accomplishments associated with a leader's reign. The king's palace in the northern Yoruba kingdom of Ikere is distinguished by courtyard veranda pillars carved by the early twentieth-century artist Olowe of Ise. As a court artist, Olowe was a well-travelled itinerant whose architectural sculptures embellished several palaces within a sixty mile radius (Walker 1994: 93). Olowe's royal patrons included the Owa of Ijesa, the Ojomu of Obaji in Akoko and the Ogoga of Ikere (Walker 1994: 93). Olowe's first patron, the Arinjale of Ise, commissioned him to carve doors, distinguished by a high-relief three-dimensional treatment of the motifs, and verandah posts. As his fame grew, he traveled to Ikere; the veranda pillars made for the Ogoga's palace there are characterized by boldly carved elongated figures with richly textured surfaces. The iconography, determined by the king, included an equestrian image and a seated enthroned king sheltered by his wife, reinforcing important leadership concepts. While the lack of written documentation about early patronage practices in Africa is the norm, the Yoruba oral tradition of praise poetry (*oriki*) offers valuable information about artists and patrons, as seen in the following praise poem dedicated to Olowe:

Handsome among his friends
Outstanding among his peers.
One who carves the hard wood of the *iroko* tree
As though it were as soft as a calabash.
One who achieves fame with the proceeds of his carving.
Olowe, who carves *iroko* wood.
The Master carver.
He went to the palace of Ogoga
And spent four years there.
He was carving there.
If you visit the Ogoga's palace
And the one at Owo,
The work of my husband is there.
If you go to Ikare,
The work of my husband is there
Pay a visit to Igede,
You will find my husband's work there.

(Walker 1994: 100–2)

Among the Islamized Nupe to the north, the vaulted palace reception halls of nineteenth- and early twentieth-century emirs were also supported by carved wooden veranda pillars, commissioned by leaders. Unlike the figurative Yoruba veranda pillars, the Nupe pillars were decorated with abstract, geometric patterns influenced by Islamic designs. The veranda of the Etsu Pategi's palace, located south of the Niger River, is a fine extant example of this architectural tradition.

Leadership Dress: Power and Bigness

It is at the state level of political organization that we see most clearly the importance of prestige cloth as commodity and art form, used by leaders to strengthen their positions of power. Dress, a critical component of leadership art closely tied to a state's hierarchical structure, is probably the least examined of the different genres of leadership art, having been overshadowed by the attention given to sculpted regalia. Nevertheless, in those areas of Africa where centralized leadership is exercised, textile arts and differentiated clothing are highly developed. The communicative importance of cloth and dress in leadership contexts where they act as 'tracers of rank' and bolster the visual hierarchy cannot be over emphasized (Schneider 1987: 412).

As we might expect, the finest examples of artistry in a dress tradition are associated with those of the highest rank, exemplified by an eighteenth-century Kongo raffia textile tradition where the finest was made only for the king (Sieber 1972: 159). Another type,

> for the greatest noblemen, [was] made very fine, and with curious workmanship, flower'd, and beautify'd with exquisite imagery, each cloth holding about two spans and a half [about ten inches] square, which a weaver with his greatest diligence may well spend fifteen or sixteen days in working to finish it. (Barbot 1732, cited in Sieber 1972: 159)

Clothing, when combined with other types of regalia, constitutes leadership dress. 'Regalia includes the raiment that adorns a ruler, the insignia carried by a ruler and the emblematic devices that support or shelter the ruler as symbols of royal power' (Nooter 1996: 351). By its very nature leadership dress is exclusive, and in many places was controlled by strict sumptuary rules until the twentieth century. Dress ensembles, including cloth, jewelry, headgear, footwear and carried regalia items, function not only as important prerogatives of leadership, but also as active instruments of rule, essential to the exercise of leadership. As a leadership art, dress in state societies is used to present the self and construct the political persona of the wearer in public, formalized contexts that set the leader apart.

> ... dress for special occasions and ceremonial events often involves the use of particularly elaborate, precious, or exotic materials, a high degree of decorative embellishment, and/or forms that clearly depart from more mundane modes of attire. The special or ceremonial nature of the event is signalled by the adoption of dress and body ornamentation that is viewed as spectacular, either in the combination of forms, the choice of materials, or in the symbolic messages conveyed. (Kreamer 1995: 99)

In general, leadership dress demands decorative elaboration and serves as 'visual metaphors for the social, political, and at times, religious powers of rulers' (Kreamer 1995: 100). According to Herbert Cole, 'a leader adorned is a living work of art, combining performance, with visual panoply for an occasion of state' (1989: 24). However, a dressed leader reflects the power and wealth of the state, not the personal preferences of an individual. Awareness of the society's cultural expectations guide leaders in their role as art patrons when selecting attire and regalia for their office. For example, Richard Lander observed that the early nineteenth-century Alafin of Oyo 'only conformed to the whims and fancies of his people ... when he attired himself fancifully, for they preferred a ruler with a smart and gorgeous exterior' (Allison 1956: 21). A similar sentiment was expressed almost two centuries later by an Asante village chief who claimed that personally he and other chiefs did not enjoy wearing a surplus of gold jewelry and riding on palanquins because they are uncomfortable, but 'we do so because it is what is expected' (Kwarteng 1995). Image takes precedence over the personal comfort of the individual playing the role, demonstrating how a leader is guided by social expectations in his choice of proper dress.

Leadership attire is calculated and manipulated to project great political as well as spiritual power through emphasis on 'bigness.' In public settings the leader assumes classic postures evoking political authority, especially the seated posture on a throne, horse or palanquin.[3] When seated in state, it is customary for the leader to generate a substantial presence extending personal space by sitting with knees spread widely apart, a posture which enhances the leader's size, visually reinforcing the stability of his office. On horseback his voluminous robes hang down over the horse to increase his size. The way in which a leader's attire drapes and hangs on his body in these public displays amplifies his actual size, generating an illusion of monumentality.

To increase the sense of bigness, leadership dress in Africa is frequently layered. According to Eicher, the layering of garments 'provides the effects of bulk, as does the use of heavy fabric. The importance of an individual's social position may be visually reinforced by the size of his or her ensemble' (1996: 347). Through layering and the addition of regalia, the dress ensemble is expanded and enlarged, resulting in an expansive image of the dressed leader. An ensemble of enormous physical bulk not only serves to make the aggrandized image concrete but also symbolically conveys strength and wealth, becoming a visual metaphor of the leader's power. While physical bigness in body mass communicated through dress is seen as an expression of a leader's authority, metaphorical bigness conveys a leader's generosity of character as well as his position as a source of power, ready to be tapped and released when needed for the community. Thus, the leader's body, enveloped, draped, and wrapped in large quantities of cloth, expresses the authority and dignity expected of a ruler.

Bigness is seen in the elaborate and heavy dress of the Oba of Benin. For annual rituals and for secular occasions requiring full ceremonial dress, such as the annual Ugie-Erha ceremony to commemorate the Oba's father and the Oba's reception of Britain's Queen in a 1956 visit to Nigeria (Nigeria in Costume 1965: 48), the Oba wore a coral-bead costume including crown, collar, tunic and slippers. A Benin chief explained that 'when the king is wearing this heavy beaded costume, he does not shake or blink but stays still and unmoving. As soon as he sits down on the throne he is not a human being but a god' (Ben Amos 1980a: 68). In addition to the beaded regalia, the Oba wears a red cloth skirt, supported by a hoop-like armature to further increase his girth. The skirt (*iyerhuan*), formerly woven by the Owina n'

Ido, the Benin palace guild of male and female weavers, can be worn only by the political elite. The skirt is decorated with black and yellow motifs representing leopards, a reference to the Oba's praise name 'Leopard, King of the World' (Duchateau 1994: 64). A second motif represents the Oba flanked by two figures, a reference to the great weight of his ceremonial dress, which requires that the Oba be physically supported by court attendants. These figures are a visual reminder of the power hierarchy within the Benin court. In addition, the Oba may appear with a state sword completely covered with red coral beads. Red coral, associated with Olokun, the god and king of the sea, is viewed as dangerous and threatening, indicating the power of the Oba. The Oba also wears ivory armlets carved in relief, an ivory pendant and ivory tubes suspended from his waist. Referring to spiritual purity, the white of the elephant's ivory is another metaphor for the leader's great power. The beaded crown and collar worn by the Oba are depicted in Benin brass commemorative altar heads while the Oba in full leadership dress is seen on sixteenth-century Benin brass palace plaques, establishing strong visual documentation for centuries of elaborate Benin leadership dress traditions.

The Benin annual ritual cycles have been curtailed in recent years, and the creation of art objects and costumes for these occasions has diminished, but they have not disappeared (Ben Amos 1980). Regal dress has been resilient in the face of change, a phenomenon documented by Joseph Nevadomsky during the 1978–9 ceremonies marking the accession of the thirty-fifth Oba of Benin, Eredauwa, to the throne. Through dress and regalia, these ceremonies reaffirmed the solidarity of the community and the historical legitimacy of Benin leadership. Kingship 'continues to form the basis of a cosmology that orders both time and space, and it provides the bedrock upon which a keen sense of Bini ethnic identity is founded' (Nevadomsky and Inneh 1983: 47).

The aesthetic goal of bigness in leadership dress makes it no surprise that leaders and their dress ensembles across the continent often refer directly or indirectly to the great power and presence of the elephant. Regarded as invincible and all-powerful, the elephant became an apt metaphor and icon for African leaders (Ross 1992: 150). In the Cameroon Grassfields, the leader is called 'elephant,' alluding not only to his physical mass conveyed by dress, but to his power and political importance. Not only does the elephant icon appear in the arts commissioned by the nineteenth-century Fon leader, Glele, but it was reported that when Glele did things, 'they became beautiful and big' (Blier 1991: 48). In Benin an eighteenth-century leader is reputed to have been able to transform himself into an elephant (Ben Amos 1980a: 33). For the Yoruba people, rulers and elephants are regarded as sharing the same conceptual space, both are 'mighty, essentially undefinable, and beyond circumscription' (Drewal 1992: 189). The accumulated experience and wisdom of leaders and elephants is conveyed by the Yoruba proverb, 'if an elephant eats and is not satisfied, the fault is that of the forest, not the elephant' (Drewal 1992: 191).

The ivory tusk condenses many of the meanings associated with the elephant and consequently is a primary power symbol and item of leadership regalia for many African peoples. Among the Kuba, the elephant's ivory tusk is a supreme symbol of royalty, displayed only by the Kuba ruler and his immediate family (Binkley 1992: 288). When Cameroon Grassfields leaders sit in state their feet rest on ivory elephant tusks, connoting that their power is superior to that of the elephant. (Figure 4.1) This idea is further reinforced by the fact that elephants are among the motifs which form caryatid supports of Cameroon Grassfields wooden stools and thrones and decorate ceramic pipe bowls smoked by royals. Among the Asante of Ghana, a gold-handled fly-whisk fashioned from the hairs of an elephant's tail is one of the most important regalia items belonging to the Asantehene (king). The proverb, 'though the elephant tail is short it can nevertheless keep flies off the elephant,' means that despite any shortcomings the chief is prepared to solve all problems (Ross 1992: 22). In the principal Asante ancestral commemoration ceremony, Adae, an elephant skin can be placed beneath the blackened ancestral stools, signifying the power of the spirits of deceased ancestors (Ross 1992: 141). Elephant skin is also placed underneath the Golden Stool, the absolute symbol of Asante nationhood.

Lions and leopards, supreme forest predators, also occur frequently in the symbolism of leadership art traditions as metaphorical references to bigness. For example, in the Benin Kingdom, like the leopard, the Oba of Benin is believed to control physical and magical forces which he can use suddenly and with great destructiveness . . . The leopard is considered the King of the Bush Animals and embodies all that the Edo associated with ideal leadership: physical characteristics of grace, bodily proportion, and beautiful coloration, as well as qualities of good character, wisdom, and forcefulness. Most of all, however, the leopard is capable of swift and violent aggression, a quality particularly appropriate in the context of warfare. In former times, warrior chiefs wore leopard skins or cloth representations of leopard faces to frighten off enemies. (Ben-Amos 1983:51, cited in Anderson and Kreamer 1989: 77)

Actual products from the elephant and leopard are frequently incorporated into leadership regalia of African kings to symbolize power. (Figure 4.1) This practice is motivated by the desire of leaders and those in power to 'align themselves with the dangerous, unpredictable, and powerful animals of the wild' (Anderson and Kreamer 1989: 79). Bound by sumptuary laws in many parts of Africa, hunters were expected to turn over elephant ivory and leopard skins to chiefs or kings. In the Bamun kingdom of the Cameroon Grassfields, it was the ultimate right of the king to decide the distribution of a large variety of slain animals – leopard, lion, elephant, buffalo, large snakes, hippopotamus, crocodile, and hyena (Geary 1983: 110).

Metaphorically embodying the principle of bigness, special cloths are regarded as interchangeable with the skin of powerful animals. Such was the case with *khasa* strip-woven cloths, made from goat wool by Fulani weavers in Mali and traded to the Asante court from Kano via the northern Ghanaian city of Salega. The Asante, who placed high value and prestige on *khasa* furnishing cloths, equated them with elephant skin, using them as ground covers (Lamb 1975: 106) and to fashion umbrellas (McLeod 1981: 109).[4] *Khasa* cloths have been observed as a covering for the Asantehene's palanquin and as 'a house of cloths' for the king's funerary bed (Lamb 1975: 146).

Finally, *bigness* as an aesthetic principle, can be seen in the costumes of African masqueraders, relating to power and leadership. In some, the metaphorical attributes and qualities of the elephant extend into the realm of spiritual forces controlled by or allied with secular and religious leaders. In the Yoruba city of Abeokuta the masquerade type *Egungun erin* (see Chapter 3 and Figure 3.2) through reference to the elephant (*erin*), and its imposing height and impressive bulky costume of cloth, visually underscores the wealth and prestige of owners and their lineages (Wolff 1981). Other examples of masqueraders that incorporate the aesthetic of bigness make use of a composite assemblage of materials including animal skins, cowrie shells, beads, cloth, fur and feathers. These include the Kuba of Zaire *Moshambooy* and *Mukenga* masqueraders, and the elephant masqueraders of the Bamilike of the Cameroon Grassfields. The headpieces and costumes of these masqueraders dress powerful spirits with leadership functions. In the Bamilike kingdom of the Cameroon Grassfields, members of a palace regulatory association perform in composite headpieces made of stitch-dyed indigo *ndop* cloth panels decorated with beads that fall over the dancer's chest, suggesting the form of elephants' trunks (Geary 1992: 253). A relationship to the political elite is further emphasized by the addition of leopard skin to the back of the costume. This combined force of a beaded elephant representation with the actual skin of a leopard and royal *ndop* cloth serves to visually reinforce the great political authority of the king, who draws on the power of both the elephant and the leopard for his rule.

Among the Kuba, masks and costumes belonging to the trilogy of royal masqueraders, recounting the legend of Bushong cultural heroes belonging to the ruling dynasty, resemble the dress of the Kuba king in the profusion of weighty, prestigious beadwork, densely assembled in a labor-intensive process.

The bead-covered Mukenga mask of the northern Kuba-related peoples features the same interlacing designs found in the king's embroidered raffia dress and a conical projection representing the elephant's trunk. The Mukenga mask primarily appears at funerals of initiated title holders who belong to high ranking clans (Binkley 1992: 284). Some Mukenga masks made before 1880 incorporated actual elephant skin into the face panel, reflecting the fact that the region's wealth was directly tied to its control of the ivory trade (Binkley 1992: 285).

Kente Cloth and Asante Leadership Dress

While cloth and dress have not received the same attention as other types of state regalia, the wearing of Asante *kente* strip-cloth in Ghana, combined with gold regalia to energize the surrounding space of the *kente*-clad leader with royal urgency, is an exception. At least since the eighteenth century, the brilliantly colored *kente* cloth has come to symbolize the wealth and brilliance of the royal stool (office) of the supreme Asante leader, the Asantehene, and his paramount chiefs. During the independence period it has become tied to concepts of Ghanaian identity and nationhood. While sumptuary rules controlling the wearing of *kente* have greatly decreased in this century, certain varieties of *kente* are still reserved exclusively for royalty. During the production of one type of complex *kente* weave, *asasia*, commissioned only by the king, the weaver is sponsored in the palace and rewarded with a suitable sum.[5] Another spectacular densely woven *kente* with complex inlay twill designs, called *adweneasa* ('my skill is exhausted'), was made for the king and wealthy individuals. The dress of Asante male leaders consists of an enormous cloth, wrapped several times around the body, draped over the left shoulder while leaving the right shoulder bare. Bowdich described these colorful silk *kente* cloths in the early nineteenth century as being 'of an incredible size and weight, and thrown over the shoulders exactly like the Roman toga' (1966: 35). As a type of dress,

> wrapped garments create [an] . . . aesthetic space surrounding the body; it extends as the wearer moves and contracts as he assumes a static pose. This space enhances the body's potential for graceful movement, the ultimate expression of which occurs during dance or ritualized activity (Gilfoy 1987: 39–40).

Through the wearer's fluid movements of wrapping, unwrapping and draping the body, cloth amplifies the body to fill the surrounding space. When properly worn, *kente* cloth exhibits a clear interplay of horizontal and vertical elements, which emphasize the armature of the wearer's body, while visually expressing its mass and stability.

Kente of various types play a role in symbolizing dynastic order during the ritual of Adae, commemorating deceased rulers at forty-two day intervals. White cloths with accents of blue (an earlier style of *kente*) are worn by chiefs when making sacrifices to the blackened ancestral stools (McLeod 1981: 149). Adae worship requires that a king or chief wear a plain old cloth into the stool room and that he slip out of his sandals, while letting the cloth drop to a thick fold around his waist to demonstrate his humility before the ancestors. Prior to reappearing before his constituency, the king dons his most elaborate attire of *kente* cloth and exquisite gold jewelry, emphasizing his current position of leadership. According to Lamb, this cloth representing 'the dignity and position vested in the chief or king . . . must be glowing and brilliant to symbolize wealth and power. The king must be seen to be great and his stool must therefore be rich in cloth' (1975: 141). Adae worship with wardrobe changes becomes an aesthetic process which can be compared to the act of dressing itself 'as a dance of adjustment, with extensive wrapping and unwrapping gestures' (Cole and Ross 1977: 16).

The development of the *kente* cloth tradition resulted from an interaction of art patronage and trade. In the eighteenth century special luxury textile workshops, controlled by the court, were established within an already developed cotton weaving industry (Adler 1992: 44; McLeod 1981: 155). Since the early nineteenth century the weaving of *kente* cloth has been centered in the weaving town of Bonwire, outside of the capital city, Kumasi. While the luxury tradition of *kente* cloth dates back to the early eighteenth century, in its earliest stages it was not the colorful cloth we know today, but rather a plainer blue and white striped or checked cotton strip-woven cloth (Cole and Ross 1977: 38). It was similar to many other early West African textile traditions, including the eleventh-century archaeological Tellem cloths from Mali, blue and white striped *kyekye* cloths from Côte d'Ivoire, and blue and white checked *saki* cloth from Nigeria. An early twentieth-century observation that blue and white checked cloth was valued and worn by chiefs confirms its early use as a prestige textile (Rattray 1927: 248). On a relatively plain blue and white base weave, inlays of red silk weft blocks were added, first as accents of color, and eventually as dominant design motifs. Later large weft-faced blocks of green and yellow silk were incorporated, resulting in the elaborate and colorful *kente* cloth tradition. The process of inlaying silk on a ground weave using supplementary heddles involves overlaying one sumptuous material on another, increasing not only the density and weight of the cloth, but also its prestige and value. With the addition of the weft-floats, a relatively plain leadership cloth became more elaborate and subject to sumptuary laws.

An examination of the development of *kente* design must consider the possible reasons why prestige value was assigned to a relatively plain cloth. First, an early source for blue and white *kente* cloth was probably imported exotic prototypes from outside the African continent. We know from trade records that blue and white checked 'Guinea cloth'[6] was manufactured in India and traded into the Senegambia region during the seventeenth century. Versions of blue and white plaid and checked cloth were also produced in the nineteenth-century textile mills of Britain for the purpose of export to Africa, thus catering to an established taste preference for this type of cloth. Indigenous West African cloth industries producing checked and striped cloths also played a role in creating an Asante taste preference for blue and white cloths. Several writers have suggested blue and white cloth from Bondoukou, Côte d'Ivoire as a likely source for early blue and white *kente* cloth (Rattray 1927; Lamb 1975; Gilfoy 1987; Adler 1992). Another possible source of early *kente* design was the blue and white checked *saki* cloth gowns made by Nupe weavers in Nigeria and traded via Kano to Gonja state in northern Ghana along the kola nut route (see Chapter 6). Salega, a Muslim town in Gonja state, functioned as an important cloth entrepot for *saki* cloth and gowns which were traded southwards into Kumasi.[7] The idea of Nupe *saki* cloth as a likely prototype for early forms of Asante *kente* is supported by the value which the Asante attach to *saki* gowns, which were exchanged for kola nuts.[8] The silk from North Africa, used in the weaving of *kente*, also entered Ghana along this same trade route from Kano (Gilfoy 1987: 35). Asante trade connections with India, Europe, Côte d'Ivoire and Kano were well-established by the eighteenth century, suggesting that blue and white prestige cloths from all of these sources may have converged, serving as prototypes for the early forms of Asante *kente* cloth.

The Asante receptivity to imported cloths from a variety of sources therefore becomes clear. The earlier, plainer versions of *kente* and the more elaborate types continued to develop as the Asante aesthetically responded to cloth traditions from elsewhere. While *kente* cloth became increasingly refined in pattern complexity and technical virtuosity over the course of the nineteenth and twentieth centuries through the art patronage practices of the king and paramount chiefs, the foundation of *kente* development is grounded in early trade connections.

Silver Jubilee Festival The strength of the *kente* tradition was demonstrated in August 1995 when the Silver Jubilee of the reigning Asantahene was held. The festival, a very elaborate version of an Adae ceremony in which the blackened ancestral stools belonging to former rulers were 'washed' with sacrifices, was held in Kumasi to honor Nana Otunfo Ware II's twenty-five-year reign. For this occasion the king chose an older checkerboard style of *kente* cloth, composed of alternating blocks of blue and white checks enhanced by red and gold silk weft blocks. Festivals like the 1995 Jubilee provide the most spectacular performance context for a rich display of dress and regalia. The Jubilee was a grandiose event marked by a sea of hundreds of umbrellas, each sheltering a paramount chief and members of his entourage.

During the festival, approximately one thousand richly attired chiefs and queen mothers gathered to honor the Asantehene, expressing the political and social solidarity of the Asante people in a grand regal procession. (Figure 4.2) Critical to the festival's visual lavishness was the vast array of hand-woven and factory cloth worn by participants, encompassing a rainbow of colors. The paramount chiefs, swathed in colorful *kente* cloth and weighted down with gold necklaces and armlets, moved in dignified stately movements accompanied by assistants to support the weight of their arms. As an aesthetic manifestation of the leader's bigness, this practice was reminiscent of one reported almost two centuries earlier by Bowdich, who described the gold armlets as so heavy that the chief's arms had to by supported by the heads of boys (1966: 35).

The order of participants as the procession unfolded reflected the political hierarchy of the Asante state, with important paramount chiefs followed by their divisional chiefs and village chiefs, all with queen mothers. For each cluster of chiefs and queen mothers, retainers carried stools and cushions. The procession culminated with the appearance of the Asantehene himself, carried on a palanquin and accompanied by the Golden Stool, a gold-leaf covered state drum, and a treasury box. While the Asantehene and some of the paramount chiefs were dressed in *kente* cloth, the majority of the festival participants wore light colored handwoven and commercial cloths of white and blue to signify the happiness and joy of the occasion (Kwarteng 1995). The wearing of *kente* was reserved for only the most important participants, because for any event the politically senior leader must be the 'most sumpt-uously attired ... it [being] improper for a lesser chief to surpass a higher one' (Cole and Ross 1977: 23).

Leadership Arts and the Marketplace

Leadership arts are not exempt from the marketplace, particularly as the political power of indigenous rulers has declined and sumptuary laws have weakened since European contact. It is characteristic of centralized state societies that the art patronage of leaders and traders shape art traditions. The art patronage practices of state leaders and wealthy traders are character-

Figure 4.2. Kente cloth-clad Asante paramount chief and entourage in 1995 Silver Jubilee Festival, Kumasi, Ghana. Source: Stephen Howard.

ized by two distinct arenas of exchange, with different demands voiced for the same art product. The same type of luxury product may be produced to meet the prestige needs of state leaders as well as the commercial demands of the marketplace. This results in a phenomenon where the processes of art patronage and trade interact, and the boundaries between commissioning patrons and consumer patrons become blurred. Depending upon which patron role is emphasized at the time when production of a luxury good is initiated, the same artform may function as an item of leadership dress and regalia or as an economic commodity.

While it is not uncommon for the same type of art product to be produced on a commission basis for a state leader or to be stockpiled for the market-place for resale, the products themselves may be distinguished by qualitative differences. In general, higher quality and more elaborate designs are found in the prestige product specially commissioned by a state leader in comparison to products intended for resale in the market. For example, in the Cameroon Grassfields clay pipes made for the local weekly markets were relatively simple in design while special-ordered clay pipes made for rulers had elaborate imagery (Northern 1984: 57). Similarly, Grassfields artists carved wooden stools for both kings and the marketplace and the Benin carving guild made elaborated wooden and ivory regalia for the palace and wooden plates, spoons and mortars for the marketplace. This two-track production strategy, tied to two distinctively different arenas of exchange, has kept many African art traditions viable as cultural change has affected indigenous patronage. This is seen in the arrival of a new kind of outgroup patron for the African artist – the foreign patron (European and American) (see Chapter 3).

The Emergence of Foreign Art Patronage for Leadership Arts

In the colonial and independence periods, the art patronage demand from outgroup foreign tourists has become increasingly important in some state societies. The quality and sometimes spectacular visual appeal of leadership arts has, from the beginning, attracted the eye of European visitors and expatriates. Demand from outgroup foreign patrons has played a critical role in ensuring the continuing vitality of certain art traditions, and in some cases boosted an art industry's production.

Beginning in the colonial period, the political powers of African indigenous rulers became increasingly circumscribed. Associated with a decline in political power was a decline in royal patronage of the arts. Artists who had been dependent on the patronage of leaders turned to new markets, leading to a relaxation in rules regarding sumptuary control over certain forms of state regalia. As a result, outgroup foreign patronage has developed in a way that co-exists with court patronage, and in some cases, replaces court patronage altogether. The art tradition, in these cases, begins to shift directions to accommodate the demands of foreigners.

The Fon tradition of appliquéd wall hangings from the Republic of Benin demonstrates how a transition from court patronage to marketplace demand occurred. During the precolonial nineteenth century a Fon guild of tailors based in the capital of Abomey produced appliqué banners exclusively for the court (Adams 1980: 28). In the late eighteenth century the Fon leader, Angonglo, had brought tailors from Porto Novo to Abomey, commissioning them to create appliqué banners illustrating military episodes to function as espionage maps (Adams 1980: 37; Blier 1993: 428). It became customary for successive kings to determine banner motifs symbolizing the accomplishments of their own reigns. The nineteenth-century Fon king, Gezo, for example, selected motifs for his state banners inspired by his personal divination signs, including the bull buffalo and the tree of prosperity (Adams 1980: 40). Shortly after the establishment of French colonial rule in 1898 the tailors started to diversify, expanding their production to meet the needs of a growing foreign market, including colonial officers and travelers. The process continued to escalate and a half century later the products of the tailor's guild had become exclusively commercial in efforts to cater to the taste of outgroup foreign patrons, a shift which continued in the independence period (Adams 1980: 37). One interesting result of this shift in patronage was in the way tailors selected symbols and motifs for the banners. In the precolonial period individual kings determined the banner motifs; during the colonial period, tailors began combining the motifs of different kings on the same banner, resulting in 'summarizing cloths,' a creative adaptation to the new patronage situation (Adams 1980: 37). The Fon appliqué cloth tradition,

> once an elitist art embedded in a local culture, . . . became a product offered aggressively to anonymous buyers at the Abomey market, to itinerant traders for their African markets and finally to international exporters to Europe and America. (Adams 1980: 37)

Similar changes occurred in the Fon metal sculptural traditions associated with leadership. During the colonial period, the unique life-size iron figures and wooden figures overlaid with hammered sheets of silver and brass representing Fon kings gave way to small mass-produced cast brass narrative genre scenes. This is another example of how change in the local patronage base, where court patronage is replaced by patronage of colonially appointed local chiefs and foreign tourists, reshapes an older tradition (Blier 1993: 429).

Dress and other leadership arts play a critical role in maintaining the political system in African state societies, supporting inequities of rank while defining and structuring a state's power relations. In the Nigerian case studies that follow in Part II we will go beyond the broad presentation of art patronage and leadership presented here to examine how cloth and dress reveal the complex interrelationship between art patronage, leadership and trade in a regional context. We will see in the Hausa, Nupe and Yoruba states, that leaders and traders emerge as twin pillars of power, the former political and the latter economic. It is the political and economic power of leaders and traders that has given rise to two of the most important art patron roles throughout much of Africa. Both leaders and traders are responsible for commissioning, controlling and distributing large quantities of art products. In the remaining chapters (5 to 8) the dynamics and processes that link leaders, traders and terminal consumers will be revealed in a more focused examination of particular cloth and dress patronage and consumption practices operating in the Hausa, Nupe and Yoruba state societies of Nigeria.

Notes

1. The use of the term 'guild' in the literature on African art may be an overstatement and an attempt to apply a western concept to an African situation. See discussion of Nupe guilds in Chapter 6.

2. See Chapter 2 for a discussion of the patronage of Hausa builders by wealthy Hausa merchants.

3. For further discussion of these classic postures see Thompson (1974) and Cole (1989).

4. In the early nineteenth century the British traveler to Ghana, Bowdich, reported umbrellas made of leopard skin (McLeod 1981: 109).

5. According to Lamb (1975), *asasia* has not been made since World War II.

6. 'Guinea' referred to the trade target site of the Guinea Coast of West Africa.

7. According to McLeod (1981: 153), Salega was under Asante control in the mid eighteenth century during which time it produced cotton for the Asante.

8. Some Hausa weavers and embroiderers of *saki* cloth had emigrated to Salega to produce cloth and gowns for Muslim Ghanaian chiefs. The Asante name for the blue and white checked pattern, *asambo*, means 'guinea fowl breast,' while the Hausa term, *saki*, refers to the mottled appearance of guinea fowl plumage, further reinforcing a conceptual and stylistic relationship between *saki* cloth and *kente*.

Part 2

The Development of Hausa, Nupe and Yoruba Cloth and Dress Traditions

5

Historical Context of Leadership, Trade and Art Patronage

The Hausa, Nupe and Yoruba are geographically contiguous ethnic groups historically organized into pre-industrial states with strongly defined systems of leadership. There are no significant geographical barriers between the groups.[1] The Hausa are located in the arid Northern High Plains savannah that merges into the southern edges of the Sahara. Historically, the seven Hausa city states were dependent on trans-Saharan trade. Hausa commodities have been traded throughout the region and beyond for centuries. The society is stratified with differences in rank and occupation marked by a system of titled offices. The Hausa accepted Islam and Islamic culture early and actively spread the religion to the south through trade routes. Their language, belonging to the Chadic family, is related to Arabic. Due to their trade activities, the Hausa language has been used as a lingua franca in the region for centuries.

Bordering the Hausa to the south, the Nupe live in the savannah lowlands of the Niger River. The Nupe are geographically and culturally transitional between the Hausa and the Yoruba of the southern forest. Linguistically, the Nupe language belongs to the Kwa family (closely related to Yoruba), but Hausa is widely spoken as a second language in Nupeland. Contact with the north exposed the Nupe to many influences from the Islamic world, whereas contact with the south opened up trading relations with Europe. Due to their intermediary position along a north–south continuum of diverging trade routes, the Nupe on the Niger River were a gateway culture, channeling ideas and art products in both directions.

The Yoruba homeland extends from south of the Niger River to the coast with savannahs in the north changing to rain forest in the south. Yoruba kingdoms are among the oldest in sub-Saharan Africa with over fifty Yoruba kingdoms existing before European contact. Moreover, the Yoruba have been urbanized longer than any other sub-Saharan people. A rich tradition of leadership and ritual arts, now counted with the world's great art traditions, developed in these early cities. With European contact, the Yoruba became major players in the north–south interregional trade, moving the commodities of Europe into the network. While separated by language and some cultural traditions, the three groups have had a great deal of intercultural exchange through trade, war and the encroachment of Islam. Interregional trade routes have throughout this time served as arteries tying Hausa, Nupe and Yoruba centers of artistic production together, facilitating outgroup patron-artist transactions.

Trade is particularly important to our understanding not only the interconnectedness of the region, but also the nature of artist-patron interactions within and between these ethnic groups. As we shall see, the small city-states of this region were drawn into larger mega-states where power revolved around control of local and long distance trade. The Sokoto Caliphate which integrated the Muslim Emirates of the Hausa and Nupe, and the Oyo Empire, enveloping many Yoruba kingdoms, did not emerge until interregional trade was well-developed. Speaking of Yoruba kingdoms, historian Ade Obayemi remarked on this relationship, which is equally true of Emirates.

> ... Accounts of European travellers and merchants ... mention the preoccupation of the rulers of the various great states with trade ... Such involvement ... would have given them access to slaves and superior weapons, as well as control over the distribution of luxury goods to the rural population. These benefits would have been sufficient to enable them to develop hegemonies over the small and mini-state polities of the surrounding countryside. (1976: 258)

Such a socioeconomic context provides a rich background for examining the relationship between leadership, trade, art patronage and the creative transformation of art traditions.

Characteristics of Western Sudanic States

Powerful centralized societies have existed in West Africa for many centuries. A series of empire states, including Ghana, Mali and Songhay, waxed and waned in the region of the Upper Niger River of the Western Sudan region in the period between the eighth and sixteenth centuries AD. These early states arose in response to growing trans-Saharan trade opportunities linking North and West Africa. In the process, 'trade stimulated a higher level of political organisation, while the emergence of extensive states accorded more security to trade routes' (Levtzion 1976: 116). Towns in the Sahel area below the Sahara became entrepots of trade where commodities from the savannahs and rainforests (such as gold and ivory) were traded for goods (such as salt, copper and cloth) brought across the Sahara. Strong centralized leadership emerged when local leaders moved to extend their control over the lucrative trade.

A close relationship between rulers and traders grew due to the efforts of both to regulate the supply and demand of commodities. Through their active involvement in the trans-Saharan trade the Western Sudan states became conduits for Islam. Since the eighth century, northern traders, primarily Muslim, spread Islam along the trade routes. In the emergent states, local traders and political elites accepted Islam, greatly facilitating interregional trade relationships. Islam also provided a model for state structures so that Koranic law was established and hierarchical bureaucracies, specialized ministries and titled offices soon appeared in the Western Sudan states. Armies were established with an emphasis on horse cavalry. The adoption of Islam was also an important stimulant for the development of an early demand for tailored prestige clothing tied to leadership in the region (Adler 1992: 30). A tenth-century Arab traveler in the Western Sudan, Al Bakri, observed that 'among the people who follow the king's religion [Islam] only he and his heir apparent . . . may wear sewn clothing' (Levtzion and Hopkins, cited in Gilfoy 1987: 81).[2] When Ibn Battuta visited ancient Mali in 1352, he observed a powerful state where the king was dressed in splendid robes and gold ornaments and rode an embellished horse (Sieber 1972).

Early Links Between the Hausa, Nupe and Yoruba

Trade played a particularly important role in connecting the Hausa, Nupe and Yoruba city states through the centuries. The Hausa, poised on the edge of the Sahara, played a role similar to that of the early Western Sudan states, moving the commodities of the south into the trans-Saharan trade routes. The Nupe, positioned between the Hausa and the Yoruba, also took an active role in this movement. Similarly, the Yoruba moved their own commodities to the north and trade goods to the coast. Raka, a nineteenth-century northern Yoruba city on the commercial frontier, was described as 'a great place of trade between the interior and the coast'(Mason 1981: 61). It has been suggested that Hausa-Nupe trade relations developed out of thirteenth- and fourteenth-century exchanges of North African horses and horse equipment for Nupe eunuch slaves (Law 1977, Isichei 1983: 87). In the following centuries as trade products diversified, the Nupe became integrated into the interregional trade network. Yoruba involvement in trade exchanges with the Hausa probably also began with the import of horses and horse equipment sometime in the sixteenth century, when the Yoruba kingdom of Ile Oyo became a cavalry state (Isichei 1983: 87).

War was another reason for intense interaction in the region. From the viewpoint of the arts (as we saw in Chapter 4), wars resulted in artists from one group being captured and resettled as slaves among another group, a phenomenon that significantly impacted art traditions of the captor. In the seventeenth and eighteenth centuries, for example, Hausa slaves were often purchased by the Yoruba, who placed them in domestic service. Among these slaves were skilled artists, including weavers and leatherworkers, who no doubt were responsible for the transmission of these northern technologies to the Yoruba.

A third factor responsible for interregional unity was the adoption of Islam, first by a small political elite and later by larger sectors of the population. Islam was first introduced to the Hausa in the fourteenth and fifteenth centuries by Mande clerics from Mali. In those Hausa states, deeply involved in trade, such as Kano, the ruling class and traders embraced Islam, partly as a strategy to reinforce trading relations with the Mali Empire to their west. Accompanying the spread of Islam throughout the western and central Sudan by traders and koranic scholars was the men's treadle loom. After an introduction to Kano in the fifteenth century by Mande clerics from Mali, the treadle loom technology was dispersed to the south, first to the Nupe and later to the Yoruba peoples. On the basis of the association of weaving with Islam, the Nupe region and the Oyo Empire may have been producing strip-woven cloth by the seventeenth century (Kriger 1990: 39). The Muslim presence in Nupe and Yoruba country dates back several centuries; in the mid-seventeenth century, Muslims in Yoruba country looked to Hausaland for Islamic inspiration and advice (Adamu 1978: 129). However, conversion to Islam by Yoruba kings and political elite was slow. For over two centuries (AD 1600 to 1800) the Oyo Empire controlled the smaller Yoruba kingdoms reaching from the Niger River to the southern coast. In the early 1800s, the process of Islamization in the Central Sudan intensified due to the jihads (Muslim wars of conquest) staged by the Fulani people who had migrated into the area and intermingled with the Hausa as early as the seventeenth-century. The Fulani, in the name of Islam, established a theocracy, the Sokoto Caliphate, which incorporated the Hausa, Nupe and northern Yoruba as emirates into a single political entity.

For our purposes of analyzing the patterns of art patronage and trade, the Oyo Empire and Sokoto Caliphate are of particular concern. Prior to 1800, the Yoruba and Nupe peoples had some interaction when the Oyo Empire was controlling much of the Yoruba area. The collapse of the Oyo Empire in the early nineteenth century overlapped with the rise of the Sokoto Caliphate, so that the northern Yoruba, Nupe and Hausa formed a single powerful political structure. Patterns of trade and requirements of gift exchange within the Caliphate linked a vast area of Nigeria from Kano in the north to Ilorin in the south.

The Yoruba Oyo Empire and Northern Nupe Neighbors before 1800

Between 1100–1450 AD the Yoruba city state of Ile-Ife, believed to be the point of origin of the Yoruba people, reached its height as the political, economic and religious center of the Yoruba world. At this time, it was a viable part of the long-distance trading system linking the Yoruba to their northern neighbors. Art production was highly developed in the ancient city, and art industries supplied goods for both local and long distance trade. The kings (*oni*) of Ife were major art patrons who commissioned leadership regalia for their office. Through their sponsorship as patrons, they contributed to the development of a sophisticated tradition of cast brass and terracotta sculpture used in the commemoration of royal ancestors. Moreover, Ile-Ife was the first Yoruba state where beaded royal regalia was produced for the king (Drewal and Mason 1998). A deified former Ile Ife ruler, Obalufon is associated with the invention of beads and the establishment of the bead-working industry. Oral tradition indicates that the Adiyanrun of Obalaayan compound at Ilode formerly made crowns for the Ife court. Today, the Buraimoh Osunwusi of Olosara is one of the few compounds producing beaded crowns in Ife (Drewal and Mason 1998: 54, 62). Visual evidence, dating from the eleventh to the fourteenth century in the form of brass figurative statues and heads depicting kings wearing beaded crowns and jewelry, confirms an early elaborate dress tradition. Subsequent Yoruba leaders looked to the Oni of Ife as the supreme leader, receiving from him the right to rule and wear the beaded crown, a royal prerogative produced by the Ife workshop. Crowns and other items of beaded dress and regalia continued to be commissioned from Ife in later centuries by Yoruba kings who ruled the sixteen kingdoms that recognized the religious authority of the King of Ile Ife. Since the late nineteenth century the northern Ekiti town of Efon-Alaye has been a major center of beaded regalia production. Efon-Alaye bead artists from the Adesina family are credited with developing the glass seed bead style of crowns, commissioned by rulers throughout Yoruba country (Drewal and Mason 1998: 62). (Figure 5.1)

By the sixteenth and seventeenth centuries, Ile-Ife began to decline as a center of trade and political power, although it retained its importance as the 'Holy City of the Yorubas' (Eyo and Willett 1980: 42). Ife's fall was largely

Figure 5.1. Yoruba oba's beaded tunic, Kingdom of Owo, late nineteenth century. Source: New Orleans Museum of Art. Robert P. Gordy and Carrie Heiderick Funds.

due to a shift in the major trade routes. Under the impetus of the increasing demands of the European transatlantic slave trade, trade routes to the southern coast became increasingly important. By the late sixteenth century, the Yoruba center of power shifted from Ile Ife to the northwestern city state of Ile Oyo, the capital of the Oyo kingdom, which had better access to the southern coast (Shaw 1978: 163–6). The Alafin (king) of Oyo controlled trade, and the city became a focus for production of commodities for leadership and commerce. For the next two centuries (c. 1650–1832), the history of the Yoruba became synonymous with the history of the growth of the Oyo Empire. By the eighteenth century the Oyo Yoruba had extended the boundaries of Yoruba culture to its present westernmost limit, reaching its greatest extent and power in the 1780s (Law 1977: 254).

The history of the Oyo Empire would be incomplete without considering Yoruba interactions with the Nupe. War, conquest, tribute and trade have tied the two peoples together for centuries (Law 1977: 207–17). The Nupe's early status as a gateway culture was recognized by historian Michael Mason:

> Despite the ever-widening web of social and commercial relationships which was gradually spread over Nupe from the north, we must not lose sight of the fact that Nupe culture, especially prior to the nineteenth century, was firmly wedded to that of its neighbors in the area of the Niger. (1981: 10–11)

It has been suggested that from 1450–1850 that the Nupe and Yoruba may even have been indistinguishable (Dupigny 1920: 42). An early connection between the two peoples is recounted in Yoruba history. It is asserted that the legendary fourth Yoruba King of Oyo, Shango (who after his death was deified to become the god of thunder and lightning), was the son of a Yoruba father and a Nupe mother. By the first half of the eighteenth century the territory controlled by Oyo, north to the Niger River, including parts of Nupe country, was part of a single economic, cultural and political complex, sharing a common language. Another area where evidence of early historical contact between the two peoples can be seen is in religious practices. The Yoruba Egungun ancestral masquerade (discussed in Part I and later in this chapter) may have been introduced to the Yoruba by the Nupe (Johnson 1921). Whichever direction the Egungun cult may have moved, it became firmly established in the Oyo Empire, from where it spread to other Yoruba regions after Oyo's collapse during the nineteenth century.

The commercial importance of the Nupe can be attributed in part to their domination over the Niger River traffic, the cheapest way to transport bulky goods over long distances (Mason 1981: 64). Before the nineteenth century Kulfo and other Nupe towns situated along the Niger functioned as important entrepots for manufactured commodities. Kulfo, reputed as 'the greatest market town in Nupe country' and 'at all times a central point for trade in this part of the interior'(Clapperton 1966: 169, 137), was a purely commercial center where goods from the Atlantic and North Africa were imported and exported (Mason 1981: 59). The eighteenth century saw a fair amount of political and commercial contact between Nupe and Yoruba: 'The natural places where goods changed hands all around, lay in Nupe along the Niger' (Colvin 1973: 115). Also, some of the craft technologies diffused into Yorubaland by way of the Oyo Empire. Reverend Samuel Johnson remarked that 'light and civilization with the Yoruba came from the north . . . the centers of life and activity of large populations and industries were in the interior' (Johnson 1921: 40).

Although little is known of Nupe history before the Fulani conquest in the nineteenth century, it is believed that the Nupe were a powerful early Central

Sudanese state (Crowder 1978: 24). Oral tradition credits a cultural hero, Tsoede, born of a Nupe mother and an Igala father, with the unification of the Nupe kingdom during the fifteenth century (Hodgkin 1960: 25). Settling in the hamlet of Nupeko on the Niger River, Tsoede became the first sovereign to establish a dynasty of kings who reigned until the 1830s when the Nupe were conquered by the Fulani and incorporated into the Sokoto Caliphate (Nadel 1942: 406). At this time the legitimate Nupe dynasty that traced descent back to Tsoede abandoned all legal claim to rulership (Nadel 1942: 80). Today, the Emir of Pategi (Etsu Pategi), first appointed by the British, rules from the southern Nupe town of Pategi, claiming direct descent from Tsoede.

Relations were not always peaceful between the Nupe and Yoruba, and the balance of power passed back and forth. The earliest instance of Nupe invasion and conquest of the Oyo kingdom occurred during the reign of the sixteenth-century Ile Oyo king, Onigbogie (Akinjobin 1968: 29). When Ile Oyo was militarily dominated by the Nupe, many of whom were already settled in northern Yoruba territory. Robin Law has suggested that the success of the Nupe expansion south of the Niger at this time and the state-building activities of the Nupe king, Tsoede, were in part due to the Nupe adoption of cavalry. By the end of the sixteenth century, Ile Oyo had checked Nupe invasions and the Oyo kingdom became reconstituted, partly as a result of its own adoption of cavalry (Law 1978: 39). Oyo reorganized and carried out an extensive imperial expansion during the following centuries (Law 1977: 44). At this time, Nupe oral tradition recounts that the Etsu Nupe and the Alafin of Oyo met annually to exchange gifts at the Nupe frontier town of Ogodo (Mason 1981: 11). This exchange between leaders does not imply the subjection of one people by the other, but rather that diplomatic relations between the two rulers expressed by gift-giving existed (Law 1977: 148). Law believes that any control which Oyo had over the Nupe ended by the late eighteenth century and that, if anything, Oyo was subordinate to Nupe. By 1789 Oyo was paying tribute to the Nupe, having suffered defeat perhaps because of a growing inability to maintain control over a large empire (Law 1977: 150). This last defeat by the Nupe marked the beginning of Oyo's decline before its final collapse in the 1830s.

Earlier, the Oyo Empire, reached its greatest extent and influence during the reign of Alafin Abiodun (1774–1789), who was reputed to be more interested in fostering trade than in military strategies. During his reign, trade between Oyo and the north had become substantial (Law 1977: 211). Among the goods traded south were strip-woven cloth, tailored gowns and leather-work. In the nineteenth century, with an increase in the availability of European trade goods, Oyo (and the rest of the Western and Central Sudan), turned attention 'from the desert to the sea and while concentrating on its communications with the coast Oyo probably neglected its northern frontiers' (Allison 1956: 26). In 1837, no longer able to sustain the turmoil created by numerous internal civil wars and conflict with Nupe and Dahomey, the Oyo Empire fell, dividing once more into a number of independent city states. Without the overreaching authority of the Oyo Empire, warfare between the former tributary Yoruba kingdoms in southern Yorubaland broke out as each competed for power and access to the profitable European trade. For the rest of the nineteenth century the Yoruba peoples were locked into a pattern of chronic civil warfare. Villages, small towns and even cities of many thousands of people lost population as peoples fled and resettled elsewhere.

Despite social turbulence caused by these civil wars, the Yoruba were remarkably successful in maintaining an overreaching cultural identity, evident in the city states of Ilorin, new Oyo (settled by Ile Oyo refugees), Ibadan and Abeokuta. Many of the art industries formerly centered in Ile Oyo, such as weaving and leatherworking, relocated to the cities of Ilorin, Iseyin and new Oyo.[3]

Hausaland before 1800

Among the Hausa, the most influential and powerful city state was Kano.[4] As both an entrepot and production center for trade goods, Kano and its environs has served the trans-Saharan and Western and Central Sudan trade networks for over five hundred years. It is a place where long-distance trading routes converge and where a permanent trader population of diverse origins reside. According to oral traditions, people were first attracted to the Kano area as early as the sixth century due to the iron ore deposits at Dala Hill. The earliest inhabitants of Kano were descendants of a Gaiya blacksmith named Kano who settled at Dala Hill (Yahaya 1984). By AD 999 the Dala Hill area developed into a fortified city which served the political and economic needs of a small kingdom under the leadership of Barbushe, a priest-chief. Barbushe's leadership was superseded by that of Bagauda from Daura, who became the first chief (*sarki*), establishing the *sarauta* title system of administrative authority in which the chief was supported by functional and honorary title holders (Yahaya 1984).

From the eleventh to the fourteenth century Kano underwent a process of internal consolidation and gradual territorial expansion based on improved military technology, which included bows, arrows, spears and other weapons. By the end of the fifteenth century, during Sarki Rumfa's reign, Islam became the official religion of the ruling elite. Along with Islam, other skills and institutions became established, including reading and writing, *sharia* Islamic law, administration and science (Yahaya 1984). Under the influence of the Mande-speaking clerics from Mali, a class of Hausa Islamic scholars (*malamai*), emerged; the *malamai* continue to perform important spiritual and educational roles in Hausa society today.

The fifteenth century was a time when Hausaland opened trade contacts in all directions (Lovejoy 1978: 186–9). During the reign of the fifteenth-century leader, Sarki Yakubu, Kano was actively involved in trade with North Africa, exchanging slaves, cloth and agricultural products for natron, horses and equestrian equipment (Isichei 1983: 86). During the mid-fifteenth-century reign of Sarki Abdulhai Burja, Kano became part of a large long-distance trade network linking the Borno Empire in the east to Ghana in the West (National Commission 1985: 16). Trade with the Western Sudan during this period also contributed to the economic expansion of Hausaland; the Hausa exported tanned leather and reexported salt to Songhai, receiving gold in return. The Mande people from the west introduced art technologies to the Hausa at this time, including strip-weaving, leatherworking and possibly architectural vaulted construction.

By the early fifteenth century Kano had achieved immense political power and prosperity, expanding its territory through conquest. Kano's leader, Kanajeji dem Yafi (1390–1410) is credited with having introduced military equipment, including quilted cotton horse armor (*lifidi*), iron helmets and coats of chain mail (National Commission 1985: 16–17). It is thought that prior to the arrival of the Mande, the Hausa cavalry rode unharnessed ponies without saddles and stirrups. (National Commission 1985: 16–17)

In the late fifteenth century, Kano's political authority and wealth was manifest in the elaborate regalia introduced by Sarki Rumfa (1463–99), who established himself as an important patron of leadership arts. During his reign, Kano was transformed and Rumfa's court became known for its pomp and ceremony. Among the contributions associated with Rumfa's reign were the establishment of the city market; building of city walls; and along with the adoption of Islam, the building of city mosques; royal wife seclusion; month-long Ramadan fasting; and elaborate Sallah festivals marking the end of Ramadan. Certain royal regalia items exclusively associated with the Kano royal family also were introduced, such as sandals and fans trimmed with ostrich plumes, long brass trumpets (*kakaki*) and the red and green attire of palace bodyguards (Yahaya 1984: 22). In order to break with non-Islamic customs and practices, Rumfa moved the royal residence (*gida*) from Dala Hill, sponsoring the building of a new palace (Gidan Rumfa) adjacent to the city mosque.

The Nineteenth-century Sokoto Caliphate

The establishment of the Sokoto Caliphate changed the balance of power in the Central Sudan. During the Fulani jihad started in 1804, the armies of Sheik Usman dan Fodio triggered the establishment of the Sokoto Caliphate. The Hausa, Nupe and some northern Yoruba city states were conquered and became part of the Caliphate under the rule of Fulani administrators. While the Hausa state of Katsina, Kano's major competitor in trade, suffered as a result of directing too much energy toward resisting the jihad, Kano surrendered, resulting in peaceful conditions that encouraged commercial growth and prosperity. The Fulani jihad had a great impact on reshaping the configuration of trade centers in the Central Sudan. Pre-nineteenth-century market centers in Yoruba country, such as Ile Oyo, declined while new trade centers in the Caliphate, such as Islamized Ilorin in Yorubaland and Bida in Nupe country, replaced them. The Fulani jihad brought a political and religious cohesion and stability to an area that had been plagued by interstate warfare. The end result was that during the first half of the nineteenth century autonomous Hausa states, as well as those of Nupe, Ilorin, Adamawa and parts of Bornu, came under control of Sokoto's hegemony. The emergence of a pervasive Islamic ideology reinforced the development of the Sokoto Caliphate, whose states were governed by emissaries of Sheikh Usman dan Fodio. The result was not only Islamic reform, but

'a profound political, social, cultural, religious, economic, demographic, and intellectual revolution' (Adelaye 1971: 21, cited in Prussin 1986: 199).

By 1820 the Sokoto Caliphate consisted of seven major emirates, while ten others were in the process of formation (Last 1988: 562). The Caliph took the title Sarkin Musulmi, the leader of all Muslims, looking to Allah as the source of state authority (Last 1988: 563). Fulani emirate administrators settled in the local capitals and with time became 'Hausacized,' that is, they adopted the Hausa language and were absorbed into Hausa culture (M.G. Smith 1965). Today the ruling class of Hausaland are referred to as 'Hausa-Fulani.'

Encompassing a vast territory, the Fulani-ruled Caliphate, with its headquarters in Sokoto, became the ultimate art patron with different levels of patronage existing within the state. While the highest level was generated by the Caliph (paramount ruler of the Caliphate), the local Hausa-Fulani emirs and titled officials created the greatest demand. The emirs and their deputies, as custodians of the Fulani authority in their respective states, commissioned and purchased the same types of luxury art products as the Caliph himself.

At both the caliphate and emirate levels, a premium was placed on the building arts, particularly for the leader's palace and mosque. The need for luxury cloth and items of prestige dress was immense as was the demand for war equipment. In each emirate, a chief of blacksmiths was appointed whose main duty was to supervise the production of spears, swords, arrowheads and knives for the emir. Although traders were generally free to sell non-military products in the open market, in some emirates like Bida the sale of military goods was subject to state sumptuary rules. Within the Sokoto Caliphate, Kano, Bida and Ilorin, representative of the Hausa, Nupe and Yoruba cultures, provide a focus for our study of art patronage and trade.

Kano Emirate

When a Hausa literary scholar, Suleiman, was appointed the first Hausa emir of Kano (1807–19), he abandoned many of the old Hausa customs and ceremonies (National Commission 1985: 22). His reign was followed by that of Ibrahim Dabo (1819–46), a military officer from the Fulani Sullubawa clan, who held the military title of Galadiman, becoming the first Fulani emir of Kano. He reinstituted many of the earlier cultural traditions abandoned by his predecessor, while adding some innovations of his own to state regalia. These included the royal turban with two protruding ends symbolizing Allah, and the wearing of the Arabic-style burnous hooded cloak (*alkyabba*) by members of the Kano royal family (Bayero 1981; Yahaya 1984: 22). In the second half of the nineteenth century Dabo's second son Emir Abdullahi (1855–83) distinguished himself as a capable leader by encouraging trade and art industries. An active patron of the arts, he sponsored the construction of the Kano Friday mosque and a second palace, Nassarawa, in 1860 (National Commission 1985: 22).

During the nineteenth century, Kano City and the surrounding satellite villages was a thickly populated area and important center of production which went far beyond fulfilling local needs. A wide range of both rural and urban lineage-based artists produced commodities for the local and long-distance markets. The British reported in 1921 that the area around Kano City was so thickly populated that it could not produce necessary staple foods (Gazetteer 1972: 38), because human labor was needed for commodity production for local and long-distance trade markets. Most commodity production was seasonal, as farming took precedence in the wet season. In the dry season, the population of Kano City greatly increased when various kinds of artists immigrated to the city to take advantage of the demand for art products (Pokrant 1982: 88), including textiles and tailored garments, raw hides and tanned leather, and leather sandals and bags – ubiquitous commodities in long-distance trade. Pot production, calabash carving, iron, brass and silversmithing were well-developed industries that served local needs. Production of these commodities was controlled through a hierarchy of appointed chiefs (*sarkin*) that mirrored political levels. For each occupation a *sarkin* represented the concerns of the professions and channeled patronage demands to the producers. When necessary, these heads acted as tribute collectors and coordinators of large-scale production. For example, black-smiths were under a *Sarkin Makera* (head of the blacksmiths). The village *Sarkin Makera* was directly responsible to the district *Sarkin Makera* who was, in turn, responsible to the state *Sarkin Makera,* appointed by the Emir (Kiyawa 1986:73).

In the countryside there were large groups of slaves attached to royal and aristocratic rural estates, who farmed as well as engaged in art production (Johnson 1983). Nupe weavers of blue *saki* cloth (see Chapter 6) were among the slaves who produced cloth for the Kano and Sokoto courts. Some Muslim clerics and wealthy merchants, involved in the kola and cloth trade, owned smaller private estates where agricultural and art products were produced for both local consumption and the export market. Moreover, the landlords of privately owned estates received and provided shelter for long-distance traders, arranging for the purchase and sale of imported goods along with the sale of art goods produced on their own estates (Pokrant 1982: 88).

Bida Emirate

The establishment of Bida emirate followed a period of bitter civil war in the area. In 1795, civil strife broke out in Nupe country after the death of the Nupe king, Etsu Mazun. The king's sons, Jimada and Maija, divided the kingdom and ruled from the towns of Gbara and Raba.[5] In 1805 a Hausa-Fulani Muslim preacher, diviner and charm seller, Mallam Dendo, became part of Maija's court at Raba on the Niger River. With assistance from the Fulani at Ilorin in Yoruba country, Dendo overthrew Maija, reigning at Raba from 1820 to 1833. During this period, Raba developed into a prosperous commercial center. In the early 1830s the Raba market superseded Kulfo as 'one of the largest and best in the whole country' (Mason 1981: 65). While Nupe weavers, wood carvers, blacksmiths and brass-smiths residing in Zagohi, a Nupe island village across from Raba, produced commodities for the market, those manufactured in Raba, especially leather items and woven mats, were considered spectacular compared to those made in Zagohi (Lander 1965 [1832]: 198). The high quality of leather products suggests that Hausa slaves probably dominated Raba's leatherworking industry. In the early nineteenth century, Raba and Ile Oyo, the capital of the Oyo Empire, were important political and commercial centers. Located only fifty miles apart, the Nupe and Yoruba residents engaged in a fluid exchange of ideas and goods (Lander 1965 [1832]: 12–13). The proximity of Raba to Ile Oyo during this period has implications for the history of some of the Nupe art industries including stone bead polishing (*lantana*), which has a Yoruba origin. In the years following Dendo's death, Nupe country was ravaged by a series of battles between Dendo's two sons, Masaba and Usman Zaki. In the 1830s Usman Zaki forced his brother into exile and established himself as the *Etsu Nupe* in Raba. In 1857 Usman became the first Fulani Emir of Nupeland, relocating the Emirate capital from Raba to Bida, a former military camp. Three branches of the Fulani royal dynasty at Bida became established, each branch tracing descent either to one of Mallam Dendo's two sons or his nephew. Each dynastic branch had its own palace located in separate quarters of the city and controlled its own group of artists.

Masaba superseded Usman after his death in 1859; Masaba's reign was characterized by imperialistic expansion, causing the Nupe Empire to reach its maximum size between 1860 and 1900. A skilled warrior, Masaba, was particularly successful in gaining control over Yoruba territories south of the Niger River through conquest and slave raiding. As a result of these military campaigns there was a steady flow of wealth in the form of booty and tribute into Bida. Yoruba slaves were used in the Nupe army and were exchanged for horses from the north and guns from the south (Mason 1981: 196). Another dimension of Masaba is revealed in his role as major art patron, which encouraged the development of Bida art industries. Masaba transformed Bida into a significant cultural center during his reign, bringing artists from Raba and Nupe rural areas as well as Yoruba slave artists from captured territories to Bida. The slaves taken from the fringes of the Nupe Kingdom and northern Yoruba country worked both as agriculturalists and craft producers.

Economically, 'larger towns like Bida prospered because of exactions made on the villages. The villages produced and the towns dispersed of the products' (Mason 1981: 58). In some of these slave-client villages, Yoruba slaves from the Yagba region with valuable skills in textile arts were settled. The textiles produced by these slaves contributed significantly to the development of the nineteenth-century Nupe textile industry.

In the Bida area, artists were organized into professional lineage-based work groups, specializing in men's weaving, wood carving, indigo dyeing, leatherworking, brassworking, embroidery, blacksmithing and glassmaking. The oldest male member of the lineage group became the chief of the work group, responsible for receiving commissions, deciding which artists would execute the commission, organizing large-scale production, supervising and paying workers and maintaining quality control. The work group chief served as a mediator between the artists and the Emir, who ultimately controlled production and distribution.

During his reign, Masaba established a friendly trade relationship with the British. However, in 1897, when the Royal Niger Company lodged complaints against the continuing slave raids by the Nupe into their territory, military campaigns were launched and the Emirate fell, coming under the control of the British. As a result, the prosperity and power of Bida Emirate, contingent upon tribute and imperialistic expansion, began to wane in the early colonial period. The Nupe population decreased and certain art industries, such as brassworking and leatherworking, largely dependent upon the patronage of military leaders declined.

Ilorin Emirate

Ilorin, a northern Yoruba city, was a major conduit for Islam and trade with the north before 1800. By 1817, Ilorin as a city-state broke with the weakening Oyo Empire and looked north to the Muslim world. It became a powerful, prosperous capital of the southernmost emirate in the Caliphate. In 1831 the first emir of Ilorin took office and by 1836 the Ilorin army had invaded and defeated the armies of Ile Oyo marking the collapse of the Oyo Empire. Muslim Yoruba emigrated from small towns in the disintegrating Oyo Empire, resettling in Ilorin for several reasons: to take advantage of the new prosperity; to escape the civil wars and upheavals of the Yoruba successor states; and to pursue Islamic learning (O'Hear 1983). Ile Oyo weavers of strip-woven luxury cloth and potters were among the many artists who relocated to Ilorin. Also resident in Ilorin were Hausa Koranic teachers and artists who had been captured as victims of the jihad war and sold to the Yoruba peoples (Adamu 1978: 127). However, Hausa slaves generally were treated with respect by their Yoruba masters:

> They were allowed to observe their prayers and dress themselves in their own way ... the professionals among them did not lose their skills because ... they were made by their masters to perform the services. (Adamu 1978: 128)

These Hausa artists and Koranic teachers introduced northern techniques and designs, contributing to the development of the Yoruba weaving, embroidery and leatherworking industries, which flourished not only in Ilorin Emirate, but were carried to Yoruba towns such as new Oyo, Iseyin and Ede.

Ilorin continued as an important trade entrepot due to its strategic position along the north-south trade route, connecting with other Caliphate and

Yoruba markets. As a result it maintained a sizeable artist population that served large numbers of potential customers, both locally and through the long-distance trade networks (O'Hear l983: 128). Both raw materials and cheap labor were readily available to support a variety of art industries (O'Hear l983: l28). It was only at the end of the nineteenth century that Ilorin, like Bida, was targeted by the British as a barrier to their control over northern Nigerian trade. In 1897, in the same series of military campaigns that defeated the Nupe, Ilorin fell to the British.

Interconnecting Cloth Traditions

As the above brief history of the Hausa-Nupe-Yoruba region has revealed, many of the artistic traditions of these three ethnic groups are shared. Trade routes that criss-crossed the region moved art commodities freely over cultural boundaries with artists following as entrepreneurs, refugees and slaves.

While distinctions exist, historically there has been much overlap in Hausa, Nupe and Yoruba cloth traditions. The basic forms of women's weaving originated with the Yoruba, who disseminated the technology northward to the Nupe and Hausa by the early twentieth century. Women of all three groups produced a wide cotton cloth on the single-heddle upright loom. In recent years Hausa women still weave the wider cloth sold in the markets as ties to carry babies. Nupe women weavers produce cloth only on a special commission basis, while Yoruba women make a limited amount of cloth in response to ceremonial and ritual demand. All three groups have specialists who dye cloth with indigo, but only the Hausa and Yoruba make patterned indigo cloth. The term *adire* has become a blanket term referring to indigo-dyed cloth, patterned using a variety of design techniques including tie-dye, stenciling, and hand-painting (see Chapter 7). While Yoruba women dyers have produced all types of *adire* since the 1920s, Hausa male dyers in Kano only have produced *adire* since the late colonial period, selling it to rural Hausa women.

Hausa, Nupe and Yoruba male weavers produce narrow-strip cotton cloth on the treadle loom. Evidence suggests that the adoption of the treadle loom was associated with the spread of Islam, reaching the Hausa area first with later adoption by the Nupe and the Yoruba. Of the three ethnic groups, the Hausa have most fully explored the width potential of the narrow-strip format, producing an exceedingly narrow indigo-dyed prestige cloth *yan kura* (Chapter 6), and wide twentieth-century versions, *gwado* and *mudukare* (Chapter 7). The Yoruba, on the other hand, are unsurpassed in the great variety of colors, materials and designs used in creating narrow-strip cloth (Chapter 8). Despite apparent differences, the narrow-strip cloths are grounded in a single tradition of prestige cloth made of cotton and silk, shared by all three groups. We use the term 'caliphate cloth' to describe these shared types of prestige cotton and silk cloths.[6] The narrow-strip caliphate cloth tradition is comprised of the following basic cloth types:

1.   Tan and white striped cloth made from native silk and cotton, called *tsamiya* by Hausa and Nupe, *sanyan* by Yoruba;
2.   Red and white striped cloth made from either silk or cotton, called *barage* by Hausa, *baraze* by Nupe, *alaari* by Yoruba;
3.   Blue and white striped or minutely checked cloth made of cotton, called *saki* by Hausa, *zabo* by Nupe, *etu* by Yoruba;
4.   White cloth made from cotton, called *fari* by Hausa, *edekun* by Nupe, *ala* or *foo* by Yoruba.

The Hausa labels will be used in our discussion of caliphate cloth because the Sokoto Caliphate, encompassing the Hausa, Nupe and Yoruba peoples, is where such cloth first gained importance.

The Aesthetic of Layering and 'Bigness'

Traditions of dress are also shared in the three areas. The basic prestige dress of male gown ensembles and women's wrapper ensembles, are quite similar. For prestige contexts, both men and women adhere to the aesthetic of accumulative layering and 'bigness' to amplify a wearer's physical and symbolic presence (see Chapter 4). For example, Yoruba women wear wrapper ensembles composed of a rectangular wrapper (*iro*), a tailored blouse (*buba*), a headtie (*gele*), and a second rectangular cloth folded on the shoulder (*iboran*) or worn as an over-wrapper. (Figure 5.2) The items in the dress ensembles of Hausa and Nupe women correspond to those of the Yoruba with one exception – a large folded cloth worn on top of the headtie. When a full wrapper ensemble of strip cloth is worn, it adds an imposing weightiness to a woman's body. The layering of cloth, with the multiple twists and folds in wrapper and headtie, adds bulk, projecting an image of physical substance and social importance. In addition, the bulging waistline signals a woman's fertility and significant maternal role. The importance of the aesthetic of bigness is further explored here in the dress of Hausa-Fulani leaders and in the costumes of Yoruba Egungun masquerades.

Figure 5.2. Yoruba women wearing *aso-ebi* wrapper ensembles for chieftaincy celebration, Nigeria. Their *aso-oke* ensembles are made from black and gold, double-wide Super-Q cloth. Source: Al Brooks.

Hausa-Fulani Dress Ensembles

Among the Hausa, the most significant consumer group of luxury cloth is the Hausa-Fulani political elite, who activated the creation of different dress and regalia components. Today, members of the ruling aristocracy and their followers still wear 'big gowns' (*riga* and *girke*) and turbans (*rawani*) to set themselves apart from the rest of the population. A highly embroidered big gown woven from caliphate cloth or made from expensive imported cloth marks a man's membership in, or his ties to, the Hausa-Fulani ruling class. Individual distinctions are signaled by differences in cloth, in the quality of tailoring and embroidery, and by accessories. For public appearances, aristocrats carefully orchestrate their appearance. One method to impress observers is to wear several gowns at once to increase the projected size of the body. In the early twentieth century, an English colonial official in northern Nigeria described the use of layering by a Fulani leader:

The Sarikin Gando had a light green silk cape embroidered with silver lace, then a sky-blue silk robe, then a pink silk robe, then a dark blue silk robe, then a crimson one, and lastly a white silk one. As he turned the sleeves up on to the shoulder you could see them all on top of one another. (Kisch 1910: 104)

Physical bulk, achieved through accumulative layering richly decorated cloths, evokes a sensation of 'aesthetic overload'. Further impressions of layering are projected by the heavily embroidered surfaces of the big gowns, such as the huge pocket on the front of a gown. While it is said to function to hold the wearer's Koran, its main purpose appears to be decorative; it is the part of the gown on which embroiderers focus their technical and artistic virtuosity.

Each individual item of dress and regalia that contributes to the final leadership ensemble is the product of a specific patron-artist relationship, adding particular social and symbolic messages to the total ensemble. The big gowns and turbans, laden with deep cultural meaning, express the wearer's high social status and identification with Islam. Through their patronage and consumption of cloth and other forms of regalia, members of the Fulani political elite have been cultural guardians for this distinctive type of dress, ensuring the maintenance of high qualitative standards for two centuries.

The following example of a Fulani aristocrat's keen awareness of the importance of proper dress for religious and political events demonstrates his perception of the critical role played by dress on state occasions. The late Alhaji Abubakar Bayero, junior brother of the Emir of Kano and Head of Bichi District, was called upon regularly to be a living symbol of his royal position and the Islamic tradition (Perani and Wolff 1992). For Muslim activities, such as participating in the annual Sallah festivals or leading weekly prayers at the Friday mosque, Bayero wore an embroidered white *fari* gown and a white *harsa* turban to express religious piety. When receiving an important visitor or making a public appearance representing the royal family, he usually selected a colored gown. For a 1977 appearance at FESTAC, an international festival of the arts held in Nigeria, Bayero wore a blue and white striped *rigar giwa*, 'gown of the elephant,' made of *gwanda*, a variant of *saki* caliphate cloth. The name *rigar giwa* refers to the enormous size of the gown type (up to 4 yards in width) and to the high political and social importance of the wearer. In his desire for a spectacular gown to meet the protocol expected of the occasion, Alhaji Bayero turned to Nupe artists. He sent his agent to specially commission a Nupe weaver from the Hausa town of Kura to weave the cloth, and to Nupe embroiderers from the Iman's house in Bida to embellish the gown, evidence of the Hausa-Fulani awareness of the excellent reputation held by Nupe weavers and embroiderers. As a high-ranking royal and chairman of the Kano State Arts Council, his choice of the voluminous, beautifully embroidered *rigar giwa* was indeed appropriate. The fact that he wore a gown of Nupe origin for an audience of 'art connoisseurs' revealed the long-standing patronage relationship existing between Nupe artists and the Hausa-Fulani aristocracy.

One of the most impressive gowns in Bayero's wardrobe was a *girke* made of *saki* caliphate cloth. The *girke* gown is distinguished from the *riga* by inserted gussets of cloth, causing the hem to flare out. Each *saki* strip is folded and doubled prior to being edge-stitched and tailored into a gown providing a 'built-in' lining for the gown that increases its thickness and weight and causes it to stand out from the body, thus augmenting the impression of bulk. Hem and sleeves are lined with a border of striped red silk, glimpsed when the sleeves are folded back on the shoulders. The enormous pocket is embroidered with double-layered *aska-biyu* designs made of silk *tsamiya* thread. *Aska biyu* designs ('two knives'), pre-dating the beginning of the Sokoto Caliphate, are characterized by paired elongated triangles pointing downward from the top of the pocket. It is such attention to details of tailoring and embroidery that transform an otherwise ordinary market gown into an exquisite one, deserving to be classified as a 'robe of honor.' Of his *girke* gowns, Bayero remarked that 'to wear these gowns is to be different from other people. When you see them, you know this person is of the royal family' (Bayero 1981).

The bulk and heaviness of the gown of honor weighs the wearer down, enlarging his space while enhancing his dignified, immobile, monumental posture. Caliphate cloth gowns patterned with striped designs reproduce the interacting vertical and horizontal axes of the wearer's body, reminiscent of the way in which the overall grid patterning of *kente* cloth is aligned with the body's armature (Chapter 4). The stripes on the front and back central panels run vertically, while those on the wide sleeves extend horizontally along the outstretched arms of the wearer. When the sleeves are folded back over the shoulder a more dynamic pattern is created. Enveloped by caliphate cloth, the wearer's body becomes defined and framed by the striped panels of the 'big gown'. Whether standing or seated on horseback, a Fulani ruler's gown ensemble serves to visually center, stabilize and focus attention on him as a source of energy and power.[7]

Big gowns are worn with a turban, which can reach up to 4 yards in length, wound around the head several times over a small red cap, and positioned to cover the chin. The height and bulk of the voluminous turban complement the imposing size of the gown. The turban signals the wearer's Muslim identity and his accomplished pilgrimage to Mecca. The particular way in which the white *harsa* turban is wrapped and tied with two upward projecting loops and ends trailing down the back communicates the wearer's membership in the Kano royal family. This form of the turban replicates the Arabic writing of the word 'Allah', reminding the wearer that 'God is over him' (Bayero 1981).

The hooded cloak, *alkyabba*, is the final major dress item necessary to the gown ensemble of Fulani royals. (Figure 5.3) Of the items of aristocratic dress, it appears to be the most recent, probably adopted from the Middle East sometime in the late nineteenth century. Hooded cloaks are made of imported luxury cloths, such as wool, silk and velvet. They are embellished with arabesque designs of shiny floss thread, stitched on to the surface. While decorated cloaks may be commissioned and purchased from Kano embroiderers who specialize in fashioning 'Mecca-styled' clothing, they are also acquired from North Africa and the Middle East. Compared to embroidered gowns, the decoration of the hooded cloak appears to be more open to innovation. A black wool cloak in Bayero's wardrobe, for example, is distinguished by the motif of a British-styled crown, a pattern he innovated by requesting a Kano embroiderer to copy it from a Middle Eastern cloak gifted to him on a visit to Jordan. While all other items in the gown ensemble belong to the state, the hooded cloak can be passed to a leader's heir, a practice which may be explained by its more recent addition to the gown ensemble (Fosu 1982).

The full impact of Fulani-Hausa aristocratic dress ensembles is most evident in equestrian displays where a leader's own body on the elevating support of his decorated horse epitomizes aesthetic extravagance. A Fulani ruler or aristocrat wearing a turban, several layers of embroidered gowns over bulky, colorfully embroidered drawstring trousers, and a flowing cloak embellished with shiny arabesque patterns, mounted on a horse layered with multiple saddleblankets of varied materials, patterns and origins, strikes a splendid spectacle. Not only does accumulative layering enlarge the physical girth of the mounted rider, but the visual brilliance and textural complexity is enriched by a scintillating surface, sparkling and shining in a kaleidoscope of color and light. Together the horse and rider blend into a single entity, creating a powerful icon of political presence, power and authority represented in sculptural traditions across West Africa for the last millennium (Cole 1989: 116–35). Elevating the leader's visibility above the masses, the horse functions as a moving throne, reminiscent of the historical foundation of the state's power – the strength of its cavalry forces.

For Sallah celebrations, marking the end of the Ramadan month of fasting, the elaborately dressed emir is the focal point in a sea of well-dressed aristocratic title-holders, loyal servants, district officers and village heads who assemble in their hundreds to acknowledge the leader's authority in an expression of state solidarity. The Emirate's social and political structure visually unfolds during the festival procession as groups of lavishly attired mounted riders and attendants on foot parade between palace and mosque, culminating finally in the appearance of the mounted ruler under an impressive twirling state umbrella.

Figure 5.3. The late Alhaji Abubukar Bayero, Head of Bichi District in Kano State, in gown ensemble consisting of an embroidered gown made from white factory-made cloth, a *harsa* turban and a hooded cloak made from imported brown silk, Bichi, Nigeria. Source: Judith Perani and Norma Wolff.

Yoruba Egungun Ensembles

While the layered dress ensembles of the Fulani-Hausa political elite are tied to public displays associated with a Muslim context, the spectacular layered cloth costumes which dress Yoruba Egungun ancestral spirits, (see Chapter 3) perform at annual festivals to honor the ancestors and funerals to bless and punish the living, and garner prestige for the individuals and lineages sponsoring the masqueraders.[8] The cloth of the costumes plays a critical role in capturing and projecting the otherworldly spirit by enclosing it in a man-made cage of cloth. A range of cloths, including handwoven strip-cloth, velvets, damasks, wax prints and indigo resist-dyed cloths may be used for the costume.

While there are many forms of Egungun, almost all wear costumes designed to increase the sacred space occupied by the masquerader.[9] Ancestors, like leaders, are expected to appear in larger-than-life dimensions. One of the oldest types of Egungun masquerader, owned by town chiefs in the Oyo region, is called *Alago*; it is distinguished by a loose, sack-like costume constructed of imported cloth and strip weave used in shrouds. The dignified *Alago* moves slowly, trailing a cloth train extending many feet behind the masquerader to further enhance its beauty and power. The 'elephant ancestor,' *Egun erin*, (described in Chapter 3) is the largest of the Egungun in the southern Yoruba city of Abeokuta. (see Figure 3.2) Layer upon layer of beautiful cloth, often replenished on a yearly basis, with accessories that feature sparking materials such as mirrors, beads, metallic surfaces and brilliant colors, make the *Egun erin* one of the most admired of the ancestral masquerades. Bigness is further accentuated by the carved mask with elongated rabbitlike ears, making it tower over the audience. In a stately dance, the *Erin* masquerader whirls, causing cloth panels to impressively extend. Another type of Egungun, *Paka*, popular in Oyo, has a wood framework from which are suspended layers of brightly colored appliquéd cloth panels, dramatically swirled in dance to create a 'breeze of blessing' (Fitzgerald 1995: 57).

> In motion, primarily whirling, the panels fly outward on the wind, extending the ancestral apparition in space and, in effect, fanning the surrounding audience with the unseen purifying and protecting powers of the afterworld. (Drewal 1979: 195)

Religion and aesthetics come together in the construction of an Egungun costume. The fabrication of an Egungun masquerader involves a series of ritual and art patronage transactions. Initially a cult patron who becomes the 'owner' of an Egungun masquerader assumes the obligation after consultation with a diviner, who mediates an ancestor's desire to appear as an Egungun.[9] The owner then engages in a series of commissioning transactions, beginning with a tailor who specializes in costume fabrication. This often involves patchworking and the addition of elaborate appliqué and embroidered patterns to the cloth panels, each pattern adding to the masquerader's layered mystery. An indigenous medical practitioner then is commissioned to prepare the protective charms and amulets to be attached to the cloth, further empowering the masquerader. The owner commissions a wooden mask if required by the Egungun spirit. Throughout the life history of an Egungun masquerader, the owner continues to refurbish and repair it. Most important, the owner sees that periodic sacrifices and rituals are carried out to maintain and enhance the power of the costume, which essentially becomes a kind of shrine to the ancestral spirit.

In public appearances, Egungun masqueraders are the focus of admiration and awe. Like the Hausa-Fulani leaders, these personified ancestors, usually with surrounding attendants to expand their sacred arena, are visually spectacular personas. Displaying both bigness and shine in layered cloth dress with sparkling attachments, Egungun masqueraders illuminate and glorify the past.

Notes

1. See Morgan (1983) for a detailed description of the characteristics of the natural and cultural landscapes of these areas.

2. The eleventh-century existence of indigenous strip-woven cloth produced on the treadle loom is supported by the textile fragments found in the Sanga region of Mali (about 1300 km west of Kano) associated with Tellem burials. See Bolland 1992.

3. Weavers working in new Oyo today claim descent from Ile Oyo refugees (Clarke 1996: 15), as do those of Iseyin. Woodcarvers in Abeokuta also claim that distinction.

4. The *Kano Chronicle* is the most important source about early Kano history, recording information about the reigns of Kano leaders from the arrival of the legendary Bagauda in the tenth century up until the Fulani jihad in the early nineteenth century. The *Kano Chronicle* was assembled from brief histories written in Arabic during the seventeenth century, probably by Arabs residing in Kano.

5. According to oral tradition the Nupe glass industry had been established at Gbara since the fifteenth century.

6. See Perani (1992) and Perani and Wolff (1992) for detailed descriptions of the use of caliphate cloth. See Kriger (1988) for historical insights into the use of 'caliphate robes of honor' in the Sokoto Caliphate.

7. The visual emphasis on the intricately layered bulk of prestige materials, resulting

in an impression of bigness as seen in royal Hausa-Fulani gowns, exhibits a parallel with the finest examples of Asante *kente* cloth, characterized by a layering of densely worked inlaid patterns made from silk thread.

8. See special issue of *African Arts*, vol. XI, no. 3, on Egungun traditions in several regions of Yorubaland.

9. The owner of a masquerader is the person called by the ancestral spirits to create an *Egungun* costume. The owner may wear the costume and be controlled by the ancestral spirit in performance, or accompany the masquerader in ritual contexts. While only men wear the costumes, women may own them.

6

Patterns of Production and Consumption in Nineteenth-Century Luxury Cloth Traditions

Historically, the city-states of the Sokoto Caliphate and the Oyo Empire were linked through an interdependent economic network, and as a result shared cloth and dress traditions. In the fourteenth and fifteenth centuries, Islamized Mande-speaking clerics and traders from Mali introduced Islam, weaving and leatherworking technologies as well as tailored garments to the Hausa people during the course of their trade contact with the Hausa. Through the trade networks these arts spread throughout Hausaland and south through Nupe territory to the Yoruba.

By the nineteenth century, two luxury cloth traditions were particularly well-developed in the region, serving the patron needs of leaders and the marketplace, greatly contributing to the economic prosperity of the Sokoto Caliphate. These are 'caliphate cloth' (narrow-strip silk and cotton prestige cloth) produced by Hausa, Nupe and Yoruba weavers, and *yan kura* cloth (indigo-dyed and beaten narrow-strip prestige cloth), a unique Hausa art form.[1] These cloth traditions, that crossed ethnic boundaries as part of wide-scale long-distance trade and outgroup patronage, provide examples of the fluid inter-ethnic relationships between art producers, patrons and consumers in a regional context.

Since 1800, caliphate cloth and *yan kura* cloth have functioned as important mediators of cultural meaning in northern and central Nigeria, intersecting with the social, political and economic spheres of the Sokoto Caliphate. When transformed into dress, these cloth types played a critical role in supporting and communicating the Caliphate Islamic ideology. Cloth was regarded as a repository of wealth and social meaning by Fulani emirate rulers, who manipulated cloth and dress to facilitate specific social and political goals. As we have seen, the Fulani Caliph of Sokoto and the emirate rulers placed great value on the mediating function of dress to express the Muslim wearer's high social status.

The overlapping demand of leaders and the marketplace was critical in shaping the development of the luxury cloth industries. Throughout the Sokoto Caliphate commissioning-patrons and consumer-patrons including political and economic elites, traders, market agents, as well as weavers, tailors, dyers, beaters and embroiderers, were part of a complex network of luxury textile production, distribution and consumption. Textile production was complex, with a specialization of labor not discerned by early observers, such as Henrich Barth in the mid- nineteenth century. Philip Shea, an economic historian who has conducted extensive research in Kano Emirate, is the first scholar to carefully scrutinize the dynamics of cloth production and distribution in the region (Shea 1975). He has argued for an examination of the different types of linkages binding Hausa specialists who carry out the production steps of cloth manufacture to the consumers of their products, in order to better understand the dynamics of Hausa textile production (Shea 1983).

> We must look closely at the set of relations which existed between and among the various direct producers, those who organized and controlled production, and the ultimate consumers . . . What we really have to consider then, is not just technology but also configurations of production and the ability of different systems [or areas or polities] to adjust and adopt their configurations over time. (Shea 1983: 94–5)

Leader Demand and Market Demand

Both caliphate cloth and *yan kura* cloth were distributed and used for centuries over much of West Africa, particularly in the Sudan and Sahara areas. Using the treadle loom, weavers in the Sokoto Caliphate were producing caliphate cloth at least since the late eighteenth century, and *yan kura* cloth since the fifteenth century, for the ruling class and the export market. Depending upon for whom the cloths were made, they were regarded differently. Throughout the region, Hausa-Fulani leaders officially adopted a northern-styled ceremonial attire, consisting of a long flowing embroidered gown tailored of caliphate cloth (Figure 6.1), and a turban of gauzy indigo-dyed *yan kura* cloth. Over the centuries, the Hausa and Fulani developed a distinctive, impressive style of dress worn by Muslim men of status across West Africa into the twentieth century. The adoption of Islamic dress was a statement of religious piety, clearly identifying the wearer with the interests of the new Muslim states (Arnoldi l995: 127).[2] By the nineteenth century, the Hausa-Fulani political elite had generated an important source of art patronage, greatly stimulating an increase in luxury cloth production and guaranteeing high qualitative standards.

Embroidered gowns and turbans were used by state leaders to accomplish specific political goals, regarded as the ultimate gifts in a complex gift-giving system. Throughout the Sokoto Caliphate, gowns were sent by the emirates as tribute payment to the Sokoto court, where they were stored in the treasury to be used as needed. Gowns were essential to the turbanning ceremonies in which the Emir bestowed new titles on palace officials and servants, defining expected obligations and responsibilities. They were also used to seal alliances. A well-worn gown, one that passed as a gift, changing ownership as it moves through diplomatic channels, acquires a rich cultural *patina*, encoding a history of inter-emirate linkages, political alliances and obligations with each transfer of ownership.

When embroidered caliphate cloth gowns were made for the use of the political elite, special care was taken during every phase of production, from spinning and weaving to tailoring and embroidery. The highest grade of caliphate cloth was tightly woven from finely spun yarn for the Hausa-Fulani leaders.[3] These gowns were carefully tailored, lined, hemmed (see Figure 6.3) and often extensively embroidered, representing a much greater financial investment in both material and labor than the unlined, unhemmed, moderately embroidered counterparts made for the market. The embroidery of the finest gowns was done by Nupe artists. Up to five Nupe tailor-embroiderers, each specializing in a different type of stitch, might work on a single gown for a Hausa-Fulani leader or high ranking official. In the early 1900s, it was noted that a tailor using a needle made of bone spent up to two months embroidering a gown for the Emir of Bida, the Etsu Nupe (Banfield 1905). As major items of Caliphate leadership dress these gowns, distinguished by the incorporation of luxury materials and excellent workmanship, were regarded as 'robes of honor', a designator given to important high-status official garments throughout the Islamic world since the eighth century AD (Kriger 1988: 52). The palace treasuries of Islamic states might hold hundreds of these 'robes of honor' to be awarded on state occasions by political superiors to subordinates for recognition of services rendered.

Similar standards of quality were applied to the *yan kura* cloth made for Hausa-Fulani rulers, as well as for some segments of the export trade. *Yan kura* is made from *turkudi*, an extremely narrow gauze-like cotton strip-cloth, dyed with indigo. The highest quality *yan kura* requires finely spun thread and a shiny metallic-like blue-black color. *Yan kura* is mostly used

Figure 6.1. Four Nupe titled officials wearing hand-embroidered gowns of *tsamia* caliphate cloth and turbans made from red factory cloth for the 1990 Sallah festival in Bida, Nigeria. The second man from the left wears a *luru* blanket draped over his shoulder. Source: Judith Perani.

Figure 6.2. Etsu Nupe (Emir of Bida Emirate) wearing big gown ensemble with *yan kura* turban at 1990 Sallah festival in Bida, Nigeria. Titled officials, wearing embroidered gown ensembles, gather to pay homage to the emir. Source: Judith Perani.

for turbans. A turban of deeply dyed shining *yan kura* is one of the most distinctive symbols of the political elite, worn with a big gown to identify membership in a royal Hausa-Fulani family or a connection to the aristocracy. The wrapping of the head is an act of Muslim piety, 'for it is said that Mohammed himself wore a turban' (Arnoldi 1995: 127).

Several yards of fabric are wrapped around the head in numerous turns over a small red cap and positioned to cover the lower face. The *yan kura* turban (*rawani*), is worn by emirs and titled officials for a variety of different political contexts. (Figure 6.2) Like the big gowns, cloth for the *rawani* turban can be gifted to persons of lower rank. For example, the personal messenger of the late District Head of Bichi (discussed in Chapter 5) always took pride in wearing the *yan kura* turban presented to him by his superior. The white *harsa* turban, worn by royals to indicate Muslim identity, is made of undyed *turkudi* strips, although in recent years it is sometimes made from imported

Figure 6.3. Titled Nupe official mounted on horse, wearing gown of *saki* cloth lined with red *barage* cloth for 1990 Sallah festival in Bida, Nigeria. Source: Judith Perani.

cloth. In Kano State, to use *turkudi* in its undyed state as a turban is an exclusive prerogative of the royal family and certain district heads connected to the family. The white *harsa* turban, as an indicator of religious piety and status, is worn at religious activities, including leading prayers at Friday mosque and Muslim Sallah processions. On occasion, Hausa-Fulani leaders request big gowns made from white *turkudi*. However, most white *turkudi* gowns are made for the export market, as the main patrons for these big gowns are wealthy Tuareg outgroup patrons from Niger.

Ultimately, the livelihood of caliphate and *yan kura* cloth producers was tied to the market. In contrast to special commissions by rulers, in the context of the marketplace, the luxury dimension of cloth was de-emphasized as it primarily was seen as an economic commodity, woven, tailored and traded for profit. As might be expected, a wider range in qualitative standards existed in cloth produced for the local and export markets than in the cloth commissioned by leaders. Among the caliphate cloth types *saki* was the most important in trade. Rolls of blue and white checked *saki* caliphate cloth as well as gowns, made by Nupe weavers and embroiderers were distributed widely throughout the Sokoto Caliphate and traded from Kano into northern Ghana in exchange for kola nuts. *Saki* gowns were greatly prized there and seen as unfailing passports of entry into northern Ghanaian courts, commonly presented by traders as gifts to Ghanaian kings and chiefs (Adamu 1978: 60–1). In response to this demand some Nupe weavers and embroiderers and Hausa dyers even emigrated to northern Ghana to manufacture *saki* cloth for leaders (Adamu 1978: 73). *Saki* gowns were also traded east into Bornu for natron. In addition, *saki* cloth and gowns along with *yan kura* cloth moved north into the desert Tuareg markets of Niger, in exchange for salt. The Tuareg people used the indigo-dyed *yan kura* cloth for turbans, men's gowns and women's wrappers. From Niger, some *yan kura* cloth was traded to Mali and North Africa.

In the nineteenth century, leadership and market demands for caliphate and *yan kura* cloth types led to localized production centers linking the Hausa, Nupe and Yoruba into a coordinated inter-regional trade network. One such center of production and trade was Kano Emirate.

Nineteenth-century Textile Production and Trade in Kano Emirate, Nupe Country and the Oyo Empire

Kano Emirate

The city of Kano (as described in Chapter 5) was traversed by a web of trade routes and for centuries has been an important center of production, where 'commerce and manufacture go hand in hand' (Barth I 1851: 510). It has been said that Kano clothed half of West Africa in the nineteenth century (Robinson 1897). Most of the Kano cloth that entered nineteenth-century local and regional trade was not woven in the city, but in the surrounding countryside or in the Nupe and Yoruba regions. The situation today remains relatively unchanged. The surrounding countryside is where most of the cloth dyeing and beating and all of the weaving occurs. Today, only a small portion of cloth made by rural Kano weavers is sold in Kano City's major Kurmi market. Most rural weaving villages sell their cloth directly to itinerant long-distance traders who enter it into the long-distance trade.

The centuries old heterogeneous character of Kano's cloth industries continues today with Hausa, Nupe and Arab textile workers and market agents involved. The use of the term 'Kano cloth' in the literature in fact camouflaged the role played by nineteenth-century Nupe weavers in developing Kano's luxury caliphate cloth industry. Several varieties of caliphate cloth produced in Kano Emirate were made exclusively by Nupe weavers who resided in the Kano region.[4] In the nineteenth century groups of Nupe freemen weavers emigrated to Kano to take advantage of an expanding textile market, while others were taken as slaves during the Hausa-Nupe wars (Clapperton 1829: 113). This assimilation of free and slave Nupe labor into the Kano weaving industry helped to expand Kano's export textile trade, not only in direct production, but also by enlarging and cementing the network of Kano's commercial relationships with the Nupe and Yoruba to the south (Shea 1983: 106–7).

Niger River Nupe Weaving Centers and Bida Emirate

In spite of the emigration of large numbers of Nupe weavers to Kano emirate, many remained in Nupeland, maintaining the Nupe reputation as excellent textile artists. Before the Fulani conquest of Nupe in the mid-nineteenth century, Nupe weavers and embroiderers mainly lived in small towns situated along the northern and southern banks of the Niger River. Nineteenth-century travel accounts described large-scale weaving activity and high production of quality embroidered gowns in the towns of Kulfo, Raba and Egga (Clapperton: 137, 169; Lander 1965 [1832]: 197). Although accounts stressed the importance of these towns as textile production centers, they did not specify the ethnic identity of the textile artists. The riverain location suggests that both Nupe and Yoruba textile artists were involved in the Nupe textile industry.[5] Like the weaving villages in the Kano countryside, these Nupe communities were important to regional trade, serving as commercial links between the Hausa and the Yoruba.

Throughout the Sokoto Caliphate, emirate rulers purchased large stocks of embroidered gowns manufactured in Egga, Raba and Bida for palace treasuries. The southern Nupe town of Egga, near the confluence of the Niger and Benue Rivers, was especially important as a textile production center until the late nineteenth century.[6] Unlike Raba, Egga resisted Fulani rule, but still paid annual tribute to the Caliphate rulers. The Egga textile industry was directly involved in regional trade relationships, including the Ghana trade (M. Johnson 1973: 361, Whitford 1967). Egga weavers specialized in manufacturing silk gowns from unwrought red *alharini* European waste silk, imported from Tripoli via Kano, along with gowns made from indigenous *tsamiya* silk,[7] for Fulani rulers in Raba as well as for trade to other emirates (M. Johnson l973: 361).

In l857, when Bida became an emirate, skilled weavers and embroiderers were resettled in Bida. A large percentage of these weavers were former Yoruba slaves, taken captive during the early nineteenth-century Nupe-Yoruba wars. The incorporation of Yoruba weavers into the Bida weaving industry paralleled the assimilation of Nupe slave weavers into the Kano weaving industry. Throughout the Caliphate much of the volume of art productivity was made possible by slave plantation labor (Kriger 1993). Such assimilations were a strategy to centralize production, and to expand and unify Caliphate weaving industries to meet increased market demand for embroidered gowns and the intensified demand for luxury garments by Hausa-Fulani leaders. These resettlement programs also fostered interethnic and interregional linkages. By the late twentieth century, some Bida weavers still claimed Yoruba descent.

Many of the nineteenth-century Yoruba weavers resettled in Bida came from the Yagba region of northeastern Yoruba country near Egga. The northern Yoruba city of Ile Oyo already was renowned for silk cloth production in the late eighteenth century. It appears that knowledge of weaving silk was one of the special skills that the nineteenth-century Yoruba weavers introduced to the Nupe. It also seems likely that the Yoruba were the first weavers to use the treadle loom for weaving silk in this region. The resettled Yoruba silk weavers encountered a well-established Nupe tradition of cotton *saki* cloth weavers. No doubt, the latter were receptive to learning silk weaving from the newly arrived Yoruba and became proficient in weaving red silk *barage* and tan *tsamiya* caliphate cloth. This suggests that the vast majority of silk gowns exported to the northern emirates in the second half of the nineteenth century from Bida were either woven by Yoruba weavers or by Yoruba-trained Nupe weavers. The silk cloth was used for luxury gowns which were expertly stitched and decorated by Nupe tailors and embroiderers, who gained a reputation among the Hausa-Fulani elite for producing exceptional gowns, overshadowing the skills of Yoruba weavers.

Beginning with British anthropologist Nadel's research in Bida during the 1930s, scholars have perpetuated the idea that nineteenth-century Fulani leaders organized Nupe artists into craft guilds,[8] a term which has not been consistently defined or employed. Although Nadel applied the term guild to some Nupe industries (1942: 257–85), closer examination does not suggest the existence of Nupe craft guilds. Instead, the essential labor unit for Nupe artists, recognized by Nadel, was the hereditary family group (*efako*), a very common way to organize close kin for production in Africa. Nupe artist workshops, based on an extended family unit and located in the family house, recognized the oldest male member as negotiator and family representative, a position that Nadel erroneously associated with the occupational title of guild head. The family head, who was a master artist himself, represented his family of specialists (such as weavers, blacksmiths and glassworkers) whenever necessary at the Fulani court. He negotiated commissions, coordinating and overseeing production by family members to ensure that a court order was completed on schedule and that quality standards were maintained. At other times, in the absence of commissions from the court, family members worked on an individual basis although arts such as blacksmithing, brassworking and glassmaking always required group cooperation in production. Within families, it was common for individual artists to specialize and become proficient in producing certain products. In the case of textiles, a weaver might specialize in specific styles of cloth, such as *saki* or *barage*.

The Oyo Empire

By the late eighteenth century, Ile Oyo, the capital of the Oyo Empire, was already a major center for the production of *aso-oke*, the Yoruba strip cloth equivalent of caliphate cloth. As we saw in Chapter 5, the technology of strip-woven cloth production came from the north, spreading southward from the Hausa and Nupe peoples, probably becoming established among the Yoruba by the seventeenth century. Around this time, northern-styled Hausa and Nupe ready-made clothing was also being imported into Ile Oyo from northern cities, and the wearing of Muslim dress was increasingly common. Initially, the wearing of flowing northern-style embroidered robes was subject to sumptuary laws.

> In ancient times the gowns were made very plain and were of purely native manufacture. They were without embroidery on the breast and around the neck as at present; only kings and chiefs wore gowns made of superior stuffs richly embroidered. (S. Johnson 1921: 110)

In the 1820s, Clapperton and Lander remarked upon the appearance of the Alafin of Oyo, attired in a northern-styled gown (Adamu 1978: 126). By 1861, the British explorer, Richard Burton, observed that in the Yoruba city of Abeokuta the best attired people were Muslims, and a broad segment of the population was wearing tailored clothing (Adamu 1978: 126).

Nineteenth-century Muslim weavers in Ile Oyo specialized in producing both cotton and silk cloths for both local consumption and trade to other Yoruba towns and to the southern coast (O'Hear 1983: 125; Law 1977: 204–8). In 1823 J. Adams, who traded along the west coast of Africa as far south as the Congo, observed that 'the cloth manufactured in Hio [Oyo] is superior, both for variety of pattern, colour and dimensions, to any made in neighbouring countries' (Law 1977: 204). Adams may have included in his assessment the beige silk *sanyan* and scarlet silk *alaari* luxury strip-cloth manufactured in Ile Oyo at least since the eighteenth century and possibly as early as the seventeenth century. The beige and scarlet colors of *sanyan* and *alaari*, along with the deep indigo blue of *etu* cloth (the Yoruba equivalents of Hausa *tsamiya*, *barage* and *saki* cloth), are believed to possess moral as well as aesthetic qualities (Euba 1986). To this day, to wear garments of *sanyan*, *alaari* and *etu* cloth is the ultimate visual expression of ethnic pride and self worth for many Yorubas. Garments in these colors are regularly worn by kings, chiefs, priests of indigenous cults and individuals who value the traditions of the past (Wolff and Wahab 1995: 11).

As a consequence of the early nineteenth-century political upheavals and trade disruptions associated with the Fulani jihad, Ile Oyo experienced a 'severe commercial depression' (Law 1977: 281). Weavers moved from the town, resettling in new nineteenth-century Yoruba communities such as Iseyin, Ilorin and Ede where they continued to produce caliphate cloth. In particular, Iseyin quickly developed into a recognized center of *aso-oke* production, a reputation it still holds today (Wolff and Wahab 1996).

Caliphate Cloth and Caliphate Gowns

The finest 'robes of honor' which circulated in the Sokoto Caliphate were, as already described, made of the finest caliphate cloth and were heavily embossed with embroidery. The lavish embroidered gowns known today emerged from a much more modest tradition, evidenced by the few nineteenth-century examples found in European museums. The earliest tailored gowns were probably not embroidered at all, but covered with Koranic script written in ink directly onto the cloth as protective 'prayer' gowns for potentially dangerous conditions. The written script was eventually replaced with minimal stitched embroidered designs as the gowns' military function lessened, and they increasingly became associated with a ceremonial context of prestige. The fact that stitched embroidered patterns directly followed drawn designs is reinforced by the fact that many embroiderers are also Koranic scholars. The outgrowth of a ceremonial function from a military one is more easily understood once it is realized that many of the high-ranking Hausa-Fulani office holders earned their status and position through exceptional military accomplishments.

Color is a major factor in distinguishing between the types of Hausa caliphate gowns (*riga*). The colors of the oldest caliphate gowns – white, red, beige and deep blue – most likely reflect more than the availability of local dyes and imported yarn, suggesting a deep-seated intent to convey symbolic meaning. The color range of caliphate gowns can be regarded as an expression of the ritually significant tripartite color scheme discussed in Chapter 2. For the Hausa, Nupe and Yoruba, white cloth and beige-colored cloth fall into the range of 'white'. The 'red' category of gowns were first made of imported magenta silk yarn from North Africa and later with indigenous cotton and silk thread dyed locally. 'Black' caliphate gowns are those made with deep indigo-dyed yarn in a checked or striped pattern or from white cloth subjected to numerous immersions in an indigo dye vat. No doubt this triadic color scheme intersected with deeply-held cultural attitudes and beliefs about the power of certain colors to enhance purity, convey power, or offer protection. For the Hausa, red symbolizes danger, but also connotes strength and bravery. White is associated with optimism and happiness, and more importantly, symbolizes Islamic piety. Black is associated with wealth, maturity and elder status (Zarruk 1978: 65–70).

The tradition of caliphate cloth includes several types of narrow-strip cotton and silk cloths, woven by the Hausa, Nupe and Yoruba. The oldest types are *fari*, a plain white cotton cloth; *kore*, a glazed indigo cotton cloth; *saki*, a minutely checked or striped blue and white cotton cloth; *barage*, a striped red and white silk and cotton cloth, and *tsamiya*, a striped beige and white silk and cotton cloth. Caliphate cloths have a plain weave structure, measure one to four inches in width, and are either plain in color or simply decorated with an arrangement of warp-faced stripes or checks. *Fari* cloth, the first type to be fashioned into big gowns, maintained its popularity for several centuries. The requirement of white for ceremonial Muslim dress, along with the widespread use of handwoven white cloth for burial shrouds (*likafani*), created a constant and regular source of patronage for both Hausa and Nupe weavers (Lamb and Holmes 1981: 104).

A *fari* gown (*rigar fari*) is transformed into a *rigar kore* gown by dyeing it with indigo to produce a glossy surface and deep black color. In the mid-nineteenth century, the *rigar kore* was being exported by the Nupe to Kano for re-export along the long distance trade routes. By the turn of the century, Kano textile artists had begun to make the *rigar kore* (Barth 1851 I: 512). Certain Hausa villages (Dawakin Tofa, Dal and Gwarzo) in the Kano area specialized in this type of gown, directing their production and distribution to the Kanuri market in Bornu (Shea 1975). The literature has several references to wearing the black *kore* gown over a white *fari* gown, a practice called *hadi* in Hausa, meaning 'putting together things of different quality.' A 1904 photograph by Canadian missionary Banfield illustrates a Nupe Koranic scholar in such dress (Kriger 1988: 52).

One of the most commonly mentioned gowns in nineteenth-century accounts is the indigo blue *rigar saki*. *Saki* cloth is made with indigo-dyed yarns with a small amount of white yarns used to produce faint narrow stripes or checked patterns. *Saki* which means 'guinea fowl', referring to the cloth's speckled appearance that resembles the plumage of the bird, (see Chapter 4) constituted a large portion of the general output of the nineteenth-century Nupe textile industry as well as the Kano export trade. In pre-colonial Nigeria the *rigar saki* was only worn by individuals of the highest political and social stature. (Figure 6.3) Occasionally, the prestige value of *saki* cloth was further enhanced by incorporating narrow strips of unwrought red *alharini* silk into the cloth. Such gowns, known as *saki harir*, were one of the specialties of the Nupe weaving center at Egga (Allen and Thompson 1848: 100).[9]

Barage, another type of caliphate cloth was woven with red *alharini* silk. *Barage* cloth is characterized by a large white stripe often flanked by narrow black and yellow stripes set against a red silk ground. In the early nineteenth century Lander remarked that 'of the different colored *tobes* [robes] worn by men none looked as well as those of a deep crimson color on some of the horsemen' (Lander 1965 [1832]: 111). Gowns tailored from red *barage* cloth embellished with green embroidery create an impressive spectacle when worn by titled Fulani aristocrats today. Regarded as an auspicious color, red possesses protective properties, whereas green symbolizes the vigor of youth and the fertility of farm and pastoral lands (Zarruk 1978: 69). In pre-colonial Nigeria *barage* gowns were commonly presented as gifts to body guards and palace servants responsible for protecting the emir.

Gowns of beige indigenous silk yarn (*rigar tsamiya*), along with *barage* gowns, made by Nupe and Yoruba weavers, were the most highly esteemed and expensive of the caliphate gowns in Hausaland. The production of a *tsamiya* gown exemplifies the complex interdependent trade web, which has tied Hausa, Nupe and Yoruba together economically. *Tsamiya* silk, found in northern and central Nigeria, is processed from the cocoons of the *anaphe* moth and spun into yarn; both cocoons and yarn were exported from the

Kano countryside. Although some of the silk thread was sold in Kano's Kurmi Market to Kano embroiderers, the bulk was purchased by long-distance traders who carried it south to Nupe and Yoruba spinners and weavers. The Nupe and Yoruba weavers in Egga excelled in weaving *tsamiya* cloth, and Egga's reputation as a center of silk weaving was overshadowed only after the emergence of Bida Emirate (Frobenius 1968 [1913] I: 430). Unlike the Nupe and Yoruba, however, the Hausa did not develop an interest in weaving silk. Since the nineteenth century and possibly earlier, the southern-directed trade of *tsamiya* cocoons and yarn from Kano was counterbalanced by a northern directed trade route in Nupe *tsamiya* cloth and embroidered gowns. Rolls of *tsamiya* cloth were purchased by Nupe and Hausa embroiderers, who tailored the cloth into gowns and embroidered them with finely executed designs for Hausa-Fulani leaders. Some of the completed gowns were sold to Hausa traders who redistributed them along the trade routes.

The *Yan* Kura Cloth Industry

A second older luxury cloth tradition, *yan kura*, was shaped by the same art patron and market demands as caliphate cloth during the pre-colonial and colonial periods. Shortly after the Hausa adopted the treadle loom in the fourteenth century, they developed a unique product, *yan kura*, a gauzy cotton cloth made of half-inch strips stitched together. This cloth is called *turkudi* in its undyed white stage, and *yan kura* after it has been dyed numerous times and beaten with indigo powder until it turns a rich dark blue color. The production of *yan kura* cloths had grown to a huge industry in the nineteenth century, due to patronage from not only Hausa leaders but also from outgroup patrons served by long-distance trade. It has been estimated that in the nineteenth century there were at least tens of thousands, if not hundreds of thousands, of weavers and dyers in the Kano region participating in long-distance trade (M. Johnson 1983: 10), many of them involved in the *yan kura* luxury cloth industry. Passing from textile artists to landlords or household heads, some cloth was sold in local markets, but most was sold to country-based long-distance traders who resold it to terminal consumer-patrons throughout the Sahel region of West Africa, particularly the desert pastoral Tuareg. Hausa *yan kura* cloth is a good example of an art product whose production was largely fueled by the market principle. Operating as a commodity in an economic arena of value, *yan kura* had centuries of use as a valued item of exchange and as a desirable consumer good for outgroup patrons.

The *yan kura* cloth industry greatly contributed to Kano's reputation as a textile production center in the pre-colonial period. The tremendous expansion and prosperity of the *yan kura* industry was largely due to the breadth and volume of outgroup consumer-patrons of whom the Tuareg in the Sahel were among the most important. A steady but more limited source of patronage came from the nineteenth-century Hausa-Fulani emirs of the Sokoto Caliphate, who commissioned and purchased *yan kura* cloth for *rawani* turbans (Figure 6.2). This patron group primarily directed their patronage to the indigo dyers and cloth beaters residing in Kano City who were closely linked to the palace and were almost entirely dependent upon royal patronage for their livelihood. Because the political elite demanded the best, the *yan kura* destined for the nobility was woven with the finest grade of handspun thread, carefully stitched, and beaten with a heavy application of indigo powder (*shuni*) to produce a 'black cloth' with a high-gloss surface resembling burnished metal.

Yan kura for the export market was produced in eight different indigo dyeing districts in Kano Emirate (Shea 1975). The development of a large-scale dyeing industry in the southern region of Kano Emirate can be attributed to the region's high water table and plentiful supplies of high quality indigo and cultivated cotton (Hill 1977: 13). Today, the weaving and dyeing of *yan kura* is still centered in the town of Kura, and satellite villages south of Kano City, where specialist skills are passed on through a family apprenticeship system. The historical importance of Kura as a place, critical to the industry's development, is reflected in the name of the cloth type.[10] Kura weavers claim that *turkudi* weaving was begun by Koranic scholars there, reinforcing the idea that Mande clerics introduced weaving techniques to the Hausa. The nearby towns of Dawakin Kudu and Bunkure are also important indigo dyeing centers for *yan kura* cloth.[11]

The weavers residing in and around Kura specialized in producing high quality, white *turkudi* cloth from handspun cotton thread for the northern export trade. Cloth sewers stitched together lengths of *turkudi* strips, ranging in width from two and a half to fifteen yards into cloth consisting of either sixteen, seventeen, or twenty strips, the number of strips most desirable to Tuareg for use as turbans.[12] For Tuareg men, the indigo-dyed turban and face veil are major symbols of male identity. The word for wrapping the veil in the Tuareg language, *tamacheq*, is also the word for male honor (Claudot-Hawad 1993, cited in Arnoldi 1995: 134). A poorer grade of *turkudi*, sometimes woven with imported thread, was produced in Dawakin Kudu District villages for sale to poorer Tuareg consumers. Dawakin Kudu cloth was considered inferior because it did not take the indigo dye well.

The system in which *yan kura* cloth was produced and distributed involved a complex division of labor and chain of economic interactions largely controlled by Hausa and Tuareg middlemen traders operating as landlords and market agents (*fatoma*) (Shea 1975). Their monopoly over the industry was facilitated by the linkages they established between Hausa cloth producers and Tuareg cloth consumers. The market agents possessed a shrewd business sense and invested huge amounts of capital into the *yan kura* industry, thereby establishing a monopolized control over the industry. Although indigo dyers, cloth beaters and cloth sewers sometimes individually purchased *turkudi* cloth directly from the weavers to process and resale, by far the most important purchases were made by the Hausa and Tuareg landlords. Rather than using the indigo dyers in Kura, these market agents commissioned dyers in other centers such as Bunkure, to dye the *turkudi* cloth. Such a strategy prevented the Kura dyers from becoming too powerful economically, and allowed the market agents to control all phases of cloth production and distribution, ensuring that they, rather than the textile artists, would reap a large profit from the sale of *yan kura* cloth.

Market agents bought rolls of *turkudi* cloth from the weavers and then commissioned specialist cloth sewers to edge-stitch the cloth strips together. In a second act of patronage, the agents brought the cloth to indigo dyers, asking them to dye it a deep indigo 'black' color. In a final commissioning act, agents took the cloth to the cloth beaters, who used heavy wooden mallets to pound it with *shuni* (powdered indigo) to create the shiny glazed surface. Larger amounts of *shuni* produced a glossier surface, resulting in a higher price. The *yan kura* clothes were then individually folded and wrapped in tubes of paper on which the market agents wrote their initials, a kind of guarantee of high quality. The cloth was then ready to sell to long-distance Hausa traders who carried it north to the city of Agades in Niger where it was purchased by Tuareg consumer-patrons who referred to this very expensive deeply-dyed cloth, used for turbans and face-veils, as *shegga* (Lamb and Holmes 1980: 93–4).

Tuareg middlemen often maintained residences in both Kura and Agades and sometimes sent young Tuareg men to Kura from Niger to take up apprenticeships with Hausa dyers. The importance and power of Tuareg merchants is conveyed in the oral history of Kura.

> In the early twentieth century a wealthy Tuareg trader from Niger, named Maranga, used to travel with powerful charms that had the ability to kill his competitors. He came to Kura to buy *turkudi* cloth and his charms ensured him a total monopoly over the *turkudi* market. When he came, the market was his at that time. (Magangara 1981)

The centralized location of Kura and the control of production and distribution by Tuareg middlemen, who invested large amounts of capital in the *yan kura* cloth industry, made patterns of production and distribution very efficient and were critical to the economic success of the industry.

The Continuing Demand for *Yan Kura*

Although the important economic role of Tuareg market agents continued into the colonial and post-colonial periods, there was a decline in *yan kura* cloth production in the twentieth century. During the first four decades, Hausa weavers and dyers continued to produce for the same patrons and markets, including the Hausa-Fulani political elite and the northern Tuareg desert market. British colonial policies (to be discussed in further detail in Chapter 7) impacted the *yan kura* cloth industries by pressuring North African merchants to abandon trans-Saharan routes. Introducing tolls, the British stripped the North African caravan leaders of their monopoly over the trans-Saharan trade, and in 1902 Lord Lugard, the governor general of northern Nigeria, imposed a caravan tax on indigenous Hausa textiles (Fika 1978: 143–4). At the same time, the security provided by British overrule led to increased trade links to the south through Lokoja to Lagos on the coast. This opening up of these new markets led to the expansion of the Emirate's cloth and clothing industries in the early twentieth century (Fika 1978: 148–9).

The British were also interested in shifting Hausa productivity away from the creation of finished textile products to a concentration on growing cotton to be exported to the textile mills in Britain (M. Johnson 1974). To this end, the British Cotton Growers Association encouraged the completion of the Lagos/Kano railroad which occurred in 1912. Hausa weavers and Tuareg market agents, however, were able to offer the growers better prices and bought more cotton than the Association, causing the British to shift their interest from cotton to groundnut production (Fika 1978: 150–3). By the 1920s groundnuts had replaced textiles as northern Nigeria's most important export crop. The economic prosperity brought about by the groundnut boom effectively shifted Kano's productivity away from the northern trans-Saharan cloth trade, redirecting it southward into the colonial economy (Fika 1978: 207–9).

The Hausa, however, continued to produce cloth for the specialized northern market, but on a reduced scale. The Tuareg market essentially maintained its integrity and was not integrated into Nigeria's colonial economy. In the 1980s market agents in Kura still played the middleman role for the *turkudi* and *yan kura* trade. *Yan kura* producers from outside Kura brought cloth to market agents' homes, where they were provided lodging while they arranged for cloth sales to long-distance Hausa traders. In exchange, the producer paid the Kura market agent a commission. Moreover, it was common for cloth sewers, dyers and beaters with a cash surplus to buy up cloth from oneanother and sell it to market agents and long-distance traders in the *Fari* Market of Kura.[13]

In the early 1980s, changing patterns of patronage were affecting *turkudi* and *yan kura* production. Indigo dyers from the town of Dawakin Kudu reported that their cloth sold better than Kura cloth because it was cheaper; Kura weavers disagreed and claimed that Tuareg consumers preferred the higher quality of Kura *turkudi*. This contradiction is explained by the fact that the two groups were dependent upon two distinct consumer groups in the Tuareg market – respectively, the general populace and wealthy leaders and traders. In general, however, the number of weavers and dyers in both places declined, in part due to the Sahel drought and famine which forced large numbers of Tuaregs to emigrate south to Nigeria. There, in cities like Kano, they took jobs such as guards and night watchmen. These Tuareg immigrants no longer could afford *yan kura* and instead wore turbans of factory manufactured cloth, dyed with indigo in an attempt to imitate the costly *yan kura* cloth.[14]

In 1981, specialists in all phases of *yan kura* cloth production stressed to the authors that they never had actual contracts with consumer-patrons; instead, they claimed that traders and market agents purchase what is available. The patrons were aware of the distinct quality differences in *yan kura* cloth, depending upon such criteria as yarn (handspun or factory-made), density of weave structure, finesse of sewing, and the amount of *shuni* indigo powder applied. Keeping the financial resources of the two tracks of Tuareg terminal consumers in mind, market agents and traders purchased *yan kura* of both the higher and lower quality. Although there has been a decline in demand for *yan kura* during the independence period, Kura's reputation is still associated with the prestigious *yan kura* cloth industry; in 1990 the authors were told that approximately fifty active *turkudi* weavers resided in Kura. Overall, the production steps and processes, the appearance of the final cloth product, and the patron roles of Tuareg middlemen and consumer-patrons who historically have sustained the industry, have remained essentially unchanged for the last five hundred years.

The Continuing Demand for Caliphate Cloth and Embroidered Gowns

While the *yan kura* cloth industry was localized in the rural Kano area and largely controlled by wealthy Tuareg agents, caliphate cloth production was based in both urban and rural centers throughout the Sokoto Caliphate. Unlike Hausa *yan kura* cloth producers, the artists specializing in the different production phases of caliphate gowns were ethnically mixed, including Hausa, Nupe and Yoruba weavers and embroiderers. Moreover, the caliphate cloth industry lacked an established system where middlemen controlled different phases of production. Instead, weavers sold rolls of narrow-strip cloth directly to Nupe and Hausa embroiderers, and sometimes to Hausa traders who resold cloth to embroiderers living in other parts of the Caliphate. The embroiderer/ tailors transformed caliphate cloth strips into embroidered big gowns. Depending upon the source of patronage, royal leaders or the marketplace, embroidered gowns were personalized by a qualitative attention to detail in which embroiderers would 'take time' when producing for royalty while making standardized less elaborate gowns for the marketplace.

In the Hausa and Nupe area, embroiderers edge-stitched the strips of cloth together and tailored it into a variety of big gown styles. A group of embroiderers, each specializing in a single stitch, then covered the gown's front and back with intricate designs. This very labor-intensive work might take several months to complete. As we have seen, Nupe embroiderers in the city of Bida were esteemed throughout the Caliphate for their exceptional skill; it was not uncommon for cloth woven elsewhere to be brought to Bida for embroidery, especially when a Hausa-Fulani ruler desired the best. Because of their skill, some Bida embroiderers were encouraged by Fulani courts in Sokoto, Kano and Katsina to relocate, resulting in an on-going relationship between Hausa-Fulani leaders and Nupe embroiderers. Nupe gown embroiderers have produced the highest quality gowns in the last century and a half, maintaining a consistent, conservative approach to gown design. In contrast, Hausa embroiderers, in the independence period, have been more receptive to experimentation, a tendency echoing recent trends in Hausa weaving (discussed in Chapter 7).

Examples of experimentation were seen by the authors in the wardrobe of the Sulama, a high-ranking title-holder in the Kano court, who owned several gowns gifted to him by the Emir of Kano as well as gowns he commissioned himself. One of his gowns, made of white factory cloth and decorated with an elaborate arabesque of orange embroidery, was specially commissioned by him from a Hausa embroiderer. Based on the *aska biyu* (two-knife) design, the gown's design reflects the patron's desire for an original gown with an unusual decoration, conveying prestige (Sulama 1990). This commission exemplifies a high-ranking patron's request for an innovative variation of a well-established design. The embroidery pattern's name, 'Mercedes,' suggesting the higher price the patron was willing to pay, reinforces both the message of prestige and the contemporary nature of the novel design.

In general, British colonial policies appear to have had a negligible impact on the production of caliphate cloth for the Hausa-Fulani political elite in the early colonial period. In fact, the British policy of indirect rule, where Hausa-Fulani emirs were retained as administrators of colonial policy, may have contributed to an increase in patron demand by the Hausa-Fulani political elite for luxury items such as embroidered gowns and turbans. To effectively administer the vast geographical Caliphate region, the British even created some new positions for indigenous rulers, such as the position of Emir of Pategi in southern Nupe country.

The colonial economy also encouraged the rise of a new patron type. The British emphasis on the development of the Hausa groundnut industry led to the emergence of a nouveau riche class of wealthy Hausa groundnut merchants. Anxious to invest in the traditional symbols of status and to express personal prestige and wealth, this group of merchants became an important patron category for finely embroidered gowns and the gear for embellished horses. Strict nineteenth-century sumptuary rules, restricting certain regalia to Hausa-Fulani rulers, began to relax, and new opportunities for wealthy, influential private citizens to commission and purchase prestige items increased. From these wealthy commoners emerged a powerful and prosperous group of self-motivated patrons whose competitive spirit and pursuit of the spectacular pushed artists to explore their creative potential, with the goal of maximizing their patrons' prestige (see Chapter 3). Within the parameters of tasteful restraint, as demanded by adherents to the Islamic faith, the secularization of what had been exclusively leadership art forms led to an unprecedented aesthetic florescence for a limited but demanding market.

In the late colonial period, royal patronage for caliphate cloth began to decline, ceasing altogether during the independence period.[15] First affected were the urban weavers of caliphate cloth in Sokoto, Kano, Bida and Ilorin, who had honed their skill to produce the highest quality of cloth for the Hausa-Fulani ruling class. The previously close relationship between urban caliphate cloth weavers and their royal patrons appears to be the main reason for the demise of urban weaving centers during the independence period. Although members of the Hausa-Fulani and Nupe-Fulani ruling class still wear embroidered caliphate gowns on ceremonial occasions, they seldom commission new state gowns but instead wear old gowns from their personal collections and palace treasury. Robes of lesser quality are purchased from the market when needed for gift-giving occasions. A reserve of caliphate cloth weavers still exist in smaller rural communities scattered throughout the Hausa countryside, such as the Nupe weavers residing in Kura.

While rural-based weavers occasionally produced cloth for the Fulani court, their production was never restricted by the narrow patronage demands of the ruling class. Unlike their urban counterparts, rural caliphate cloth weavers also produced cloth for the market on a regular basis. As a result, in contrast to urban caliphate cloth weavers, the rural caliphate cloth weavers continued to find a demand for their products. Also, because of their physical and social distance from the Hausa-Fulani court, rural caliphate cloth weaving centers were not constricted by the leaders' conservative requests. Perhaps even more important is the fact that, historically, rural Hausa weavers had always directed their production to a more diverse patron mix than their urban counterparts, a strategy which assured survival. In the twentieth century, as local patronage demands changed, the rural-based caliphate cloth weavers began production of new styles of cloth that were specifically designed to please outgroup patrons. These weaving innovations along with those of Yoruba cloth dyers and designers are the focus of Chapter 7.

Notes

1. The shiny black cloth produced in Kano Emirate is called *yan kura* after the Hausa production center of Kura. See Shea 1975: 56.
2. Both muslim and non-muslim Yoruba adopted northern dress for prestige purposes.
3. Colleen Kriger's technical analysis of selected nineteenth-century gowns made of caliphate cloth supports the idea that high cloth density was the most important variable to judge high quality woven cloth. She found that nineteenth-century embroidered gowns have a much higher thread count than their twentieth-century counterparts (Kriger 1993).
4. *Saki* cloth weavers in the Hausa town of Kura claim a Nupe descent. (Interviews with *saki* weavers in Kura, 1981.)
5. Many of the textiles collected by the British sponsored 1841 Niger Expedition and now in the Museum of Mankind in London, can be attributed to Yoruba female and male weavers.
6. In 1841 the Niger Expedition made a collection of samples of strip woven cloth and cloth produced on the upright loom. These cloths with warp-striped and checked designs constitute the earliest dated collection of men's and women's weaving from the Nupe and Yoruba peoples. The majority of textiles collected by the Expedition were cheap Yoruba imports from Ijebu, traded at the Nupe market at Egga.
7. Indigenous *tsamiya* silk is not a filament silk, but requires spinning.

8. Nadel's research focused on those art industries that required a high degree of cooperation among family members in the production process. These industries included blacksmithing, brassworking and glassworking.

9. See Chapter 7 for a discussion of a more recent modification of *saki harir*, incorporating strips of red cotton and *yan kura* cloth.

10. *Yan kura* is also known as *dan kura* ('son of the town of Kura').

11. See Philip Shea (1983) for a discussion of how Bunkure replaced Kura as a dyeing center in the twentieth century.

12. The most expensive and elegant Tuareg veils in Niger consisted of nearly 100 strips of cloth (Kristyne Loughran Bini as cited in Arnoldi 1995: 134).

13. The Kura cloth market is called the *Fari* ('white') because of the preponderance of undyed white *turkudi* cloth for sale.

14. Factory-made navy blue '*yan kura* cloth' is currently included in the Tuareg display at the Field Museum of Natural History, Chicago, Illinois.

15. In 1981 caliphate cloth was no longer woven in Kano City. Caliphate cloth was still being made in Bida in the late 1970s, but by 1990 men's weaving was no longer done. In the late 1970s and early 1980s no caliphate cloth weavers were active in Ilorin (O'Hear 1991).

7

Continuity and Change in Twentieth-Century Cloth Traditions

At the turn of the twentieth century, the area of Nigeria was experiencing increasing foreign influence with the establishment of British colonialism. This resulted in cultural, political and economic change that introduced competitive imported products, transforming consumer demands. In this chapter we see how the flourishing textile industries of the area met these challenges. Hausa and Yoruba cloth producers succeeded in maintaining viable traditions into the independence period (1960) by adapting their products to the needs and demands of indigenous art patrons, unlike many other Nigerian art industries that became increasingly dependent on unreliable outgroup foreign tourists and expatriates. While Nupe male weavers were less successful in adapting their product to appeal to the larger market, embroiderers maintained a reputation for superior embroidery. Although Nupe weavers had played a critical role in the development of the flourishing luxury caliphate cloth industry in the nineteenth century, patron demand had greatly declined by the mid-twentieth century. In the early independence period a small number of caliphate cloth weavers worked on a special commission basis in Bida, but by 1990 the production of strip-woven cloth had ceased altogether. In contrast, the decades following World War II saw a florescence in cloth made on the upright loom by Nupe women. While this trend continued into the 1980s, with many new cloth patterns created as a result of the influx of imported cotton and shiny floss yarn, by 1990 the explosion in new cloth types and designs had ceased. A few women continued to weave on commission for special occasions such as family weddings.

The British Impact

The end of the nineteenth century saw the seeds of British colonialism sown in the homelands of the Hausa, Nupe and Yoruba, an event that was to have a far-reaching influence on production and patronage demands for textiles. The Berlin Conference of 1885 convened by the major European powers, ceded the Niger Territory to Great Britain. The British presence was increasingly felt in their efforts to establish control over economic production and trade. The Royal Niger Company, already active in the coastal trade, was given a royal charter in 1886, establishing trade relations with the Nupe and Hausa. British intervention in the Yoruba civil wars was intensified when trade routes to the southern seaports became blocked. By 1895 Yorubaland belonged to the British Southern Protectorate and the Royal Niger Company was actively engaged in trade in the north. In 1901 the British launched an offensive in the north to extend their control. After the fall of the Sokoto Caliphate in 1903, the Northern Protectorate, including the Hausa, Nupe and Ilorin Yoruba was established. The British, who up to that time had been largely confined to the coastal areas, dependent upon Yoruba middlemen for northern products, were now able to exert more control over northern trade. In 1914 with the amalgamation of the two Protectorates, the Hausa, Nupe and Yoruba were for the first time united into a single political entity, the Protectorate of Nigeria. The historical background, cultural similarities and degree of contact with the West of the three ethnic groups were recognized by the British when they divided Nigeria into smaller provinces. The boundaries of the Northern Province, which included the Hausa and Nupe, dipped south below the Niger River to include the Yoruba sub-groups who had been part of the Sokoto Caliphate, including Ilorin. The rest of Yorubaland that had once been a part of the Oyo Empire was incorporated into the Southern Province.

With the establishment of British hegemony, colonial policies impacted the weaving industries. While British attempts to change weaving technology, control distribution and redirect weavers to other professions were largely unsuccessful, the availability of European materials and products influenced consumer tastes, and affected the very look of indigenous cloth. Yoruba and Hausa weavers responded quite differently to the changing habitus but both succeeded in maintaining viable weaving traditions into the twentieth century.

As we have seen, throughout the nineteenth century Kano, Nupeland and northern Yorubaland were numbered among the great weaving centers that supplied cloth for the extensive long-distance trade routes linking all of West Africa (M. Johnson 1974: 180–1). However, imported cotton trade cloth from England was playing an increasingly important role in this trade. Recognizing the importance of the existing trade routes, the British injected their own consumer goods into these arteries. In the period 1900–1914 cotton piece goods were the 'largest single item' of consumer goods sent to British colonies (M. Johnson 1974: 178). With the establishment of British hegemony over many areas of West Africa, the cotton mills of England sought to increase their export market while increasing importation of cotton from Nigeria. In 1889 the Governor of Lagos, Alfred Moloney, suggested that Manchester cottons should replace indigenous cloth and free weavers to work in cotton production; he reasoned that their wages would allow them to buy reasonably-priced cloth imported from England (M. Johnson 1974: 181–2). Such thinking reflects the British colonial policy of seeking markets for their own goods at the expense of indigenous industries. This tactic, dubbed 'cotton imperialism' by economic historian Marion Johnson (1974), was clearly stated by Frederick Lugard, High Commissioner of the Protectorate of Northern Nigeria.

> Reduced to its crudest expression, the desire of the importing merchant [of British goods to Nigeria] would no doubt be to see native industries other than the production of raw material for export, crushed, in order that they may be superseded by imported manufactures ... (Lugard 1904, cited in M. Johnson 1974: 183)

Lugard implemented this policy by imposing a system of caravan tolls designed to increase the cost of indigenous cloth, so that import cloth would be more competitive in the market (M. Johnson 1974: 182–3). This policy affected indigenous weaving industries to the degree that while a number of female and male weavers abandoned their looms as consumers were attracted to the cheaper imported cloth, many weavers continued to be sustained by the ongoing demand for indigenous luxury cloth by the political elite. At the same time, it was a period of innovation for the more tenacious indigenous textile artists, who experimented with the new imported materials of production.

The Emergence of Modern Hausa Cloths

As we have seen, the Hausa weaving industry developed in a rural setting, with the majority of weavers spread throughout the countryside surrounding the large urban centers of Kano, Zaria and Sokoto. Those weavers who resided in the large cities worked mainly for the courts of nineteenth-century emirs and the Caliph of Sokoto. As royal patronage slowly waned in the early colonial period, rural weavers, while experiencing some decline in overall demand, remained relatively productive. Although imported cloth competed with indigenous handwoven cloths for the purchasing power of Hausa cloth users, the complex marketing network into which rural Hausa weavers directed their production was diverse enough to accommodate and support their ongoing production. While the cheaper imported cloths did compete with certain categories of Hausa weaving, they did not affect the court's reduced but steady demand for high quality caliphate cloth, needed for the embroidered gowns which supported the Caliphate's historical legacy and Islamic ideology. The negative impact from imported cloth was not experienced by indigenous caliphate cloth weavers until after World War II.

In recent years, visitors to Hausa weaving communities in the countryside of Kano Emirate have been astonished at the variety of handwoven cloth types seen in the local markets. Some of these cloths have been woven for centuries, while others originated during the colonial period. At first glance, the more recent cloths seem quite distinctive in comparison to the older cloths. While maintaining the stripe design format of caliphate cloths, some of the newer cloths are much wider, decorated with designs made of imported yarn, and are either more loosely or densely woven than earlier forms of Hausa strip-woven cloth. Nevertheless, these newer cloths share an aesthetic and formal affinity with their nineteenth-century forerunners. The established centuries old caliphate cloth tradition constitutes the foundation from which the newer styles emerged, as seen in stylistic features shared by the old and new cloths.

An important factor contributing to the dynamic character of the Hausa textile industry was the willingness of certain weavers to adopt new techniques and materials introduced by the British. Also, imported yarn from England was used increasingly during the last decades of the colonial period. Wider heddles and multicolored, factory-made imported yarn encouraged weavers to develop new textile styles. Equally important to the continued success of the Hausa weaving industry, was the determination and ingenuity of textile market agents and traders to increase outgroup patronage by introducing new cloth styles into pre-existing distant markets. As the royal and aristocratic patron need and market demand for certain types of cloth began to decline in the twentieth century, Hausa weavers and textile marketing agents demonstrated remarkable adaptability and flexibility in adjusting their production and marketing strategies to target indigenous groups of outgroup consumers, particularly the pastoral Bororo Fulani and nomadic Tuareg peoples of Niger. Long distance traders (*fatake*) and resident landlord/merchants (*fatoma*) continued to be directly involved with cloth production, contributing to the financing and organization of production.

The result was that rural-based caliphate cloth weavers of Kano Emirate actually flourished during the late colonial and early independence periods. The success of these weavers can be explained in part by their willingness to adopt the technology and raw materials, including the factory-made yarn, imported by the British. These adaptations stimulated the creation of a number of new styles of cloth including wide *saki* and *luru* and broad loomed *mudukare* and *gwado* cloths. These new styles of cloth will be examined more closely, paying particular attention to the interaction of weaver, art patron and market agent, which encouraged their production.

Wide *Saki* Cloth

The Hausa town of Kura, a major center of *yan kura* cloth production, was also a center of caliphate cloth weaving. While the *yan kura* weavers (described in Chapter 6) are Hausa, the Kura caliphate cloth weavers claim Nupe descent. Grandfathers of the elderly Nupe weavers were taken as slaves by the Hausa in the late nineteenth-century Hausa-Nupe wars. Although the children of these slaves gained freeman status during the early colonial period, they remained in Kura and continued to produce cloth for Hausa patrons. During this period other weavers emigrated from Nupe country to Kura to take advantage of new patronage opportunities.

These Nupe weavers in Kura specialized in making one inch wide densely woven *saki* bands of handspun and commercial cotton yarn for men's gowns. They also wove silk and cotton red and white *barage*, white *fari*, and blue and white *gwanda* (a wider variant of *saki*) caliphate cloth for gowns worn by the Fulani political elite. Nupe weavers of Kura claim that during the colonial period, gowns of *saki* and *gwanda* cloth were regularly ordered for 'turbanning' installation ceremonies by Fulani emirs from a wide geographical region, including Kano, Katsina, Sokoto, Bornu, Gwanda and Abuja. During this same timespan, recognizing a potential market for cloth wrappers needed by rural Hausa women, these Kura weavers began to modify the narrow *saki karamin* ('small *saki*') of one inch width into a wider version of three to four inches, *saki babban* ('big *saki*'). For the latter, factory-made yarn was used for both warp and weft, resulting in a much looser weave density. These lighter weight *saki* cloths became popular with rural Hausa women who wore them as wrappers for marriage and children's naming ceremonies. The most expensive and prestigious wrappers were embellished with thin woven bands of magenta colored silk *(alharini)*, or magenta cotton *(kudi)*.[1] The resulting wrappers, known as *saki dan kudi* ('money cloth'), appropriately reflected their wearers' relative wealth and high social status. By the mid-colonial period Kura caliphate cloth weavers were therefore producing these two types of *saki* cloth for three distinct patron groups: Fulani leaders and aristocrats, rural Hausa women, and resident Hausa traders who resold the wide *saki* cloth to long-distance Hausa traders who in turn moved the cloth along to its final destination of terminal consumer-patrons – the pastoral

Bororo Fulani and the nomadic Tuareg people of Niger. After the Second World War when cheap, factory cloth was readily available, Kura caliphate cloth weavers began to experience a decline in patron demand from two of these patron groups – the Fulani elite and rural Hausa women – consequently, the weavers became increasingly dependent on outgroup patronage.

Luru Cloth

Another important product from the looms of twentieth-century Hausa weavers is *luru*, a tapestry cloth, woven in dense cotton strips to use in blankets (see Figure 6.1). *Luru* cloth strips, varying in width from 6 to 10 inches, are white with colored stripes and decorative motifs. They were produced in the towns and villages south and northwest of Kano City, in the countryside around Katsina, and in the Gombe region (Lamb and Holmes 1980: 105). Each of these regions specialized in different widths, motifs and color combinations. The production of heavy *luru* blankets dates back to the early colonial period in the Hausa villages of Riman Rake and Chiroma, located in Bichi District northwest of Kano City. At this time the majority of Riman Rake weavers and all Chiroma weavers shifted their production away from caliphate cloth, concentrating production on *luru* blankets and other broad loomed cloths.[2]

Luru blankets were woven with cotton warp yarn and wool weft yarn in the Katsina region during the 1930s (Lamb and Holmes 1980: 112). However, in the post-Second World War period, *luru* blankets have been made from factory warp yarn and thick handspun cotton weft yarn. The early use of wool suggests an influence from woolen Fulani *khasa* blankets, woven by settled Fulani weavers in the Niger River inland delta region of Mali. The fact that former caliphate cloth weavers began producing *luru* blankets, probably after seeing Fulani *khasa* blankets which were traded to Kano from Mali, suggests that the *luru* blanket grew out of the tradition of white *fari* caliphate cloth, becoming overlaid with an influence from the structure and surface design of 'exotic' imported Fulani blankets. In any case, Hausa *luru* blankets appear to have emerged from a base tradition of much older established Hausa and Fulani prototypes, developed in a novel way. In the Bichi area, for example, white woven strips were crossed with inlaid black or blue bands containing lozenge patterns while framing fields containing small, colorful triangular designs. The interpretations of individual weavers can result in distinctive designs, contributing to a weaver's reputation.[3]

Most often Chiroma and Riman Rake *luru* weavers sold their blankets to local traders who resold them in the Bichi market to long-distance Hausa traders. These traders carried the blankets to markets in Niger where they were purchased by Fulani and Tuareg peoples for use as covers to protect against the cold and mosquitoes. Also, *luru* blankets were occasionally purchased in the Bichi market by messengers of Fulani emirs who give them as gifts to titled officials, visiting dignitaries and foreigners. The traders who deal directly with the weavers generally buy whatever the weavers produce, but there are exceptions. For example, when terminal consumers desired the highest quality of *luru*, the traders who represented their needs, requested *luru menyene*, a blanket type which is longer, heavier and more finely woven than is generally produced for trade. Although weavers claim that patrons do not specify design innovations, they are capable of creating and copying new designs. A Hausa trader in Kano City's Kurmi market reported that 'if a patron came with a special request, I would send my contacts to go to the place where the weavers live and ask them to do the things they have never done before for me, like the *luru* with special decorations.'

Broad loom Cloths

During the post-Second World War period, Hausa weavers of *fari* and *saki* cloth began to experiment with weaving even wider widths of cloth (24 to 30 inches) on a broad double treadle loom. These loosely-woven cloths (*gwado* and *mudukare*) are made with factory yarn. The two main catalysts triggering the development of a broad loom Hausa weaving tradition in the late colonial period were a declining demand for caliphate cloth and the establishment of British Textile Training Centres in the Hausa area. Resident British Textile Officers worked on the principal that if the width of the handwoven cloth was increased, weavers would experience an increase in productivity. A colonial resident wrote that the purpose of the new textile centers was 'to demonstrate and teach what the Government believes to be better methods not only to induce weavers to produce more cloth, but better cloth' (D. Clarke 1996a: 17). In attempts to replace indigenous textile industries the British opened the first two training centers in the Yoruba towns of Oyo and Ado-Ekiti in 1947, and two years later established similar centers in Kano and Sokoto (Clarke 1996a: 17). A few European floor looms were set up at these centers and weavers were trained to use them. In a short time the weaving apparatuses of these looms may have been copied and adapted to the indigenous treadle loom. Except for the width of the heddles, the indigenous looms based on the European prototype essentially remained unchanged.[4]

Overall, the colonial effort to update indigenous technology met with varied success. Among the Yoruba only a few broad loom weavers were successful for more than a few years. Their products reflected a European aesthetic which did not appeal to local consumers, so that their level of success directly corresponded to the degree of demand for cloth by the colonial government. When government patronage disappeared, those trained to operate the European-style looms could not sustain production on their own (D. Clarke 1996a: 17). In contrast, Hausa weavers to the north fared better, not only adopting the wide loom technology but creating new cloths to accommodate the changing taste preferences of established outgroup consumer patrons mentioned earlier. Fortunately for the Hausa weavers, they were able to channel the new broad loom cloths through well-established trade networks made possible by the stable economic relationships that weavers sustained with Hausa market agents and traders. The long-distance Hausa traders functioned as mediators between the weavers and terminal consumers, communicating the taste preferences and desire for cloth styles of distant consumers back to the producers.

Technological change also played a role in the success of broad loom weaving in the Hausa area. The period when Hausa weavers began to experiment with producing wider widths of cloth coincided with increased trade with Britain following World War II. This trade made available pre-dyed, factory yarn to Hausa weavers. While it is difficult and laborious to weave with handspun cotton yarn on the new wider loom, imported yarn is easier to manipulate. A group of younger rural Hausa weavers, trained in weaving caliphate cloth, became convinced that it was more efficient and cost-effective to weave the wider cloths. The younger weavers were more receptive to experimenting with new cloth types and designs than the older generation of caliphate cloth weavers, who were locked into a more rigid system of producing luxury cloths to meet the prestige demands of the Fulani political elite. The conservative taste patterns of the indigenous elite had ensured continuity in the caliphate cloth tradition for almost two centuries. In contrast, the younger generation of weavers, responding to changing economic opportunities, became increasingly interested in weaving cloth to be sold for everyday domestic use. A farmer who weaves increases his income significantly. They were not as affected by the aesthetic restrictions that imposed constraints on the older generation of weavers.

The most successful of the Hausa broad loom cloths innovated during the late colonial period – *gwado* and *mudukare* – draw upon the aesthetics of strip-woven caliphate cloth; both cloths have a plain ground color and narrow warp-face stripes. New to these cloths is the addition of weft-float patterns, a feature shared with women's cloth but not caliphate cloth. *Gwado*, woven in many parts of Hausa country, comes in several varieties such as *gwado dan fari* (a plain white cloth sometimes woven with thin blue warp stripes) and *bunu* (a plain, dark indigo blue cloth). *Gwado dan fari* has replaced strip-woven *fari* cloth for use as burial shrouds in many places. A version of dark *bunu* cloth, known as *kafi dosa*, has a deep blue shiny surface punctuated by pale blue warp and weft stripes. There is some evidence that *kafi dosa* cloth began to replace the older indigo dyed *yan kura* cloth for use as wrappers by the nomadic Tuareg women of Niger in the 1980s. *Gwado bakin*, another version of *bunu* cloth woven in Chiroma and Riman Rake, has a ground pattern of warp-faced indigo stripes, embellished with brightly colored weft float designs made of shiny synthetic yarn. In the 1980s *gwado bakin* cloth was in the process of replacing wide *saki* cloth for wrappers worn by nomadic Tuareg and Fulani consumer patrons of Niger. As part of this shift in taste preference toward a more decorative wide loom cloth, weavers in Chiroma innovated yet another variety of *gwado*, called *jajadaja*, with red and pale blue warp stripes set against a deep indigo ground color. Broad loom weavers regarded *jajadaja* cloth as an effective substitute for an older style of prestige *sokoto dan kudi* wrapper (*saki* cloth with bands or red silk or cotton) popular with rural Hausa and nomadic Fulani women. *Jajadaja* cloth, exemplifies an innovation developed by broad loom weavers as a cheaper, more cost-effective cloth that could be substituted for a more expensive prototype desired by patrons.

Mudukare is a second major type of broad loom cloth made by Hausa weavers, woven expressly for pastoral Fulani patrons since the late colonial period. Broad loom *mudukare* cloth is based on an older strip cloth called *bale*, made of handspun yarn with very thin black, red and blue stripes set against a solid ground color. *Mudukare*, like other broad loom cloths, is now made with commercial yarn. *Mudukare* weavers, concentrated in the countryside around Kano and Wudil (a town east of Kano,) directed their production to Hausa traders who carried the cloth to pastoral Fulani peoples in Niger and northern Cameroon. Fulani women and girls wore the cloth as wrappers and blouses for special occasions such as initiation and marriage ceremonies. Fulani men had the cloth tailored into sleeveless smocks and shorts. Apart from the demand for *mudukare* for use in everyday and ceremonial dress, Fulani men also presented *mudukare* cloth as gifts to their wives upon marriage and childbirth (Lamb and Holmes 1980: 107).

The centers of *mudukare* production tended to specialize in weaving different varieties. Weavers in Chiroma and Wudil made a lavender cloth with thin red and black warp stripes and weft-float insets of contrasting red and green wool and gold lurex thread, geared to appeal to the Fulani aesthetic preference in dress. The Bororo Fulani patrons responded positively to the new cloth due to their proclivity for decorating their bodies and coiffures with colorful, shiny materials, including buttons, safety pins, aluminum strips, and most recently, brightly colored plastic strips.

Hausa weavers innovated weft-float designs on the broad loom *gwado* and *mudukare* cloths as a strategy to attract the purchasing power of young pastoral Fulani patrons. While some cloth woven by Hausa women incorporated weft-float designs, this decorative technique had not been practiced by male Hausa weavers until it was adopted as a design technique by the broad loom weavers. One Chiroma broad loom weaver aptly summarized this design strategy by claiming 'decorations attract customers'.

The adoption of the broad heddle loom is an excellent example of how an innovation draws upon tradition but also has repercussions throughout the whole set of relations linking producers, traders, market agents and the ultimate consumers. The success of the male weavers of broad cloth, however, had negative consequences on women weavers. The broad heddle loomed cloth produced by male weavers is strikingly similar in appearance to the wide cloth products of the Hausa woman's upright loom.[5] Because the new broad loom allowed for more efficient and quicker production, it was relatively easy for the wide cloth of the men's loom to quickly overshadow that of the woman's upright loom. Traders must have played a role in encouraging the shift. Foreseeing the possibility of their own increased financial prosperity, market agents and traders no doubt encouraged young Hausa male weavers to adopt the broad loom technology. While pastoral Fulani patrons had been purchasing cloth woven by Hausa women since the early colonial period, the male broad cloth weavers began to capture the majority of ingroup and outgroup pre-existing markets for wide cloth. Hausa women were unable to compete with broad loom male weavers, causing women's weaving eventually to cease in many parts of Hausaland. In Chiroma, for example, women stopped weaving around the time the broad loom became established among male weavers. Yet, in some areas of Hausa country, Hausa women weavers continued to produce baby blankets of cotton and brightly colored lurex thread for rural Hausa women and pastoral Fulani women.

Factors of Change in Hausa Cloth Industries

Several factors appear to have converged during the late colonial period to facilitate the innovation and successful marketing of new types of Hausa cloth. The relative stability of the Hausa caliphate cloth market from the pre-colonial to the late colonial period helps to explain the stylistic continuity and conservatism characteristic of the narrow-strip cloth industry for centuries. On the other hand, threats to market stability in the mid-twentieth century became an incentive for change, when the stage was being set for

Nigeria's emergence as an independent nation state. The Fulani political elite realized that without the indirect rule policies of the colonial government their political authority would recede even more. This no doubt was a factor in the decline in demand for caliphate cloth by the Fulani political elite at this time. Post-Second World War imports were a second factor as elites augmented their wardrobes with embroidered gowns of imported damasks, which were lighter to wear and still prestigeful. The gradual reduction in demand by this important patron group for caliphate cloth triggered an incentive for change among the younger generation of Hausa weavers. These young weavers, who had a professional commitment to full-time production during the annual dry season as a cash activity, were ready to diversify their production by experimenting with new strip cloth types for the pre-existing outgroup markets.

Two conditions necessary for a textile industry to survive, according to John Picton, are an inventive tradition and market demand (1992: 46).

> . . . traditions vary enormously in their creative expectations. Some are certainly conservative in that the replication of existing forms is expected. Other traditions permit and perhaps encourage exploration in form and medium: it is within such traditions that we can expect to find innovative development. (1992: 39)

Continuing demand is equally important. The northern market demand for Hausa cloth was already in place. The Hausa traders who carried cloth from the various branches of the Hausa textile industry to the northern markets played a critical role in transmitting the taste preferences of the terminal cloth consumers in Niger back to the Hausa producers in Nigeria. Hausa weavers only had to test these markets with their new products using established traders and market agents as facilitators. Equipped with new materials and updated technology, young Hausa weavers were well-positioned to explore the full potential of the narrow strip textile tradition leading to a sense of renewed vitality in the late colonial Hausa textile industry. It has been observed that Hausa weavers

> seemed able to adapt, adopt, or devise patterns to suit any demand which their commercial expertise might detect. They have the potential to adopt themselves to economic and cultural change. (Lamb and Holmes 1980: 119)

Inspired, and willing to experiment with an established textile tradition firmly rooted in Hausa culture, a young generation of post-Second World War Hausa weavers made a successful transition from the colonial to the independence era.

By 1990 further shifts in patronage patterns for Hausa indigenous hand-crafted products were evident as Western imports and commodities of modern industries encouraged by the State and Local Governments became readily available. Yet, handwoven cloth remained competitive because of: perceived needs of indigenous and expatriate patrons for Hausa craft products; mutually beneficial relationships between weavers and traders; continuation of the established long-distance trade networks; lack of employment in the modern sector for unschooled and semi-literate individuals; local perceptions of part-time craft production as a ready source of supplementary cash income beyond that generated by basic subsistence activities; and low opportunity costs for craft production, including acquisition of skills as part of family socialization, equipment and raw materials.

The question of how long Hausa textile industries can continue to compete successfully against the flood of manufactured cloth and changing patterns of taste is particularly tied to the factors of perceived needs of contemporary patrons, the nature of transactions between weavers and patron-traders, and the continuation of the established long-distance trade networks. Today, as in the past, Hausa weavers and the terminal consumer patrons for their cloth are isolated from one another, linked through a complex trade network. Traders and market agents communicate the needs of distant consumer patrons back to the Hausa producers in Nigeria. Ultimately, however, it is the group of distant consumer patrons, who buy cloth from the traders for their own use, that is the determining factor controlling the dynamics of continuity and change in Hausa strip-woven and broad loom cloths. Decisions by remote consumer patrons to buy or not buy feeds back through traders to the weavers, affecting production strategies. The stability of the economic relationship between weavers, traders and market agents, is critical if Hausa weavers are to be able to meet future desires of distant secondary consumer patrons. Hausa weavers have historically always perceived an economic advantage to dealing directly with traders. Transactions are often long-standing, based on mutual trust, allowing for some flexibility in payment. A weaver, for example, may leave cloth with the trader or be paid on the spot, depending upon the financial fortune of either at the time. Also, a trader tends to support the weaver with whom he has an established relationship by ordering and paying ahead or buying stockpiled cloth. The weaver is thus guaranteed an immediate reward for his time and effort. In some cases, where the raw materials for manufacture such as yarn are costly, the trader may subsidize production by furnishing the weaver with the necessary materials needed for manufacture. Finally, market agents and traders who buy and stockpile cloth for market resale provide a service to their customers by making cloth available on a year-round basis. While cloth production by

Hausa farmers waxes and wanes according to the season, traders ensure that a good cloth product mix, both in terms of type and quality, is available in the marketplace at all times. The result is that both weavers and consumer patrons benefit from working through a middleman. This successful system which has been in place in the Kano region for centuries, most likely will carry over into the twenty-first century, assuring an ongoing viability in the Hausa weaving industry for decades to come.

Twentieth-century Developments in Yoruba Cloth Production

As with the Hausa, the increasing availability of trade cloth, known as *aso oyingbo* (whiteman's cloth) in Yorubaland, had a major impact on indigenous textile industries. Not only was import cloth competitive in the local markets, but it also greatly influenced Yoruba dress traditions. The soft cotton factory-printed cloth introduced a broad spectrum of colors and designs, was lighter in weight, more comfortable to wear and sew, and easier to care for (Renne 1995: 181). Imported damasks, velvets, satins and silks gained popularity for prestige garments. Indigenous cloth was increasingly rejected as the wearing of tailored clothing of *aso oyingbo* 'became an integral part of 'civilized' behavior' (Renne 1995: 182) and consumer decisions became increasingly tied to fashion.[6] Certain patterns and colors of imported cloth gained popularity, first in the urban areas, selling well before being replaced by a new fashion. Despite the competition from imported cloth, Yoruba textile artists, like Hausa weavers, selectively exploited opportunities created by British colonialism. Male weavers of *aso-oke* narrow-strip cloth readily accepted the new fibers and industrial dyes provided through British trading firms but rejected attempts by the Colonial government to introduce European broad loom weaving (D. Clarke 1996).

The Emergence of *Adire* Production

Adire, an indigo resist-dyed cloth made with factory-made cotton shirting, takes two forms: *adire oniko* which is tie-dyed and *adire eleko* where starch paste is applied as the resisting agent. (Figure 7.1) The prototype for *adire* is tie-dyed *kijipa*, a cloth woven by Yoruba women on the upright loom. The Yoruba city of Abeokuta in southern Nigeria, a major *adire* production center, is where *adire* first emerged around 1910. Abeokuta *adire* dominated the market through the colonial period (Afolabi 1988, Byfield 1993, Keyes-Adenaike 1993). At this time, Abeokuta also was a center for cotton growing and weaving. Women dyers not only catered to the needs of local spinners and weavers who wanted their cotton yarns dyed but were also called upon to refurbish *kijipa* clothing that had lost color by redyeing the cloth and adding tie-dyed patterns. With the increasing presence of British trading firms that sold imported white cotton shirting, women dyers found a new 'canvas' for their art.[7] The imported cloth was cheap due to the colonial government's policy of taxing local handwoven cloth and not their own imported products. The soft, smooth white shirting stimulated the invention of more elaborate patterning techniques in indigo-resist dyeing (Afolabi 1988: 5–6).

Adire eleko, in which starch paste is applied through free-hand painting or with stencils also was produced when the industry first developed. The handpainted or stenciled designs mimicked the fashionable factory printed cloths of the period, while retaining the indigenous aesthetic with regard to motifs and color. The indigo blue of *Adire* appealed to traditional Yoruba taste, while the motifs reflected contemporary concerns. The women effectively indigenized European import cloth by dyeing it with indigo, thereby allowing 'a much wider cross-section of the population to participate in the rapid evolution of fashion' (Byfield 1993: 45). Of the indigenous Yoruba cloth of the early colonial period, only *adire*, which blended old and new in response to the changing cultural milieu, could compete in the expanding world of fashion.

While some *adire* patterns stabilized and were reproduced in quantity, innovation was encouraged and new motifs and patterns constantly emerged. New designs gave dyers a market advantage in the competitive world of fashion (Byfield 1993: 132).

> Women often hid new creations from their competitors with the hope of creating a flurry of interest among buyers . . . Dyers closely guarded new designs and only brought then out on market day. A new design only provided a slight advantage because by the next market day other dyers would have copied it. (Byfield 1993: 148)

Like factory cloth, *adire* often reflected current events, especially those associated with the colonial regime. A pictorial cloth first made in the 1930s was *Oloba*, also known as 'Coronation Cloth,' with a central medallion depicting the British monarchs, King George V and Queen Mary, celebrating their Silver Jubilee (Barbour and Simmonds 1971). A popular cloth still made today, *Ibadan Dun* (the city of Ibadan is sweet), included in its motifs a representation of the columns of the British-built city hall.

In the early twentieth century, *adire* was extremely common as a trade cloth outside of the Yoruba area because it was comparatively cheap. While

Figure 7.1. Yoruba market girl wearing wrapper made of *adire eleko* cloth, Abeokuta, Nigeria. Source: Norma Wolff.

good quality *adire* with hand-painted designs could be expensive, *adire* with stenciled or tie-dyed designs was one of the least expensive colored cloths available as far away as Ghana (Eades 1980: 36–7). Yoruba indigo-dyed *adire* was sought after throughout the coastal areas of West Africa from Nigeria to Senegal and was carried across the trade routes of the Sahel to the north. In the 1920s, at the height of *adire* production, the largest number of buyers were Senegalese wholesale merchants who came to Abeokuta, buying as many as 2000 wrappers in one day (Byfield 1993: 149).

The government's ban on the import of cloth during the Second World War negatively affected production, but ingroup patronage demand for women's wrappers continued. In the 1960s rural markets were flooded with indigo-blue clad women while in urban areas *adire* was increasingly seen as 'poor people's cloth' made by elderly non-literate women with few economic options (Byfield 1993: 6). The continuing flooding of the market with cheap cloth not only from Europe, but also from Asia and Nigeria's own textile mills, led to the eventual collapse of the industry by the late 1970s. In addition, cloth made with commercial dyes in a range of colors using the resist techniques of *adire*, became popular during the Nigerian civil war (1967–9) when a government ban on the import of cloth was enforced (Picton 1995b: 17).

A renaissance in *adire* occurred in the late 1980s when it was 'considered the queen of fashion' by elites in the capital city of Lagos (Byfield 1993: 6).[8] *Adire* became increasingly popular as younger textile artists began to experiment with making wax batiks with newly available Indantheran dyes imported from Europe. The dye-fast qualities and deep hues of these dyes were perceived as superior to indigenous dyes (Craftspace Touring 1992). The brightly colored hand-crafted batiks became a mainstay in the Yoruba fashion world of the 1990s.

The Importance of Patronage to Continuity in Textile Traditions

The late twentieth century has seen a lively revival in Yoruba handcrafted textiles compared to the Hausa and Nupe regions where with the exception of cloth made for outgroup patrons, overall production significantly declined. As relevance wanes, patronage and market demands drop and so too do the number of artists involved in the manufacture and processing of cloth. Textile producers, like all artists, expect something back from their activity—money, barter, prestige or a combination of such. Without sufficient patronage weavers and other textile artists turn to other occupations and do not train the next generation. Without a market for their products, young people increasingly pursue employment opportunities offered in the modern sector. This has happened in the Hausa and Nupe regions. At the same time, Yoruba weaving and dyeing industries based on indigenous techniques, with the addition of new materials and technologies have flourished, and new types of textiles are continually emerging. Why? The answer lies in the nature of Yoruba culture and the kind of patron support for cloth industries. A primary reason for the continuing Yoruba cloth production is tied to the ongoing perceived cultural relevance which indigenous textiles continue to have for the majority of the population, as indicators of personal, social and ethnic identity.

Although Yoruba textile artist faced many of the problems mentioned for the Hausa and Nupe, a different dynamic was at work in southern Nigeria in the first half of the twentieth century. While Hausa and Nupe cloth production continued to be oriented toward the more conservative needs of outgroup pastoralists and Muslim elites which supported the trade networks that had been in place for centuries, Yoruba *adire* and *aso-oke* textile artists were involved in a larger arena of global exchange, involving links to other West African countries made possible by the British trade network. The exposure of the Yoruba to British culture and trade goods intensified the rate of change, leading to the emergence of new patterns of taste and indigenous innovative cloth types such as *adire* based on imported British designs. Contemporary *aso-oke* evolved from the longstanding caliphate cloth traditions. *Aso-oke*, unlike the Hausa forms of caliphate cloth, appealed to a broad spectrum of Yoruba patrons. The internal dynamics of this insatiable patron demand for contemporary *aso-oke* and the willingness of Yoruba weavers to respond to patrons' needs to stay abreast of the latest fashions are discussed more fully in Chapter 8.

Notes

1. Magenta *kudi* cloth made in one-half inch wide strips by Nupe weavers in Kura and Sokoto, also was alternately edge-stitched with strips of *yan kura* to produce blue and red wrappers and blouses for rural Hausa, and pastoral Fulani and Tuareg women.

2. Chiroma weavers claim that they have not woven either *fari* or *saki* cloth since the 1950s, and only one elderly Riman Rake weaver was still making wide *saki* cloth in 1990 for traders who purchased the cloth to resell to rural Hausa women and pastoral Fulani women. Personal communication with Chiroma and Riman Rake weavers, 1981 and 1990.

3. A Riman Rake weaver, Musa, claimed that his designs could be identified anywhere, indicating the pride weavers take in individual expression. (Personal communication, 1981).

4. An alternative suggestion for the origin of the double treadle broadloom is that it spread into Hausaland in its present form from the Kanuri area to the northeast in the first half of the twentieth century (Meek 1925, Lamb and Holmes 1980: 115-117, and Deafenbaugh 1989: 175).

5. Some types of women's cloth are also labeled *gwado* (Lamb and Homes 1980: 261).

6. See Renne (1995) for an account of the impact on a northern Yoruba village.

7. Other import cloth was also tested. Experiments with making *adire* with imported velvets and brocades were abandoned early because of the high cost of these cloths (Afolabi 1988: 6).

8. This was due to a government ban on the import of prestige cloths to stop the outflow of Nigerian currency.

8

The Fashionable World of the Yoruba

The survival and revitalization of the Yoruba *aso-oke* tradition in the late twentieth century has been closely tied to broad-based ingroup patronage. Market demand for aso-oke has remained strong because the cloth appeals to the Yoruba pride in ethnic identity. The initial impact from the British on *aso-oke* cloth production was relatively slight with local demand remaining high due to a strong patronage base. The wearing of *aso-oke* was not tied exclusively to the ruling class; all adult Yoruba wore it for ritual and ceremonial occasions. Colonial influence was most apparent in the introduction of factory yarns. Yoruba weavers quickly recognized advantages to using imported yarn which was easier and faster to weave than hand-spun yarn, thereby increasing production.[1] They readily experimented with the new fibers, expanding their color palette with pre-dyed yarn and imported dyes and by the 1930s, were regularly using machine-spun yarn (Clarke 1996b: 94). Nevertheless, taste preferences in *aso-oke* colors remained conservative with indigo, red, tan and white being prominent through the mid-1960s (Bray 1966: 76–7), although colorful cotton and rayon yarns were used for contrasting warp stripes and weft-float patterns (Clarke 1996b: 99). Coinciding with independence in 1960, *aso-oke* production became oriented toward self-motivated wealthy urban consumers, influenced by the colorful range of imported printed textiles for sale in the marketplace.

The viability of the *aso-oke* industry, like other successful handwoven cloth traditions in West Africa, especially was associated with the rise of this new 'middle-class' elite that accompanied the colonialism expansion of cash incomes and increases in population and living standards (M. Johnson 1978: 267–8). Clothing from handwoven cloth, in particular, has been adopted by wealthy urbanites as visible symbols of prosperity, status and pride in ethnic heritage. Like the Asante *kente* weaving industry (see Chapter 4), the Yoruba *aso-oke* industry has benefitted from the self-motivated patronage of wealthy urbanites. According to M. Johnson:

An elite demand depends partly on fashion, partly on political and religious attitudes, and very little on price; indeed, any attempt to reduce prices might prove self-defeating, since part of the demand depends on the expensiveness of the product (1978: 267).

Traditionally, Yoruba weavers were organized into kin-based production groups in which the master weavers controlled production and distribution. The use of family members as the labor force allowed production costs to remain low. Also, rather than relying on long-distance traders for distribution, master weavers often acted as their own market agents, carrying cloth to specialized periodic cloth markets in central Yorubaland.[2] To this day, the marketing of the bulk of *aso-oke* is in the hands of weaver-traders (Figure 8.1) who sell it in regional markets to both large and small-scale traders who in turn resell it in secondary markets throughout Nigeria as well as other areas of West Africa. The overlapping roles of producer-weaver and trader-patron is critical here for it guarantees continual transactions between producer and consumer, which ensure quality control and feedback resulting in a rapid turnover in designs.[3] In short, Yoruba *aso-oke* weavers have their fingers on the pulse of fashion through ongoing interactions with their elite consumer-patrons. The result is that thousands of patterns are available at any one time in the markets with new ones being added almost on a daily basis. 'In a tradition that enables and encourages choice between options innovation in pattern and design will be a matter of extending the range of options' (Picton 1992: 46).

The Yoruba desire to be attired in the most current fashion reflects a larger cultural pattern of receptivity to innovation. Compared to many other African peoples, the Yoruba are unusually open to innovations introduced from within and from outside their society while at the same time being tenacious about retaining a strong sense of cultural identity. An ongoing demand for new styles of indigenous cloth is coupled with a strong sense of 'Yorubaness.' *Asha*, the Yoruba word for 'tradition' or 'cultural heritage,' encapsulates the dynamic nature of the culture; it has a core meaning of 'selection' (*sha*, 'to pick or select many or several things from a collection or an available range of options' (Abiodun 1994: 40).[4] *Asha* is a wellspring which reflects the flexibility of Yoruba culture, a compilation of the past and present that can incorporate change without losing its cultural heart or core. The Yoruba live in a world where 'nothing is constant except change' (Lawal 1997). Yoruba textile artists, responding to the ever-changing concerns of consumer-patrons, continually expand upon the basic tradition to create relevant contemporary products.[5] New materials and technologies, new motifs, new contexts for the use of cloth and new types of patrons have encouraged cloth and clothing producers to continue to experiment and innovate.

Figure 8.1. Yoruba master weaver and cloth trader in his shop which stockpiles stacks of *aso-oke* cloth, Iseyin, Nigeria. Source: Judith Perani and Norma Wolff.

In the contemporary Yoruba world, one can see every kind of dress and fabric being used. Yorubas still put on their distinctive ethnic dress, choosing from robes and wrappers made from caliphate cloth of hand-spun cotton or silk or strip cloth woven from machine-spun cotton, viscose (similar to rayon and silk), or reflective lurex. Forms of handcrafted resist-dyed cloth using indigo or bright-colored imported dyes compete with factory-printed textiles such as wax prints and fancy prints,[6] as well as a plethora of other types of machine-woven fabrics from Europe, Asia and local textile mills. Western imported clothing, varying from business suits to blue jeans and t-shirts also are commonly seen. The continuous onslaught and adoption of new styles of *aso-oke* cloth into the current Yoruba fashion scene clearly exemplifies the Yoruba ability to draw upon their indigenous culture (*asha*) while adapting to new cultural conditions.

Most handcrafted woven and decorated Yoruba cloth, past and present, is used by Yorubas for clothing; patrons seek out those cloth and clothing styles which best reflect their life style. Elders among the Yoruba have seen tremendous change in the look of the textiles used for everyday and prestige garments. *Aso-oke* has gained a *shiny* new look with the utilization of new yarns. Indigo-dyed *adire* has been largely replaced by brightly colored cloth dyed with imported chemical dyes. Moreover, totally new artforms have appeared as Yoruba artists push the boundaries of textile arts to create fine arts for an international audience. Economic and social change, the introduction of new technologies, and shifting patterns of taste and fashion in a fast-changing society have all played a part.

Economic and Social Change

Since the late 1970s a series of events has significantly affected the stylistic direction of Yoruba textile traditions. Without certain economic restrictions established by the Nigerian federal government beginning in the late 1970s, the efflorescence of indigenous cloth production might have been more limited. From the mid-1960s to the late 1970s during Nigeria's oil boom, the Yoruba's fashion world was tied to global markets. The truly wealthy were able to patronize famous designers of Europe such as Christian Dior, Nina Ricci and Gucci (Byfield 1993: 6). Robes and wrapper ensembles, still a popular form of dress, were made from the most expensive imported textiles. In the 1970s 'lace,' an imported cotton/synthetic cloth with eyelet embroidery (and rhinestone attachments in some cases) was the height of elite fashion. Lower income people satisfied their needs for prestige cloth with factory damasks, brocades and wax prints. In 1978 the federal government, disturbed by the cash outflow to Europe, put a ban on the import of 'lace' and other prestige clothes and goods. In the 1980s, devaluations of the Nigerian currency further narrowed patronage for legally and smuggled imported prestige clothes to only the most wealthy. The result was that local hand-crafted cloth was competitive as a source for everyday and prestige clothing.[7] Patronage turned inward, and there was a renewed demand for *adire*-derived cloth and *aso-oke*. In 1986 the federal government's Structural Adjustment Programme (SAP), facilitated the revitalization of the handcrafted textile industries. While there has been a great deal of criticism of the effects of the SAP, it had a positive affect on the *aso-oke* industry.

> The growth of the [*aso-oke*] industry, no doubt, remains one of the positive consequences of the Structural Adjustment Programme (SAP) imposed in 1986 to revamp the ailing economy. Self-reliance and inward-looking ideas are some of the guiding philosophies of SAP. In the textile industry, *Aso-oke* weavers are great beneficiaries of the programme as the prices of imported clothing materials have become very expensive. (Moloye 1991: 8)

In the 1980s as *aso-oke* and *adire* became increasingly desirable cloths for fashionable dress, the patronage base for these industries expanded. The market for hand-crafted textiles allowed for the development of a larger workforce. While the establishment of free primary education in the Yoruba region beginning in 1956 had drawn away apprentices of dyers and weavers, new government programs in the 1980s drew them back. Following the implementation of SAP, the increased demand for handcrafted cloth opened up new opportunities for self-employment. In 1987 the federal government, recognizing the potential of craft production as a means of promoting employ-ment and self-reliance, developed programs such as the National Open Apprenticeship Scheme (NOAS). Apprenticeship in cloth weaving, dress-making and tailoring were included in the possible training programs open to individuals after leaving primary or secondary school (Aboaba 1997). This resulted in a huge increase in the number of male and female 'fashion designers' in Yorubaland by the early 1990s. It also led to a revolution in the long-standing gender division of labor in Yoruba weaving. Young women striving for self-reliance quickly found that the woman's upright single-heddle loom slowed production.[8]

Until this time, the weaving of narrow-strip cloth had been a male mono-poly. Some of the early female pioneers who wanted to learn *aso-oke* weaving faced a cultural sanction and male weavers were reluctant to train them.

> A weaver in Oshogbo told me that she apprenticed herself to a cotton weaver in Ibadan. The old man was reluctant to accept her, because it meant breaking a

taboo. But he had little work and needed money. When he had started to teach her he said: 'Please don't pay me any money until you have completed your apprenticeship. Because if anything happens to you now, the people will say that I should never have taught you and that I killed you through my greed.' (Beier 1993: 7)[9]

Nevertheless, women who learned taught others so that by the early 1990s women *aso-oke* weavers were established in many larger Yoruba towns. Dyeing and the production of *adire* and other resist-dyed forms of cloth also lost gender boundaries. Not only did young women return to the female-dominated craft of dyeing, but young men who learned resist-dyeing techniques in school were taking up the occupation. New forms of dyed cloth emerged due to a new clientele and the loosening of cultural prescriptions against men dyeing cloth (Byfield 1993: 7).

In part because of the linkage with the highly promoted government programs which encouraged self-reliance for individuals and the nation, a new pride in indigenous textile arts grew. Speaking of the popularity of *aso-oke* in 1990, a female master weaver in Ibadan asserted: 'We are now promoting our culture so Europeans won't come to overrule us' (Ige 1990). *Adire* evokes similar sentiments.

Introduction of New Materials and Technologies

As *adire* and *aso-oke* began to feed the expectations of contemporary fashion-minded people, there was a deliberate attempt to make it different from the cloth produced in the past. Shiny lurex yarn increasingly replaced cotton as the dominant material of *aso-oke* and colorful chemical dyes replaced the subdued indigo dye of *adire*. New techniques were introduced. Wax batiking transformed the look of *adire* and photo-stencilling allowed the transfer of pictures and designs to light-weight cloth and t-shirts. Treadle looms were modified to increase the width of *aso-oke* strips (known as '*double-wides*'), and European-style floor looms were used to produce a broadcloth *aso-oke* look-alike and other novel cloth types. These innovations have allowed textile artists of the 1990s to produce cloth and clothing for the fashionable Yoruba that is a development of the older traditions but capable of infinite variation.

Shifting Patterns of Taste and Fashion

It is impossible to discuss the production and consumption of contemporary Yoruba textiles without considering the nature of 'fashion.' The Yoruba consumption of cloth today is largely fueled by fashion, the antithesis of 'tradition.' Polhemus and Procter (1978), in their analysis of Western fashion, make a functional distinction between clothing that acts as a symbol of continuity – anti-fashion, and that which is symbolic of change – fashion. Historically, older anti-fashion styles of cloth and clothing are seen as incorporating the collective ideology of the cultural tradition and so are static and slow to change. To wear anti-fashion garments identifies an individual with the older indigenous status positions which still have some importance in the contemporary scene. In Yoruba society of the 1990s, the wearing of anti-fashion cloth and clothing is reserved for events of cultural importance, such as marriages and funerals, and is worn by those people who value their 'Yorubaness.' In many parts of Yorubaland, *etu, alaari* and *sanyan* which adhere to the older patterns of caliphate cloth, continue to be worn by kings, chiefs, priests of the indigenous cults, and by individuals who appreciate the traditions of the past. Fashionable cloth and dress, on the other hand, is linked to social mobility and the rapid social change that threatens the retention of indigenous values.

Among the Yoruba, the individual who wears fashionable styles of dress is marked as one who fully participates in the modernizing society. To be fashionable one can wear tailored clothing based on the European model; one-of-a-kind creations from fashion designers using a wide variety of cloth, including handcrafted textiles; or indigenous Yoruba dress made from the most recently imported or handcrafted textiles. Any one of these fashionable looks can be projected through the use of *adire* and *aso-oke*.

Aso-Oke as Anti-Fashion and Fashion

Aso-oke is considered an 'important cloth' by Yorubas. 'Important cloth' is expensive, prestigeful and culturally significant. As an important cloth, *aso-oke* has no equivalent in the Yoruba textile inventory. It is the ultimate visual statement of family and ethnic pride. To wear clothing made of *aso-oke* strips, particularly the older patterns, is to proclaim links with the rich indigenous culture of the Yoruba. This, however, does not mean that it does not change.

> . . . *aso-oke* is far from the cliché image of a static, convention-bound craft doomed to extinction in the face of industrial competition and changing tastes. (D. Clarke 1996b: 94)

The resilience of this textile tradition has been proven again and again as forces of cultural change inside and outside Yorubaland have tested artists' readiness to adapt to ever-changing shifts in taste, competition from outside markets, changing technologies, dwindling local supplies of raw materials, inflation, intrusive government development policies and projects, and the lure of modern sector occupations drawing away the work force. Strips belonging to the 'caliphate cloth' category of *aso-oke* are still being produced; while *sanyan*, *etu* and *alaari* may be available in markets, they are more commonly commissioned. The markets feature more fashionable cloth. *Aso-oke* of cotton, cotton and synthetic mix, lurex and viscose has been readily available in a huge variety of patterns and colors; in 1995 'literally thousands of patterns' of *aso-oke* were found in the Araromi cloth market in Oyo (Clarke 1996b: 96).

Anti-fashion Styles

Today, caliphate style cloth types – *sanyan*, *etu*, *and alaari* – are restricted in their use. According to weavers, 'proper' caliphate cloth must still be made with hand-spun thread (*aso owu riran*) and natural dyes. While examples may vary slightly through the addition of thin warp and weft stripes of additional colors, the base colors of beige, dark blue and red remain constant. Yoruba color categories parallel the three basic color terms[10] of the Yoruba language. White, or lightness (*funfun*) is represented by beige *sanyan*, black, or darkness (*dudu*) by indigo-dyed *etu*, and red (*kpukpa*) by *alaari*. A white or beige garment proclaims the moral distinction of the wearer, indigo denotes honor and dignity of high status, and red calls to mind the power of divinities and ancestors (Euba 1986: 16–7). Garments of *sanyan*, *etu* and *alaari* are still considered the most appropriate choice for expressing one's Yorubaness at occasions of great consequence, including family rites of passage, such as marriages, naming ceremonies for infants and funerals. Many of the caliphate cloth type garments have been handed down through the generations so that even a poor person may wear this prestigeful *aso-oke*; moreover, individuals lucky enough to own 'important' dress lend it freely to relatives and friends for special occasions.

Production of the time-honored cloth made with handspun yarn has become increasingly rare. Weavers say the handspun yarn is scarce, must be dyed through labor intensive techniques and is difficult to weave. The unevenness of the yarn makes it prone to tangle so that production time is increased. In addition, handspun yarn tends to produce knots that must be picked out or result in a rough textured cloth not considered of high quality. In the mid-1990s in Iseyin, the weaving town considered to be 'the home of *aso-oke*,' very few weavers produced *etu* and *sanyan* using hand-spun yarn and only for special orders. *Alaari* was not made at all because the vegetable dyes were no longer processed. The price of such cloth was significantly higher to compensate the weavers for the extra time needed for production due to the use of hand-spun yarn. To meet the continuing demand for these culturally important cloth types, some weavers now use machine-spun cotton yarn to produce cloth in the familiar colors, sometimes even using natural dyes. This cloth, sold as *sanyan*, *etu* and *alaari* in the markets, resembles the time-sanctioned types in color but varies considerably from the older types of cloth in the texture and the amount of contrasting color added as warp and weft stripes. Few consumer-patrons are concerned about differences in yarn, although weavers mark the difference in labels they use to call up the mental template needed for production. Cloth made with cotton yarns dyed to resemble the natural color of the native *sanyan* silk is called *kugu*; cloth made with indigo-dyed machine spun yarn is called *petuje*; 'adulterated *alaari*' refers to any primarily red to maroon cotton cloth.

Fashion Styles

Aso-oke used for fashionable dress is never made with hand-spun yarn. Instead, the different types of machine spun yarn (*owu eebo*) distinguish the major categories, creating distinctively different surface textures in the finished cloth. *Aso olowu*, cloth made with cotton yarn, has a matte finish, similar to the older handspun types but smoother. *Aso shain-shain* made with metal-licized plastic lurex thread, is characterized by a shiny, slightly rough surface which catches the light and glistens. *Aso siliki*, made with rayon or viscose thread, has a smoother satin-like lustrous surface. It is interesting to note that as the materials used in weaving begin to vary significantly from the native cotton and silk, English loan words increasingly are used as labels by both weavers and consumers. The use of English, the language of modernity, in labels such as *aso shain-shain* ('shine-shine') and *aso silik* ('silk') increases consumer appeal of these fashionable cloth types.

In the 1990s, *aso oke* is considered the ultimate prestige cloth for the wealthy Yoruba elite of Lagos, the fashion capital of Nigeria. In a context where ostentatious display is indulged and the Yoruba sense of *asha* underlies behavior, *aso-oke* is a significant indicator of self-expression. In Lagos and other large cities each weekend is marked by lavish celebrations and ceremonies, to which people are expected to wear their most fashionable ensembles. For members of the elite, obligations to attend weekend events can provide a scheduling and fashion dilemma. Marriages, naming cere-monies, birthday anniversaries, funeral wakes, openings of houses, businesses and schools, political appointments and coronations and their anniversaries are occasions to be seen in one's most fashionable dress as well as to observe the newest trends in cloth. It is in these contexts that new cloth patterns are launched.

Women wear *aso-oke* either as 'completes'(ensembles of wrapper (*iro*), overwrapper or shawl (*ipele*), blouse (*buba*) and head-tie (*gele*), or combine the shawl and head-tie of *aso-oke* with a wrapper and blouse of factory prestige cloth. Men may wear only a cap (*fila*) of *aso-oke* but can also wear the male 'complete' of *aso-oke*: trousers (*sokoto*), shirt (*buba*), large embroidered over-robe (*agbada* or other style) and the cap. Hosts, sponsors and members of families and clubs or organizations (*egbe*) who take an active role in a celebration or ceremony are more likely to wear the complete ensembles as *aso-ebi*. *Aso-ebi* (discussed in Chapter 2) is identical cloth used to dress people alike for the purpose of expressing group solidarity. In a 1995 funeral held by an elite family for their mother, the direct descendants all wore completes of gold *shain-shain* individualized with embroidery. The use of *aso-oke* as *aso-ebi* in contexts like this is the most common way in which a pattern gains enough attention to be copied and become a model for further innovation.(see Figure 5.2) Prior to a large family celebration, a member or delegation from the host family will place one or more large orders for *aso-oke* to be worn as *aso-ebi* by the group at the affair. The pre-production commission usually involves negotiation between family members and a cloth trader, although patrons can go directly to weavers. Because patrons attend weekly celebrations and ceremonies where fashionable *aso-oke* is worn, they are up to date about what is in vogue and are concerned that their *aso-ebi* will be admired for novelty and fashionability. This necessitates a certain amount of negotiation in the transaction between patrons, traders and weavers, all of whom share knowledge about the range of possible design and technological possibilities (Clarke 1996b: 96–7).

> The traders, many of whom belong to the same social circle as their customers, maintain a large stock, both to help customers select designs and to meet urgent orders. Customers will come with an idea in mind for a modification of another design they have seen recently, or will discuss with the trader what is currently in vogue. Some traders try to guide customers towards colour/design combinations they think will be successful but ultimately as one commented 'if they say they want it like this, I will do it for [them], but if it is not nice, I am not going to take it back.' (Clarke 1996b: 96)

Cloth traders, then, often act as mediators between the patron and the weaver, keeping a stock of 'interesting designs' for patrons to examine. Some traders devise new patterns themselves and commission weavers to make sample strips they can show to their customers. Alternatively, patrons may bring samples of *aso-oke* or describe patterns recently seen as a base for innovation. Common modifications may involve a color change, the addition or subtraction of stripes, or the alteration of stripe width (Clarke 1996b: 96). After the commissioned cloth is delivered to the patron, the new pattern is added to the samples available and may be reproduced as a market commodity. Master weavers also keep large collections of samples to stimulate commissions.

The Shain-Shain Revolution

The 1990s has been a period of rich innovation in *aso-oke* production in both weaving technology and patterns.[11] Technological innovations have come from weavers as they strive to feed the insatiable fashion market, while changes in patterns are often initiated by the patrons. Many innovations of the nineties emerged as Yoruba weavers explored the potential of lurex yarn to produce *shain-shain*. Beginning in the 1960s, according to Iseyin weavers, small amounts of lurex yarn were brought back from Egypt by Muslim weavers who had gone on the Hadj pilgrimage to Mecca. Initially small stripes of lurex were added to cotton warps to create a new look. Gradually the amount of lurex yarn available increased until the shining yarn dominated the surface of the cloth and *shain-shain* controlled the market. By 1995 Nigeria was one of the largest consumers of Japanese metallicized thread, 'officially importing over 53 tonnes in the first 8 months of 1995 alone' (Clarke 1996b: 94). Plain weave *shain-shain* is considered a lightweight modern cloth suitable for a range of clothing styles. Popular for its connotations of modernity, it is tailored in Yoruba styles as well as used for Western-style clothing. One sees it in any context where people wear formal dress.

> *Shain-shain* can be worn any time – to house openings, birthdays, burials, to church, any ceremony, Muslim holidays. They wear it because it is lighter weight. Everybody wears it. (Ige 1990)

Due to its popularity, an explosion of *shain-shain* types hit the marketplace in the early nineties. In addition to *shain-shain ordinary* or *plain*, a plain weave with lurex warp and cotton weft, innovative forms including 'ojunt-osoro,' 'jakadi,' 'sequence' and 'sandpaper' appeared. *Ojuntosoro* differs from *shain-shain plain* by incorporating twisted three- (or four-) ply weft strands of three cotton and one lurex yarn. The reflective lurex yarn appears and disappears along the surface of the cloth, sparkling more dramatically than ordinary *shain-shain*. Dubbed *ojuntosoro*, which means 'the eye is speaking,' it quickly became popular with the public and was widely copied by many weavers.[12] Interestingly, as the popularity of *ojuntosoro* grew, the label and demand for this cloth type spread more quickly than the production know-how. Some weavers who had not seen samples merely applied the label to their products without incorporating the twisted mixed weft. Another innovation, *shain-shain jakadi*, is characterized by areas of crossed lurex warp and lurex weft yarns, producing squares, rectangles and weft stripes that reflect like polished metal. *Jakadi* mimics jacquard, the most popular and expensive import cloth. By 1995 Iseyin weavers were making *shain-shain satin* with even larger areas of crossed warp and weft lurex yarns in response to the introduction of satin jacquard, an even more expensive and prestigeful import cloth. The ultimate *shain-shain* of the nineties was '*sandpaper,*' made entirely of lurex with the exception of cotton selvages to give it strength. The name clearly conveys the discomfort caused by this cloth when used as clothing, seen as a small inconvenience for being perceived at the height of fashion.

Yoruba weavers, under the stimulus of fashion demand, also explored the full potential of the treadle loom throughout the 1990s. Beginning with the six decorative techniques characteristic of *aso-oke* (warp stripes, weft stripes, ikat, open-work, carried-over threads and supplementary weft floats) (Clarke 1996b: 93), weavers readily experimented with new materials to create new decorative effects. At this time, a ribbed version of *shain-shain* cloth ('sequence' of 'shun-shun'), created by using an eight-ply cotton weft with a lurex warp, appeared (Clarke 1996b: 94). They also modified the width of the cloth and experimented with a new loom type. In 1994 'double-wide' cloth varying from 5.5 to 7.5 inches wide was being made on treadle looms modified to accommodate extra warp (Clarke 1996b: 97)[13] The wider widths caught on with the public and in 1996 the four-inch strips which had been the standard for over a century now were being referred to as 'the old type' or 'the common ones,' no longer considered fashionable (Clarke 1996b: 97). Even wider cloth made on the European broadloom to resemble *aso-oke* gained popularity. Such cloth has narrow stripes at four-inch intervals or is made to look like strip cloth by separating the warps at regular intervals to create gaps where only weft threads show on the face of the cloth.[14] It is the suggestion of strip cloth that makes the broadloom cloth fashionable. Some customers further heighten the impression of *aso-oke* by sewing a seam down the breaks in the warp or by cutting the cloth and sewing it back together (Clarke 1998).

Fashion Names

Any of the different types of fashionable *aso-oke* can catch the attention of the public and be replicated or serve as a base for innovation. When patterns gain widespread popularity, they acquire 'fashion names,'[15] such as 'sugar,' 'carpet' and 'shagari' (Nigerian Head of State). The origins of fashion names are not always clear. They may be bestowed by a group or individual who commissions the design, the weaver, or cloth traders. They may gain currency in the same way as slang enters a language, with no known ownership. Attaching fashion names aids in marketing cloth, identifying it by its most distinctive feature or by tying it to local events and personages. 'Fashion names' can pinpoint certain cloth designs in time, but they also reveal the fleeting nature of *aso oke* designs which come and go as fashion dictates.

The Yoruba practice of assigning names to striking cloth patterns for purposes of merchandising was noted by Delano in the 1930s.

> Immediately they leave the loom they are given names. European merchants who ship print clothes here for sale, on arrival give them native names, and by those names the natives know and call them. It is necessary, therefore, for the salesman to know the names of each and every cloth in his shop, otherwise he is jeopardizing his trade. The names usually refer to important events or persons in the town at the time when the cloth was first introduced. (Delano 1937: 149–50)

In 1951, the anthropologist William Bascom noted that the names of the 354 *aso-oke* samples he collected were often tied to the social clubs that had originally commissioned the cloth as *aso-ebi*. If the cloth became popular, the name 'spread the club's fame' (Boyer 1983: 42). Moreover, a number of the samples in the Bascom collection had 'regal names' referring to prominent political leaders, traditional chiefs and kings. One examples includes an innovative pattern made with handspun yarn labeled 'Kuti of Gbade Sits Down,' a reference to the coronation of the *oba* in Oyo in 1945. Such a pattern would be worn by large numbers of people who attended the coronation. Another example, labeled 'Arrival from Mecca of the King of Oyo,' was made with machine-spun thread to celebrate the hadj of the muslim Oyo king in 1950. This pattern, which incorporated tan machine-spun thread dyed to look like *sanyan* had the look of prestige needed to honor the king but was reasonable in price so that it was worn by all of the city's social clubs who gathered to meet the king on his return (Boyer 1983: 45). The linkage of certain patterns to historical events such as the coronation of a king or activities of prominent politicians is still a practice. 'Ododo Murtala' ('the flowers of Murtala') popular in the 1970s honors General Murtala Ramat Muhammed, Nigerian Head of State who was assassinated less than a year after taking office. The pattern 'Keep Right', also popular in the 1970s, was a reference to a change in national road laws. 'Abuja,' a fashion name of the 1980s, refers to the new Nigerian capital city built during this decade at great expense. It was used to label an extremely expensive double-sided reversible cloth with weft-float patterns and with time was expanded to refer to all cloths of that type. New fashion names continually emerge, gain popularity for a year or so, and then are replaced as new patterns and *aso-oke* types take over the fashion scene. As in the past, references to current events, prominent people, distinctive characteristics of the cloth and the social circumstances of the emergence of the pattern, trigger a fashion name. One new cotton and lurex cloth, reputed for keeping the wearer cool, is called 'Air Conditioner.'(Figure 8.2) This cloth utilizes the older technique for creating openwork patterns by inserting supplementary weft yarns to tie off warps, creating rows of holes across the strip. In Air Conditioner the holes are much larger than in older types of *aso-oke*.

In the 1990s *aso-oke* is more fashion driven than ever before with innovations proliferating at lightening speed. An extremely popular cloth, 'Rainbow,' identified by the juxtaposed multicolored warp stripes of at least five different colors was the source of a multitude of cloth variations. Nothing in the urban milieu escapes the observant *aso-oke* weaver as a cloth called 'Calenda,' based on the photograph of a local dignitary for a calendar, demonstrates.[16]

The Story of 'Super-Q'

A technological innovation of the 1990s provides a fascinating example of the importance of the patron in artistic change, the openness of Yorubas to incorporate innovation originating outside their own culture, and the willingness of Yoruba textile artists to adopt and shape that innovation in the context of the fashion world of the modernizing society.

In 1996, two fashionable handcrafted textiles were 'fighting it out for the top ceremonies among the wealthy of Lagos' (Clarke 1996a). Both differed significantly from *aso-oke* of past years. One was an 'imitation' *aso-oke* woven on European broadlooms. The second, the focus of this example, was 'Super-Q.'[17] Super-Q is a densely woven 51/2-inch double-wide ribbed strip cloth made with a 'silk' (rayon), cotton/synthetic mix ('Mirai') or lurex warp with an eight-ply cotton weft to create a ribbed effect. The most distinctive feature is a warp float not seen in Yoruba strip cloth before. [18] (see Figure 5.2)

The introduction of Super-Q into the Yoruba fashion scene was the achievement of a single patron – a female entrepreneurial cloth trader and owner of the Super-Q boutique in Lagos. In order to catch the eye of the fashionable elite, this woman imported strip cloth from other parts of West Africa. She sold double-wide strips made in Dakar, Senegal by migrant Ghana weavers,

Figure 8.2. Yoruba woman wearing wrapper ensemble made from 'Air Conditioner' *shain-shain aso-oke* cloth, Ibadan, Nigeria. Source: Judith Perani and Norma Wolff.

which had the advantage of being novel in the Lagos fashion world. After her new fashion became popular, she hired migrant Ewe weavers from Ghana to work in her Lagos compound and copy the designs from Dakar. As the cloth type gained popularity, other cloth traders took samples to Ghana, commissioning weavers to produce the fashionable cloth and in some cases encouraged them to migrate to Lagos. The migrant weavers established themselves in Lagos, and many in time formed their own businesses, bringing additional weavers to Lagos. By 1996 several hundred Ewe weavers had resettled in the Lagos area, producing the highly desirable Super-Q *aso-oke* for elite consumption. Through these Ewe weavers the supplementary warp float technique, prevalent in Ghana at the time, was introduced as a design feature of Super-Q (Clarke 1996b: 98). The resulting cloth mixed design features of Yoruba *aso-oke* with features of Senegalese and Ghanaian strip weaving, a product of contemporary Yoruba cross-cultural patronage.

Due to the popularity of Super-Q, cloth traders and individuals were soon placing orders with Yoruba weavers in Lagos and major weaving towns such as Iseyin, Oyo and Ilorin (Clarke 1996b, 1998). In order to produce Super-Q, Yoruba weavers were required to make a number of modifications in their production process and equipment. The reed and heddle of the Yoruba loom had to be widened to accommodate the dimensions of double-wide strips. Some Yoruba weavers also adopted the steel-toothed reed used by Ghanaian weavers to produce the tighter, thicker texture characteristic of Super-Q. Incorporating the decorative warp floats involved learning new weaving techniques as well as further modification of the loom equipment. Despite the technological demands required for weaving Super-Q, many Yoruba *aso-oke* weavers modified their looms and mastered the techniques of Super-Q. Iseyin weavers were producing it for the market by 1996: Super-Q joined the inventory of cloth types to generate additional new and fashionable cloth designs in the Yoruba area. In a further development women began to weave a cloth resembling Super-Q on the European broad loom.

Yoruba individuals, with the financial means to do so, are continually adding to their personal wardrobes, especially in the fast-moving fashion world of the large cities. With this kind of patronage, the production of contemporary forms of *aso-oke* strip-cloth is at what is probably an all-time high along with handcrafted batiks based on the older tradition of *adire* that are produced in their tons. At the same time, the Yoruba are proud of their ethnic heritage, keeping the luxury caliphate-style cloth weaving tradition alive as they commission cloth for occasions of cultural importance. As the new millennium dawns, the fashionable, Yoruba art patrons enjoy what is perhaps the liveliest cloth and dress tradition in Africa.

Notes

1. The adoption of factory thread created unforseen problems for Yoruba, Hausa and Nupe weavers. The colonial policy of discouraging modern spinning and textile mills inside British West Africa made weavers dependent upon imported yarn. Thus *aso-oke* weavers faced a crisis during World War II (1939–1945) when the colonial government banned yarn imports. A decline in *aso-oke* production followed, continuing until the 1950s when higher incomes, a surge of nationalist sentiment, the reopening of long-distance trade markets, and the reestablishment of yarn importation, invigorated the industry again (O'Hear 1987: 512).

2. These include Oje Market in Ibadan, Jankara Market in Lagos, the Ede Market and more recently Araromi Market in Oyo.

3. See Dodwell (1955); Bray (1968, 1969); Wolff and Wahab (1996) and D. Clarke (1996b, 1998) for more detailed accounts of how trade and transactions are organized.

4. The term *asha* has a broad context of use. It can refer to 'style' or 'a person's behavior or mode of work of a group of people or a period. A sense of tradition, change and continuity in Yoruba thought is reflected in the terms *asha-atijo* ('old or ancient tradition or style',) *asha-tuntun* ('new tradition or style',) and *asha-atowodowo* ('a tradition or style passed on from one generation to the next') (Abiodun 1994: 40).

5. Bastian has pointed out in her study of Igbo women's adaptation of male dress, 'what seems most "traditional" about Nigerian traditional clothing practices is their constant experimentation and co-option of outside forms and objects' (Bastian 1996: 101).

6. Wax prints are machine printed on both sides using a resin paste, while fancy prints are printed on one side only with metal rollers (Picton 1995: 24).

7. In 1992 the five yards of imported lace cloth needed for a woman's 'complete' outfit cost between 1600 and 1700 naira, while an equivalent amount of *aso-oke* cost only 500 naira (Renne 1993-unpublished paper: 22.)

8. One female entrepreneur interviewed in Ibadan in 1990 who taught young women weaving techniques recognized the problem. During the two-year training period apprentices were taught to weave on the women's upright loom only to demonstrate how slow the process was (Ige 1990).

9. A rationale often given by male weavers for excluding women from *aso-oke* weaving is that they are often pregnant and cannot fit on the benches behind the double-heddle loom.

10. See Berlin and Kay (1969) for a discussion of the significance of 'basic color terms.'

11. Clarke, in his research on the creativity of *aso-oke* weavers, reports that elderly weavers felt that the rate at which new designs emerged has been accelerating since the 1970s (Clarke 1996a).

12. Yoruba weavers have never placed emphasis on who first devises a new technique or pattern. Individuals are pleased to be copied.

13. It is very possible that the 'double-wide' of 5.5 inches was first introduced by cloth traders who traveled to Senegal and Ghana and brought back samples for Yoruba weavers to copy. (See Clarke 1996: 98).

14. This practice of imitating narrow-strip cloth on broadlooms is not new, although it has not been popular for most of the twentieth century. As early as 1841, Yoruba broadcloth made on the woman's upright single-heddle loom was being made in imitation of *aso-oke* (Clarke 1997; Kriger 1990: 44).

15. Fashion names can be applied to both factory and handwoven cloth. In the 1990s, these labels are never attached to the older caliphate cloth types of *aso-oke*.

16. Samples of these fashionable *aso-oke* patterns were collected by Wolff and Wahab (1995) during 1993 taxonomy research in Nigeria.

17. Duncan Clarke (1996a, 1997) has documented the history of Super-Q in detail. According to Clarke, this innovation, along with the increase in the width of *aso-oke*, are 'radical changes ... opening up the possibility of vast new ranges of design permutations' (Clark 1996a).

18. As pointed out by Picton and Mack (1979: 56) the use of supplementary warps is rare in Africa. Where they occur they tend to be used to bind off wefts to create openwork and with the supplementary threads floated across the surface between rows of holes for decorative affect. The *eleya* technique of the Yoruba is an example.

Postscript: To Put on Cloth

Among the Okpelle of the northern Edo area in southern Nigeria, when a man reaches the stage in life when he is ready to take on political responsibility, he goes through a ceremony called *Irhuen* meaning 'I put on a cloth.' Before this 'cloth-tying' ritual, the young male is not considered a fully socialized member of the community; he has not yet made the transition to adulthood (Borgatti 1983: 31). When a Muslim Hausa leader takes the highest political office of the land, he is 'turbanned' as he assumes the weight of responsibility. Such metaphors of cloth relating to reaching the state of being most fully human permeate African culture. The clothed body is a core symbol of the nature/culture dialectic, setting apart the unclothed 'natural' body from the cultural self. It therefore comes as no surprise that cloth and dress developed into major artforms in the societies we have examined because of their association with this universal human value. To put on cloth – to dress the human body – is tied to the most fundamental beliefs that make up the worldview of African cultures throughout the continent.

At the level of 'practice,' however, individuals and groups are unconcerned with such metaphysical issues as they act out their day-to-day activities. Human agency enters in, and the desire to consume and manipulate the meaning of cloth and dress is tempered by social roles and concepts of self. Acting within the context of socially defined roles, patrons are affected by their 'habitus' – the internalized cultural constraints that dictate the range of allowable behaviors for individuals and groups in a specific cultural context. Habitus structures behaviors in social action, but as a cultural construct, it is continually in the act of creative transformation. In other words, the 'rules of the game' are always subject to change. Lived experience is a moving target, encompassing both a need for order while providing incentives to challenge the fixed order of things (Jackson 1989: 2). In the continually changing context of lived experience, cloth and dress are used by art patrons as 'tools' to express both individual and group goals, dependent upon the circumstances of the present. The decisions of the commissioning and consuming art patron as 'actor' or 'agent' therefore inject a dynamism into traditions of cloth and dress that results in the continual reinvention of these arts. The change may be slow (artistic drift) or swift, long-lived or transient. We have given examples of these tendencies throughout this book.

In Part I of this volume, we made a case for looking at the role of 'art patron' as indispensable to any analysis of the artistic process and the development of art traditions. The meanings that attach to specific works of art in their span of existence – their life history – are in the hands of the art patron. In cumulative acts of consumption and social action, art patrons are in large part responsible for the dynamics of art traditions such as cloth and dress. They always hover on the edge of change as artistic traditions respond to their social environments. In the African context, patrons are as important as artists, if not more so, in the creative transformation of art traditions. Creativity is not confined to the artist; patrons can be equally creative through their transactions with artists and their control of the meaning of artforms in sociocultural context. In this sense, it is the patron who creates the artist.

In Part II we focused on patterns of art patronage associated with two major social roles, the political role of leader and the economic role of trader, in an examination of the complexities of patronage, production and consumption of cloth and dress in an inter-ethnic regional context. The Hausa, Nupe and Yoruba provided us with a rich example of the crucial role art patronage plays in the development and survival of textile art traditions. The importance of cloth and dress to cultural expression has been demonstrated in the centuries-old legacy of the region, where leadership and trade played an indispensable part in shaping the similarities of the interconnected cloth and dress traditions of the Hausa, Nupe and Yoruba. The same factors encouraged continuity in the textile arts despite a changing habitus that increasingly incorporated the colonial influences and modernization processes of the twentieth century. On the other hand, continuing trade and market demands, representing both ingroup and outgroup patronage, and the introduction of new technologies and production materials added a dynamic quality to speed the rate of change in the cloth and dress traditions.

As the twentieth century comes to an end, the cultural differences between the Muslim societies of the north and the more open culture of the Yoruba have led to the emergence of distinctive variations in their traditions of cloth and dress. This is because the patrons for these arts are reacting to different habitus conditions. Contemporary Hausa society has retained many elements of a conservative culture in which inherited family status, class stratification, loyalty to an indigenous leadership and Islamic prescriptions on behavior place constraints on perceptions of appropriate expressions of self that affect consumption. On the other hand, the nature of Yoruba culture is expressed by the proverb, 'Many roads lead to the market' (Lawal 1997). Love of fashion and the rewards associated with innovation have led to an excellerating rate of change in the cloth and dress traditions of the Yoruba world.

In our exploration of the dynamics of art patronage in African societies, we have expanded the Western art history model. We have shown how art patrons integrate the patronage process into a broad range of roles associated with social, economic and religious life. While the types of artist-patron transactions described here are applicable to every form of art, as demonstrated in our examples and case studies, cloth and dress is a particularly rich focus to reveal that patronage is more than economic exchange. Our framework for analysis, presented in Chapter 1 and integrated into our examples, will hopefully prove useful to researchers who want to examine the multiple levels of meaning that artworks take on through social action and human agency. The importance of cloth as a 'social skin' and the key role that dress plays in creating the 'culturally-constituted body' have provided us with a particularly rich arena of study.

Bibliography

Abiodun, R. (1994a), 'Introduction: An African(?) Art History: Promising Theoretical Approaches in Yoruba Art Studies', in R. Abiodun, H.J. Drewal and J. Pemberton III (eds), *The Yoruba Artist: New Theoretical Perspectives on African Arts*, Washington and London: Smithsonian Institution, pp. 1–34.

Aboaba, Y.A. (1998), 'The National Directorate of Employment and Apprenticeship Programs in Weaving in Oyo State', *CON/TEXT: Research Reports of the Consortium for Indigenous Textile and Clothing Research*, no. 1.

Adams, M. (1980), 'Fon Appliquéd Cloths', *African Arts*, vol. XIII, no. 2, pp. 28–41.

—— (1993), 'Women's Art as Gender Strategy Among the We of Canton Boo', *African Arts*, vol. XXVI, no. 4, pp. 32–43.

Adamu, M. (1978), *The Hausa Factor in West African History*, Zaria and Ibadan: Ahmadu Bello University Press and Oxford University Press.

Adepegba, C.O. (1995), *Nigerian Art: Its Traditions and Modern Tendencies*, Ibadan: Jodad Publishers.

Adler, P. (1992), *African Majesty: The Textile Art of the Asante and Ewe*, New York: Thames and Hudson Ltd.

—— and Barnard, N. (1992), *Asafo! African Flags of the Fante*, London: Thames and Hudson Ltd.

Afolabi, A. (n.d.), *Adire in Abeokuta: The Fluctuating Fortunes of the Indigenous Textile Industry in South Western Nigeria in the Twentieth Century*, Iogun State University, Department of History.

Aherne, T.D. (1992), *Nakunte Diarra: Bogolanfini Artist of the Beledougou*, Bloomington: Indiana University Art Museum.

Akinjobin, I.A. (1966), 'The Oyo Empire in the 18th Century – a Reassessment', *Journal of the Historical Society of Nigeria*, vol. III, no. 3, pp. 449–60.

Akinwumi, T.M. (1990), *The Commemorative Phenomenon of Textile Use among the Yoruba: A Survey of Significance and Form*, PHD thesis, Institute of African Studies, University of Ibadan.

Allen, W. and Thompson, T.R.H. (1848), *A Narrative of the Expedition to the River Niger in 1841*, vol. II, London: Thomas Nelson Ltd.

Allison, P. (1956), 'The Last Days of Old Oyo', *Odu*, no. 4, pp. 16–27.

Anderson, R.L. (1989), *Art in Small-scale Societies*, 2nd edn, Englewood Cliffs, NJ: Prentice-Hall.

Anderson, M. and Kreamer, C.M. (1989), *Wild Spirits, Strong Medicine: African*

Art and the Wilderness, New York: The Center for African Art.

Antiri, J.A. (1974), 'Akan Combs', *African Arts*, vol. 8, no. 1, pp. 32–5.

Appadurai, A. (1986), 'Introduction: Commodities and the Politics of Value', in A. Appadurai (ed.), *The Social Life of Things: Commodities in Cultural Perspective*, Cambridge: Cambridge University Press, pp. 3–63.

Aradeon, S. (1987), 'The Architecture of a Hausa Master Mason', *The Nigerian Field*, vol. 52, pp. 3–18.

Aremu, P.S.O. (1982), 'Kijipa Motifs, Colour and Symbols', *Nigeria Magazine*, no. 140, pp. 3–10.

Arnoldi, M.J. (1995), 'Wrapping the Head', in M.J. Arnoldi and C.M. Kreamer (eds), *Crowning Achievements: African Arts of Dressing the Head*, Los Angeles: UCLA Fowler Museum of Cultural History, pp. 127–37.

—— and Geary, C.M. and Hardin, K.L. (eds) (1996) *African Material Culture*, Bloomington and Indianapolis: Indiana Univeristy Press.

Aronson, L. (1980), 'Patronage and Akwete Weaving', *African Arts*, vol. XIII, no. 3, pp. 62–66, 91.

—— (1992), 'Ijebu Yoruba *Aso Olona*', *African Arts*, vol. XXV, no. 3, pp. 52–63.

Babayemi, O.S. (1994), 'The Role of Oriki Orile and Itan in the Reconstruction of the Architectural History of the Palace of Gbongan', in R. Abiodun, H.J. Drewal and J. Pemberton III (eds), *The Yoruba Artist*, Washington, DC: Smithsonian Institution Press, pp. 143–7.

Baker, S.W. (1892, orig. 1862), *The Albert N-Yanza: Great Basin of the Nile and Explorations of the Nile Sources*, London: Macmillan and Co.

Banfield, A.W. (1905), *Life Among the Nupe Tribe in West Africa*, Berlin, Ontario: H.S. Hallman.

Barbour, J. and Simmonds, D. (eds), (1971), *Adire Cloth In Nigeria*, Ibadan: The Institute of African Studies, University of Ibadan.

Barth, H.(1851), *Travels in North and Central Africa 1849–1850*, vols. I–V, London: Longmans Green & Co.

Bastian, M.L. (1996), 'Female *"Alhajis"* and Entrepreneurial Fashions: Flexible Identities in Southeastern Nigerian Clothing Practice', in H. Hendrickson (ed.), *Clothing and Difference: Embodied Identities in Colonial and Post-Colonial Africa*, Durham and London: Duke University Press, pp. 97–132.

Bastin, M.L. (1984), 'Ritual Masks of the Chokwe', *African Arts*, vol. XVII, no. 4, pp. 40–44, 92–3.

Baxandall, M. (1972), *Painting and Experience in Fifteenth Century Italy*, London: Oxford University Press.

Bay, E.G. (1985), *Iron Altars of The Fon People of Benin*, Atlanta: Emory University Museum of Art and Archaeology.

Bayero, Abubukar (1981), personal communication, Bichi, Kano State, Nigeria.

Beier, U. (1993), *Yoruba Textile Art*, Bayreuth: Iwalewa.

Ben-Amos, P. (1975), 'Professionals and Amateurs in Benin Court Carving', in D. McCall and E. Bay (eds) *African Images*, pp. 170–88.

—— (1977), 'Pidgin Languages and Tourist Arts,' *Studies in the Anthropology of*

Visual Commuunication, vol. 4, no. 2, pp. 128–39.

—— (1978), 'Owina N'Ido: Royal Weavers of Benin', *African Arts*, vol. XI, no. 4, pp. 48–53.

—— (1980a), *The Art of Benin*, London: Thames and Hudson.

—— (1980b), 'Patron-Artist Interactions in Africa,' *African Arts*, vol. XIII, no. 3, pp. 56–7.

—— (1983), 'The Power of Kings: Symbolism of a Benin Ceremonial Stool', in P. Ben-Amos and A. Rubin, *The Art of Power, The Power of Art: Studies in Benin Iconography*, UCLA Museum of Cultural History, Monograph Series no. 19.

Bentor, E. (1995), 'In Search of the Artist: Ukara Cloth of Southeastern Nigeria', paper presented at the Triennial Symposium on African Art, New York.

Berglund, A.-I. (1976), *Zulu Thought-patterns and Symbolism*, London: C. Hurst.

Berlin, B., and Kay, P. (1969), *Basic Color Terms: Their Universality and Evolution*, Berkeley and Los Angeles: University of California Press.

Berreman, G.D. (1962), *Behind Many Masks: Ethnography and Impression Management in a Himalayan Village*, Ithica, NY: Society for Applied Anthropology.

Biebuyck, D. (1969), 'Introduction', in D. Biebuyck (ed.), *Tradition and Creativity in Tribal Art*, Berkeley and Los Angeles: University of California Press, pp. 1–23.

Binkley, D.A. (1992), 'The Teeth of Nyim: The Elephant and Ivory in Kuba Art', in D.H. Ross (ed.), *Elephant: The Animal and Its Ivory in African Culture*, Los Angeles: UCLA Fowler Museum of Cultural History, pp. 277–91.

Blier, S.P. (1988), 'Words about Words about Icons: Iconologology and the Study of African Art', *Art Journal*, vol. 47, no. 2, pp. 75–87.

—— (1990), 'King Glele of Danhome. Part One: Divination Portraits of a Lion King and Man of Iron', *African Arts*, vol. XXIII, no. 4, pp. 42–53, 93–4.

—— (1991), 'King Glele of Danhome. Part Two: Dynasty and Destiny', *African Arts*, vol.XXIV, no.1, pp. 44–55, 101.

—— (1993), 'Melville J. Herskovits and the Arts of Ancient Dahomey', in R.L. Anderson and K.L. Field (eds), *Art in Small-scale Societies*, Englewood Cliffs, NJ: Prentice Hall, pp. 425–44.

—— (1995), *African Vodun: Art, Psychology, and Power*, Chicago and London: The University of Chicago Press.

—— (1998), *The Royal Arts of Africa: The Majesty of Form*. New York: H.N. Abrams.

Bohannan, P. (1968), *Tiv Economy*. Evanston: Northwestern University Press.

Bohannan, P. and Curtin, P. (1988), *Africa and Africans*. Prospect Heights, Ill: Waveland Press.

Bohannan, P. and Dalton, G. (1962), *Markets in Africa*, Evanston: Northwestern University Press.

Bolland, R. (1992), 'Clothing from Burial Caves in Mali, 11th–18th Century', in *History, Design, and Craft in West African Strip-woven Cloth*, Washington, DC: National Museum of African Art, pp. 53–81.

Borgatti, J. (1979), 'Dead Mothers of Okpella', *African Arts*, vol. XII, no. 4, pp. 48–57.

—— (1982), 'Age Grades, Masquerades, and Leadership among the Northern Edo', *African Arts*, vol. XVI, no. 1, pp. 36–51.

—— (1983), *Cloth as Metaphor: Nigerian Textiles from the Museum of Cultural History*, Los Angeles: UCLA Museum of Cultural History.

Bourdieu, P. (1977), *Outline of a Theory of Practice*, London: Cambridge University Press.

—— (1980) *The Logic of Practice*, Stanford: Stanford University Press.

Bowdich, T.E. (1966, orig. 1819), *Mission from Cape Coast Castle to Ashantee*, 3rd edn, London: Cass.

Boyer, R. (1983), 'Yourba Cloths with Regal Names', *African Arts*, vol. XVI, no. 2, pp. 42–5.

Bravmann, R. (1972), 'The Diffusion of Ashanti Political Art', in D. Fraser and H.M. Cole (eds), *African Art and Leadership*, Madison: University of Wisconsin Press, pp. 152–72.

—— (1973), *Open Frontiers: The Mobility of Art in Black Africa*, Seattle: University of Washington Press.

Bray, J.M. (1966), *The Industrial Structure of a Traditional Yoruba Town*, MA thesis, University of Ibadan.

—— (1968), 'The Organization of Traditional Weaving in Iseyin, Nigeria', *Africa*, vol. 38, pp. 270–9.

—— (1969), 'The Economics of Traditional Cloth Production in Iseyin, Nigeria', *Economic Development & Cultural Change*, vol. 17, pp. 540–51.

Brett-Smith, S.C. (1982), 'Symbolic Blood: Cloths for Excised Women', *RES* 3, pp. 15–31.

Bruner, E.M. (1986), 'Experience and Its Expressions', in V.W. Turner and E.M. Bruner (eds), *The Anthropology of Experience*, Urbana and Chicago: University of Illinois Press, pp. 3–30.

Byfield, J. (1993), *Women, Economy, and the State: A Study of the Adire Industry in Abeokuta (Western Nigeria), 1890–1939*, PhD dissertation, Graduate School of Arts and Sciences, Columbia University.

Callaway, H. (1981), 'Spatial Domains and Women's Mobility in Yorubaland, Nigeria', in Ardener, S. (ed), *Women and Space: Ground Rules and Social Maps*, London: Croom Helm.

Cannizzo, J. (1983), 'Gara Cloth by Senesse Tarawallie', *African Arts*, vol. XVI, no. 4, pp. 60–4.

—— (1989), *Into the Heart of Africa*, Toronto: Royal Ontario Museum.

Chambers, D.S. (1970), *Patrons and Artists in the Italian Renaissance,* London: Macmillan & Co. Ltd.

Chaudot-Hawad, H. (1993), *Les Touaregs: Portrait en Fragments*, Aix-en-Provence: Edisud.

Clapperton, H. (1829), *Journal of a Second Expedition into the Interior of Africa from the Bight of Benin to Sokoto*, Philadelphia: Carey, Lea & Carey.

Clarke, D. (1996), 'Colonial Intervention and Indigenous Responses: The Introduction of European Broad Loom Weaving in Oyo Town', *Kurio Africana*, vol. 2, no. 2,

Department of Fine Arts, OAU, Ife.

—— (1996), 'Creativity and the Process of Innovation in Yoruba Aso-Oke Weaving', *Nigerian Field*, vol. 61, pp. 90–103.

—— (1997), *The Art of African Textiles*. San Diego: Thunder Bay Press.

—— (1998), 'An Urban Maze: The Interaction of Weaving Traditions in 1990s Lagos', *CON/TEXT: Research Papers of the Consortium for Indigenous Textiles and Clothing Research*, no. 1.

Cole, B. (1983), *The Renaissance Artist at Work: From Pisano to Titian*, New York: Harper & Row.

Cole, H.M. (1989), *Icons: Ideals and Power in the Art of Africa*, Washington, DC and London: Smithsonian Institution Press.

—— and Aniakor, C. (1984), *Igbo Arts: Community and Cosmos*, Los Angeles: Museum of Cultural History.

—— and Ross, D.H. (1977), *The Arts of Ghana*, Los Angeles: University of California Press.

Colvin, Lucie (1973), 'The Commerce of Hausaland, 1780–1833', *Aspects of West African Islam*, Dan McCall and Norman Bennett (eds), Vol V, Boston University Papers on Africa, pp. 101–135.

Cordwell, J. (1983), 'The Art and Aesthetics of the Yoruba', *African Arts*, vol. XVI, no. 2, pp. 56–9.

Costentino, D.J. (1991), 'Afrokitsch', in S. Vogel (ed.), *Africa Explores: 20th Century African Art*, New York: The Center for African Art, pp. 240–55.

Costin, C.L. (1993), 'Textiles, Women, and Political Economy in Late Prehispanic Peru', *Research in Economic Anthropology*, vol. 14, pp. 3–28.

Craftspace Touring (1992), *Yoruba Textiles, West African Cloth Culture* [exhibition catalogue], Birmingham, England: Craftspace Touring.

Crowder, M. (1978), *The Story of Nigeria*, London: Faber and Faber.

d'Azevedo, W.L. (1958), 'A Structural Approach to Esthetics: Toward a Definition of Art in Anthropology', *American Anthropologist*, vol. 60, no. 4, pp. 702–14.

—— (1973a), 'Approaches to Non-Western Art', in W. d'Azevedo (ed.), *The Traditional Artist in African Societies*, Bloomington: Indiana University Press, pp. 425–34.

—— (1973b), 'Introduction', in W. d'Azevedo (ed.), *The Traditional Artist in African Societies*, Bloomington: Indiana University Press. pp. 1–15.

—— (1973c), 'Mask Makers and Myth in Western Liberia', in A. Forge (ed.), *Primitive Art and Society*, London: Oxford University Press, pp. 126–50.

—— (1973d), 'Sources of Gola Artistry', in W. d'Azevedo (ed.), *The Traditional Artist in African Societies*, Bloomington: Indiana University Press, pp. 282–340.

—— (ed.) (1973), *The Traditional Artist in African Societies*, Bloomington: Indiana University Press.

Delano, I.O. (1937), *The Soul of Nigeria*, London: T. Werner Laurie Ltd.

Dilley, R. (1986), 'Tukulor Weavers and the Organisation of Their Craft in Village and Town', *Africa*, vol. 56, no. 2, pp. 255–85.

Dodwell, C.B. (1955), 'Iseyin, the Town of Weavers', *Nigeria Magazine*, no. 46, pp. 118–39.

Domowitz, S. (1992), 'Wearing Proverbs: Anyi Names for Printed Factory Cloth', *African Arts*, vol. XXV, no. 3, pp. 82–7.

Douglas, M. (1962), 'Lele Economy Compared with the Bushong', in P. Bohannan and G. Dalton (eds), *Markets in Africa*, Evanston: Northwestern University Press, pp. 211–33.

—— (1967a), 'Raffia Cloth Distribution in the Lele Economy', in G. Dalton (ed.), *Tribal and Peasant Economies*, Garden City, N.J.: Natural History Press, pp. 103–22.

Drewal, H.J. (1979), 'Pageantry and Power in Yoruba Costuming', in J. Cordwell (ed.), *The Fabrics of Culture*, The Hague: Mouton, pp. 177–93.

—— (1984), 'Art, History and the Individual: A New Perspective for the Study of African Visual Traditions', in C. Roy (ed.), *Iowa Studies in African Art* I, Iowa City: University of Iowa, pp. 87–101.

—— (1992), 'Image and Indeterminacy: Elephants and Ivory among the Yoruba', in D.H. Ross (ed.), *Elephant: The Animal and Its Ivory in African Culture*, Los Angeles: UCLA Fowler Museum of Cultural History, pp. 187–207.

—— and Mason, J. (1998), *Beads, Body and Soul: Art and Light in the Yoruba Universe*, Los Angeles: UCLA Fowler Museum of Cultural History.

Duchateau, A. (1994), *Benin: Royal Art of Africa*, Houston: The Museum of Fine Arts.

Dupigny, E.G.M. (1920), *Gazetteer of Nupe Province*, London: Waterloo.

Eades, J.S. (1980), *The Yoruba Today*, Cambridge: Cambridge University Press.

Edwards, J.P. (1992), 'The Sociological Significance and Uses of Mende Country Cloth', in *History, Design, and Craft in West African Strip-woven Cloth*, Washington, DC: National Museum of African Art, pp. 133–68.

Eicher, J.B. (1969), *African Dress: A Select and Annotated Bibliography of Subsaharan Countries*, East Lansing: Michigan State University African Studies Center & Dept. of Textiles, Clothing & Related Arts.

—— (1996), 'Africa. Dress', in J. Turner (ed.), *The Dictionary of Art*, London: Macmillan Publications Limited, vol. I, pp. 347–51.

—— and Erekosima, T.V. (1981), 'Kalabari Cut-thread and Pulled-thread Cloth: An Example of Cultural Authentication', *African Arts*, vol. XIV, no. 2, pp. 48–51.

—— and Erekosima, T.V. (1989), 'Kalabari Funeral Rooms as Handicraft and Ephemeral Art', in B. Engelbrecht and B. Gardi (eds), *Man Does Not Go Naked*, Basel: Ethnologisches Seminar der Universitat und Museum for Volkerkunde, pp. 197–205.

—— and Erekosima, T.V. (1993), 'Kalabari Funerals: Celebration and Display', *African Arts*, vol. XXI, no. 1, pp. 38–45.

—— and Roach-Higgins, M.E. (1992), 'Definition and Classification of Dress: Implications for Analysis of Gender Roles', in R. Barnes and J.B. Eicher (eds), *Dress and Gender: Making and Meaning in Cultural Contexts*, New York and Oxford: Berg, pp. 8–28.

Eisenstadt, S.N., and Roniger, L. (1984), *Patrons, Clients, and Friends: Interpersonal Relations and the Structure of Trust in Society*, New York: Cambridge University Press.

Etienne, M. (1980), 'Women and Men, Cloth and Colonization: The Transformation of Production-Distribution Relations among the Baule (Ivory Coast)', in M. Etienne and E. Leacock (eds), *Women and Colonization: Anthropological Perspectives*, New York: Praeger, pp. 214–38.

Euba, T. (1986), 'The Human Image: Some Aspects of Yoruba Canons of Art and Beauty', *Nigeria,/* vol. 54, no. 4, pp. 9–21.

Eyo, E., and Willett, F. (1980), *Treasures of Ancient Nigeria*, New York: Alfred A. Knopf.

—— (1981), [comment on] 'Hunting Horn', in S. Vogel (ed.), *For Spirits and Kings*, New York: Metropolitan Museum of Art, pp. 64–7.

Fagg, William (1981), 'Hunting Horn', in *For Spirits and Kings*, Susan Vogel (ed.), New York: Metropolitan Museum of Art, pp. 64–67.

Feeley-Harik, G. (1989), 'Cloth and the Creation of Ancestors in Madagascar', in A.B. Weiner and J. Schneider (eds), *Cloth and Human Experience*, Washington, DC: Smithsonian Institution Press, pp. 73–116.

Ferguson, D.E. (1973), *Nineteenth Century Hausaland: Being a Description by Iman Imoru of the Land, Economy and Society of His People*, unpublished PhD thesis, UCLA.

Fika, A.M. (1978), *The Kano Civil War and British Overrule 1882–1942*, Ibadan: Oxford University.

Fischer, E. (1978), 'Dan Forest Spirits: Masks in Dan Villages', *African Arts*, vol. XI, no. 2, pp. 16–23.

Fitzgerald, M.A., with H.J. Drewal and M. Okediji (1995), 'Transformation through Cloth: An Egungun Costume of the Yoruba', *African Arts*, vol. XXVIII, no. 2, pp. 54–7.

Foss, S.M. (1979), 'She Who Sits as King', *African Arts*, vol. XII, no. 2, pp. 45–50.

Fosu, K. (1982), *Emblems of Royalty (Kayan Sarauta): Exhibit of Items from Palaces of the Emir of Zaria, Etsu Nupe, Lamido of Adamawa, Shebu of Borno, Sultan of Sokoto*, 6-20 December, Zaria, Nigeria: Department Of Fine Arts, Ahmadu Bello University.

Fraser, D. (1972a), 'Art and Leadership: An Overview', in D. Fraser and H. Cole (eds), *African Art and Leadership*, pp. 295–328.

—— and Cole, H.M. (eds) (1972b), *African Art and Leadership*, Madison: The University of Wisconsin Press.

Frobenius, L. (1968, orig. 1913), *The Voice of Africa*, vol. I, London: Benjamin Blom.

Geary, C. (1983), *Things of the Palace: A catalogue of the Bamum Palace Museum in Foumban (Cameroon)*, Wiesbaden: Franz Steiner Verlag GMBH.

—— (1988), *Images from Bamun. German Colonial Photography at the Court of King Njoya. Cameroon, West Africa, 1902–1915*, Washington, DC: Smithsonian Institution Press.

—— (1992), 'Elephants, Ivory, and Chiefs: The Elephant and The Arts of the Cameroon Grassfields', *Elephant: The Animal and Its Ivory in African Culture*, D.H. Ross (ed.), Los Angeles: UCLA Fowler Museum of Cultural History, pp. 229–57.

—— (1993), 'Art and Political Process in the Kingdoms of Bali-Nyonga and Bamun (Cameroon Grassfields)', in R.L. Anderson and K.L. Field (eds), *Art in Small-scale Societies*, Englewood Cliffs, NJ: Prentice Hall, pp. 84–102.

Ghaidan, U.I. (1971), 'Swahili Art of Lamu', *African Arts*, vol. V, no. 1, pp. 54–7.

Giddens, A. (1976), *New Rules of the Sociological Method: A Positive Critique of Interpretive Sociologies*, New York: Basic Books.

Gilfoy, P.S. (1987), *Patterns of Life: West African Strip-weaving Traditions*, Washington, DC and London: The National Museum of African Art by The Smithsonian Institution Press.

Glaze, A.J. (1981), *Art and Death in a Senufo Village*, Bloomington: Indiana University Press.

Grabar, Oleg (1992), *The Mediation of Ornament*, Princeton, N.J.: Princeton University Press.

Griaule, M., and Dieterlen, G. (1954), 'The Dogon of the French Sudan', in D. Forde (ed.), *African Worlds: Studies in the Cosmological Ideas and Social Values of African Peoples*, London: Oxford University Press for the International African Institute, pp. 83–110.

A Guide to the Gidan Makama Museum Kano (1985), Lagos: National Commissions for Museums and Monuments.

Guimbe, Y. (1998), personal communication, Athens, Ohio.

Hardin, K.L. (1993), *The Aesthetics of Action: Continuity and Change in a West African Town*, Washington, DC and London: Smithsonian Institution Press.

Haskell, F. (1963), *Patrons and Painters: A Study in the Relations between Italian Art and Society in the Age of the Baroque*, New York: Knopf.

Heathcote, D. (1973), 'Hausa Women's Dress in the Light of Two Recent Finds', *Savanna*, vol. 2, no. 2, pp. 201–16.

—— (1974), 'Aspects of Style in Hausa Embroidery', *Savanna*, vol. 3, no. 1, pp. 15–40.

—— (1977), 'Hausa Embroidered Dress', *African Arts*, vol. V, no. 2, pp. 12–19, 82.

Hendrickson, H. (1996a), 'Introduction', in H. Hendrickson (ed.), *Clothing and Difference: Embodied Identities in Colonial and Post-Colonial Africa*, Durham and London: Duke University Press, pp.1–16.

—— (ed.) (1996b), *Clothing and Difference: Embodied Identities in Colonial and Post-Colonial Africa*, Durham and London: Duke University Press.

Herskovits, M., and Herskovits, F. (1958), *Dahomean Narrative*, Evanston: Northwestern University Press.

Hilger, J. (1995), 'The *Kanga*: An Example of East African Textile Design', in J. Picton (ed.), *The Art of African Textiles: Technology, Tradition and Lurex*, London: Barbican Art Gallery, Lund Humphries Publishers, pp. 44–5.

Hill, P. (1977), *Population, Prosperity and Poverty: Rural Kano 1900–1970*,

Cambridge: Cambridge University Press.

Himmelheber, H. (1960), *Negerkunst und Negerkunstler*, Braunschweig: Klinkhardt and Biermann.

Hodgkin, T. (1960), *Nigerian Perspectives*, London: Oxford University Press.

Hodler, B.W. (1980), 'Indigenous Cloth Trade and Marketing in Africa', *Textile History*, vol. II, pp. 203–10.

Ige, (Mrs) A. O. (1990), Field Interview, Ibadan, June 25, 1990.

Irwin, Robert (1997), 'Colour Theory and Symbolism', *Islamic Art in Context*, New York: Perspectives Prentice Hall and Harry Abrams, pp. 196–198.

Isichei, E. (1983), *A History of Nigeria*, London: Longman.

Jackson, M. (1989), *Paths Toward a Clearing: Radical Empiricism and Ethnographic Inquiry*, Bloomington and Indianapolis: Indiana University Press.

Jegede, D. (1984), 'Patronage and Change in Nigeria Art', *Nigeria Magazine*, no. 150, pp. 29–36.

Johnson, B.C. (1986), *Four Dan Sculptors: Continuity and Change*, San Francisco: The Fine Arts Museums of San Francisco.

Johnson, M. (1973), 'Cloth on the Banks of the Niger', *Journal of the Historical Society of Nigeria*, vol. 6, no. 4, pp. 353–63.

—— (1974), 'Cotton Imperialism in West Africa', *African Affairs*, vol. 73, no. 291, pp. 178–87.

—— (1978), 'Technology, Competition and African Crafts', in C. Dewey and A.G. Hopkins (eds), *The Imperial Impact: Studies in the Economic History of Africa and India*, London: Athlone Press, pp. 259–69.

—— (1979), 'Ashanti Craft Organization', *African Arts*, vol. XIII, no. 1, pp. 60–3, 78–82.

—— (1980), 'Cloth as Money: The Cloth Strip Currencies of Africa', *Textile History*, vol. II, pp. 193–202.

—— (1983), 'Periphery and the Centre: the 19th Century Trade of Kano', in B.M. Barkindo (ed.), *Studies in the History of Kano*, Nigeria: Heinemann Educational Books, pp. 127–46.

Johnson, S. (1921), *The History of the Yorubas*, Lagos: C.M.S. (Nigeria) Bookshops.

Joseph, Marjory L. (1984), *Essentials of Textiles*, 3rd edn, New York: Holt, Rinehart & Winston.

Kalihu, R.O.R. (1991), 'Leatherwork in Oyo: Access to Material as a Factor in the Origin of an African Craft', *African Notes*, vol. 15, nos. 1–2, pp.105–12.

Kapferer, B. (1976), 'Introduction: Transactional Models Reconsidered', in Kapferer (ed.), *Transactions and Meaning: Directions in the Anthropology of Exchange and Symbolic Behavior*, Philadelphia: Institute for the Study of Human Issues, pp. 1–22.

Kasfir, S.L. (1980), 'Patronage and Maconde Carvers', *African Arts*, vol. XX, no. 2, pp. 67–70.

—— (1985), 'Art in History, History in Art: The Idoma Ancestral Masquerade as Historical Evidence', *Boston University African Studies Center Working Papers*.

—— (1992), 'African Art and Authenticity: A Text with a Shadow', *African Arts*, vol. XXV, no. 2, pp. 40–53.

Kempers, B. (1992), *Painting, Power and Patronage: The Rise of the Professional Artist in Renaissance Italy*, London: The Penguin Press.

Kisch, M. (1910), *Letters and Sketches from Northern Nigeria*, London: Chatto and Windus.

Kiyiwa, I.A. (1986), 'Economic Activities and Social Organisation in Traditional Kano', *Kano Studies*, n.s., vol. 2, no. 4, pp. 70–80.

Kopytoff, I. (1986), 'The Cultural Biography of Things: Commoditization as Process', in A. Appadurai (ed.), *The Social Life of Things: Commodities in Cultural Perspective*, Cambridge: Cambridge University Press, pp. 64–91.

Kreamer, C.M. (1995), 'Spectacular Hats for Special Occasions', in M.J. Arnoldi and C.M. Kreamer (eds), *Crowning Achievements: African Arts of Dressing the Head*, Los Angeles: UCLA Fowler Museum of Cultural History, pp. 99–125.

Kriger, C. (1988), 'Robes of The Sokoto Caliphate', *African Arts*, vol. XXI, no. 3, pp. 52–7, 78–9.

—— (1990), 'Textile Production in the Lower Niger Basin: New Evidence from the 1841 Niger Expedition Collection', *Textile History*, vol. 21, no. 1, pp. 31–56.

—— (1993), 'Textile Production and Gender in the Sokoto Caliphate', *Journal of African History*, vol. 34, pp. 361–401.

Kwarteng, Nana (1995), personal communication, Athens, Ohio.

Lamb, V. (1975), *West African Weaving*, London: Duckworth.

—— and Holmes, J. (1980), *Nigerian Weaving*, Lagos: Shell Petroleum Development Company of Nigeria.

Lamp, F. (1978), 'Frogs into Princes: The Temne Rabai Initiation', *African Arts*, vol. XI, no. 2, pp. 38–49.

Lander, R. (1965, orig. 1832), *The Niger Journal of Richard and John Lander*, Robin Hallett (ed.), New York: Praeger.

Last, M. (1988), 'The Sokoto Caliphate and Bornu', in *General History of Africa: Africa in the Nineteenth Century Until the 1880s*, vol. 5, London: UNESCO and Heinemann, pp. 555–99.

Laver, J. (1969) *Modesty in Dress*, Boston: Houghton Mifflin Company.

Law, R. (1977), *The Oyo Empire c. 1600–1836: A West African Imperialism in the Era of the Atlantic Slave Trade*, Oxford: Clarendon Press.

Lawal, B. (1997), personal communication.

Levtzion, N. (1976), 'The Early States of the Western Sudan to 1500', in J.F.A. Ajayi and M. Crowder (eds), *History of West Africa*, 2nd edn, vol. 1, New York: Longman, pp. 114–51.

—— and Hopkins, A.G. (1981), *Corpus of Early Arabic Sources for West African History*, Cambridge and New York: Cambridge University Press.

Lock, M. (1993), 'Cultivating the Body: Anthropology and Epistemologies of Bodily Practice and Knowledge', *Annual Review of Anthropology*, vol. 22, Palo Alto: Annual Reviews Inc., pp. 133–55.

Lovejoy, P. (1978), 'The Role of the Wangara in the Economic Transformation of the Central Sudan in the 15th and 16th Centuries', *Journal of African History*, vol.

XIX, no. 2, pp. 173–93.

MacGaffey, W. (1993), 'The Eyes of Understanding: Kongo Minkisi', in *Astonishment and Power*, Washington, DC and London: National Museum of African Art by The Smithsonian Institution Press, pp. 19–103.

Mack, J. (1980), 'Bakuba Emboridery Patterns: A Commentary on their Social and Political Implications', in D. Idiens and K.G. Ponting (eds), *Textiles of Africa*, Bath: The Pasold Research Fund Ltd, pp. 163–74.

Magangara, Mallam Danladi (1981), personal communication from turkudi weaver, Kura, Kano State, Nigeria.

Mahar, C. (1992), 'An exercise in Practice: Studying Migrants to Latin American Squatter Settlements', *Urban Anthropology and Studies of Cultural Systems and the World Economic Development*, vol. 21, pp. 275–309.

Maquet, J. (1986), *The Aesthetic Experience: An Anthropologist Looks at the Visual Arts*, New Haven and London: Yale University Press.

Mason, M. (1981), *The Foundations of the Bida Kingdom*, Zaria: Ahmadu Bello University Press.

Masquelier, A. (1996) 'Mediating Threads: Clothing and the Texture of Spirit/Medium Relations in Bori (Southern Niger)', in H. Hendrickson (ed.), *Clothing and Difference: Embodied Identities in Colonial and Post Colonial Africa*, Durham and London: Duke University Press, pp. 66–93.

Matory, J.L. (1994), *Sex and the Empire That Is No More: Gender and the Politics of Metaphor in Oyo Yoruba Religion*, Minneapolis: University of Minnesota Press.

McCracken, G. (1986), 'Culture and Consumption: A Theoretical Account of the Structure and Movement of the Cultural Meaning of Consumer Goods', *Journal of Consumer Research*, vol. 13, pp. 71–84.

McLeod, M.D. (1981), *The Asante*, London: British Museum Publications Ltd.

McNaughton, P.R. (1982), 'The Shirts that Mande Hunters Wear', *African Arts*, vol. XV, no. 3, pp. 54–8.

Meek, C.K. (1925), *The Northern Tribes of Nigeria: An Ethnographical Account of the Northern Provinces of Nigeria*, London: Oxford University Press.

Merriam, A.P. (1968), 'Basongye Raffia Basketry', *African Arts*, vol. II, no. 1, pp. 14–7, 73.

—— (1977), 'The Arts in Anthropology', in S. Tax and L. Freeman (eds), *Horizons of Anthropology*, 2nd edn, Chicago: Aldine Publishing Company.

Messenger, J.C. (1973), 'The Carver in Anang Society', in W. d'Azevedo (ed.), *The Traditional Artist in African Societies*, Bloomington: Indiana University Press, pp. 101–27.

Michelman, S.O., and Erekosima, T.V. (1993), 'Kalabari Dress in Nigeria: Visual Analysis and Gender Implications', in R. Barnes and J.B. Eicher (eds), *Dress and Gender: Making and Meaning*, Providence and Oxford: Berg, pp. 164–82.

Moloye, O. (1991), 'Between Tradition and Change: A Perspective of the Yoruba Traditional Aso-Oke', unpublished paper, Central States Anthropological Society Annual Meetings, March 1991.

Morgan, W.T.W. (1983), *Nigeria*, London: Longman.

Morton-Williams, P. (1956), 'The Atinga Cult Among the Soutwestern Yoruba', *Bulletin I.F.A.N.*, vol. 8, pp. 315–34).

Moughtin, J.C. (1985), *Hausa Architecture*, London: Ethnographica.

Mount, M.W. (1973), *African Art: The Years Since 1920*, Bloomington and London: Indiana University Press.

Mount, S.D. (1980), 'African Art at the Cincinnati Art Museum', *African Arts*, vol. XIII, no. 4, pp. 40–6.

Nadel, S. (1942), *Black Byzantium*, London: Oxford University Press.

—— (1954), *Nupe Religion*, London: Kegan Paul.

National Commission for Museum and Monuments (1985), A Guide to the Gidan Makama Museum Kano.

Nevadomsky, J., and Ekhaguosa, A. (1995), 'The Clothing of Political Identity', *African Arts*, vol. XXVIII, no. 1, pp. 62–73.

—— and Inneh, D.E. (1983), 'Kingship Succession Rituals in Benin. Part I: Becoming a Crown Prince', *African Arts*, vol. XVII, no. 1, pp. 47–54.

Nicklin, K. and Salmons, J. (1984), 'Cross River Art Styles', *African Arts,* vol. XVIII, no. 1, pp. 28–48.

Nigeria in Costume (1965), Lagos: The Shell Company of Nigeria.

Nigerian Institute of Social and Economic Research (NISER) (1990), *Report of World Bank/Niser Project on Education and Training for Skills and Income in the Urban Informal Sector in Sub-Saharan Africa: The Case of Urban Informal Sector of Ibadan City, Nigeria*, Ibadan: NISER.

Northern, T. (1984), *The Art of Cameroon*, Washington, DC: Smithsonian Institution Traveling Exhibition Service.

Nooter, N.I. (1996), 'Africa. Regalia', in J. Turner (ed.), *The Dictionary of Art*, vol. 1, London: Macmillan Publishers Limited, pp. 351–55.

Obayemi, A. (1976), 'The Yoruba and Edo-speaking Peoples and their Neighbours before 1600,' in J.F.A. Ajayi & M. Crowder (eds), *History of West Africa*, Vol. 1, 2nd edn, New York: Columbia Univrsity Press, pp. 196–263.

Offonry, H.K. (1987), *Investment in Goodwill: The Story of a Nigerian Philanthropist*, Owerri: New Africa Publishing Co. Ltd.

Oguntona, T. (1981), *The Oshogbo Art Workshops: A Case Study of Non-formal Art Education in Nigeria*, PhD dissertation, University of Wisconsin-Madison.

O'Hear, A. (1983), 'The Economic History of Ilorin in the Nineteenth and Twentieth Centuries: The Rise and Decline of a Middleman Society', unpublished PhD thesis, University of Birmingham.

—— (1987), 'Craft Industries in Ilorin: Dependency or Independence?', *African Affairs*, vol. 86, pp. 505–21.

—— (1990), 'The Introduction of Weft Float Motifs to Strip Weaving in Ilorin', in D. Henige and T.C. McCaskie (eds), *West African Economic and Social History*, Madison: African Studies Program, University of Wisconsin, pp. 175–88.

—— (1991), personal communication.

Okrah, K. (1997), personal communication, Athens, Ohio.

Onwuejeogwu, M. (1971), 'The Cult of the Bori Spirits Among the Hausa', in M. Douglas and P. Kaberry (eds), *Man in Africa*, New York: Doubleday & Co., pp. 249–306.

Ortner, Sherry B. (1984), 'Theory in Anthropology since the Sixties', *Comparative Studies in Society and History*, no. 26, pp. 126–66.

Peek, P. (1980), 'Isoko Artists and Their Audiences', *African Arts*, vol. XIII, no. 3, pp. 58–61.

Perani, J. (1992), 'The Cloth Connection: Patrons and Producers of Hausa and Nupe Prestige Strip-weave', in *History, Design, and Craft in West African Strip-woven Cloth*, Washington, DC: National Museum of African Art, pp. 95–112.

—— (1980), 'Patronage and Nupe Craft Industries', *African Arts*, vol. XIII, no. 3, pp. 71–5, 92.

—— and O'Connell, P. (1974), 'Traditional Bandi Crafts', paper presented at the Symposium on Liberia, Bloomington, Indiana.

—— and Smith, F. T. (1998), *The Visual Arts of Africa: Gender, Power, and Life Cycle Rituals*, Upper Saddle River, N.J.: Prentice Hall.

—— and Wolff, N.H. (1992), 'Embroidered Gown and Equestrian Ensembles of the Kano Aristocracy', *African Arts*, vol. XXV, no. 3, pp. 70–81, 102.

—— and Wolff, N.H. (1996a), 'Patronage: Contexts of Production and Use', in J. Turner (ed.), *The Dictionary of Art*, vol. I, London: Grove's Dictionaries, pp.240–43.

—— and Wolff, N.H. (1996b), 'Traders as Intermediaries'. in J. Turner (ed.), *The Dictionary of Art*, vol. I, London: Grove's Dictionaries, p. 251.

Picton, J. (1980), 'Women's Weaving: The Manufacture and Use of Textiles Among the Igbirra People of Nigeria', in D. Idiens and K.G. Ponting (eds), *Textiles of Africa*, Bath: The Pasold Research Fund Ltd.

—— (1992), 'Tradition, Technology, and Lurex: Some Comments on Textile History and Design in West Africa', in *History, Design, and Craft in West African Strip-woven Cloth*, Washington, DC: National Museum of African Art, pp. 13–52.

—— (1995a), *The Art of African Textiles: Technology, Tradition and Lurex*, London: Barbican Art Gallery, Lund Humphries Publishers.

—— (1995b), 'Technology, tradition and lurex: The art of textiles in Africa', in J. Picton (ed.), *The Art of African Textiles: Technology, Tradition and Lurex*, London: Barbican Art Gallery, Lund Humphries Publishers, pp. 9–30.

—— and Mack, J. (1979), *African Textiles*, London: British Museum Publications Ltd.

Plumer, C. (1970), *African Textiles: An Outline of Handcrafted Sub-saharan Fabrics*, East Lansing: Michigan State University African Studies Center & Dept. of Human Environment & Design.

Pokrant, R.J. (1982), 'The Tailors of Kano City', in E. Goody (ed.), *From Craft to Industry*, Cambridge: Cambridge University Press, pp. 85–132.

Polakoff, C. (1978), 'Crafts and the Concept of Art in Africa', *African Arts*, vol. XII, no. 1, pp. 22–3.

Polhemus, T., and Procter, L. (1978), *Fashion and anti-fashion: Anthropology of clothing and adornment*, London: Thames and Hudson.

Priebatsch, S., and Knight, N. (1978), 'Traditional Ndebele Beadwork', *African Arts*, vol. XI, no. 2, pp. 24–7.

Prussin, L. (1986), *Hatumere: Islamic Design in West Africa*, Berkeley: University of California Press.

Rattray, R.S. (1927), *Religion and Art in Asante*, Oxford: Clarendon Press.

Ravenhill, P.L. (1980), *Baule Statuary Art: Meaning and Modernization*. Working Papers in the Traditional Arts, no. 5, Philadelphia: Institute for the Study of Human Issues.

—— (1996), *Dreams and Reverie: Images of Otherworld Mates Among the Baule, West Africa*, Washington and London: Smithsonian Institution Press.

Renne, E.P. (1995), *Cloth That Does Not Die: The Meaning of Cloth in Bunu Social Life*, Seattle: University of Washington Press.

—— (n.d.), 'The Decline and Resurgence of Women's Weaving in Ekiti, Nigeria', unpublished paper.

Robinson, C.H. (1897), *Hausaland, or Fifteen Hundred Miles through the Central Sudan*, London: Sampson, Low.

Robinson, G.A. (1982), *Cloth-weaving Technology in Yorubaland: Iseyin as a Case Study*, original essay, BA (Honours), History and Archaeology, University of Ibadan.

Ross, D.H. (1979), *Fighting With Art: Appliquéd Flags of the Fante Asafo*, Los Angeles: Regents of the University of California.

—— (1984), 'The Art of Osei Bonsu', *African Arts*, vol. XVII, no. 2, pp. 28–40.

—— (1992), 'Imaging Elephants: An Overview', in D.H. Ross (ed.), *Elephant: The Animal and Its Ivory in African Culture*, Los Angeles: UCLA Fowler Museum of Cultural History, pp. 1–39.

Rovine, V. (1997), '*Bogolanfini* in Bamako: The Biography of a Malian Textile, *African Arts*, vol. XXX, no. 1, pp. 40–52.

Ryder, A.F.C. (1965), *Materials for West African History in Portuguese Archives*, London: Athlone Press..

Saad, H.T. (1985), 'The Role of Individual Creativity in Traditional African Art: The *Gwani* (Genius) amongst Master Builders of Hausaland', *Nigeria Magazine*, vol. 53, no. 4, pp. 3–16.

Salmons, J. (1977), 'Mammy Wata', *African Arts*, vol. X, no. 3, pp. 8–15.

—— (1980), 'Funerary Shrine Cloths of the Annang Ibibio, South-east Nigeria', *Textile History*, vol. II, pp. 119–41.

Scheflen, A.E. (1974), *How Behavior Means*, Garden City, NY: Anchor Press/ Doubleday.

Schiltz, M. (1982), 'Habitus and Peasantisation in Nigeria: A Yoruba Case Study,' *Man*, vol. 17, pp. 728–46.

Schneider, J. (1987), 'The Anthropology of Cloth', *Annual Review of Anthropology 1987*, Palo Alto: Annual Reviews Inc., pp.409–48.

Shaw, T. (1978), *Nigeria: Its Archaeology and Early History*, London: Thames and Hudson.

Shea, P. (1975), 'The Development of an Export Oriented Dyed Cloth Industry in Kano Emirate in the Nineteenth Century', unpublished PhD thesis, University of Wisconsin.

—— (1980), 'Kano and the Silk Trade', *Kano Studies*, n.s. vol. 2, no. 1, pp. 96–111.

—— (1983), 'Approaching the Study of Production in Rural Kano', in B.M. Barkindo (ed.), *Studies in the History of Kano*, Nigeria: Heinemann Educational Books, pp. 93–115.

Sieber, R. (1972), *African Textiles and Decorative Arts*, New York: The Museum of Modern Art.

—— (1973), 'Ede: Crafts and Survey', *African Arts*, vol. VI, no. 4, pp. 44–9.

—— (1973), 'Approaches to Non-Western Art', in W. d'Azeved (ed.), *The Traditional Artist in African Societies*, Bloomington: Indiana University Press, pp. 425–434.

Siegmann, William C. and Cynthia E. Schmidt, *Rock of the Ancestors: Namoa Koni*, Suakoko, Liberia: Cuttington University College.

Smith, F.T. (1982), 'Fra Fra Dress', *African Arts*, vol. V, no. 3, pp. 37–42.

—— (1987a), 'Death, Ritual and Art in Africa', *African Arts*, vol. XXI, no. 1, pp. 28–9.

—— (1987b), 'Symbols of Conflict and Integration in Frafra Funerals', *African Arts*, vol. XXI, no. 1, pp. 46–51.

Smith, M.G. (1965), 'The Hausa of Northern Nigeria', in J.L.Gibbs (ed.), *Peoples of Africa*, New York: Holt, Rinehart and Winston, pp. 119–55.

Spencer, A.M. (1982), *In Praise of Heroes: Contemporary African Commemorative Cloth*, Newark, NJ: The Newark Museum.

Spring, C. (1993), *African Arms and Armor*, Washington DC: Smithsonian Institution Press.

Steiner, C.B. (1985), 'Another Image of Africa: Toward an Ethnohistory of European Cloth Marketed in West Africa, 1873–1960', *Ethnohistory*, vol. 32, no. 2, pp. 91–110.

—— (1991), 'The Trade in West African Art', *African Arts*, vol. XXIV, no. 1, pp. 38–43.

—— (1994), *African Art in Transit*, Cambridge: Cambridge University Press.

Stokstad, M. (1995), *Art History*, 2 volumes, New York: Prentice Hall & Abrams.

Sulama (1990), Personal Communication.

Taylor, F.W., and Webb, A.G.G. (1932), *Customs of the Hausa*, London: Oxford University Press.

Thieme, O.C., and Eicher, J. (1985), 'The Study of African Dress', in I.M. Pokomowski, J.B. Eicher, M.F. Harris and O.C. Thieme (eds), *African Dress II: A Select and Annotated Bibliography*, East Lansing, MI: African Studies Center, Michigan State University, pp. 1–16.

Turner, T.S. (1980), 'The Social Skin', in J. Cherfas and R. Lewin (eds), *Not Work Alone: A Cross-cultural View of Activities Superfluous to Survival*, London: Temple Smith, pp. 112–40.

Turner, V. (1967), 'Color Classification in Ndembu Ritual: A Problem in Primitive Classification', in V. Turner, *The Forest of Symbols*, Ithaca and London: Cornell

University Press.

Ugwu-Oju, D. (1997), 'Aso-ebi', in P. Galembo, *Aso-ebi, Cloth of the Family: Benin City, Nigeria, Christmas and New Years 1991–1994*, pp. 7–16.

Vansina, J. (1972), 'Ndop: Royal Statues among the Kuba', in D. Fraser and H.M. Cole (eds), *African Art and Leadership*, Madison: University of Wisconsin Press, pp. 41–53.

—— (1978), *The Children of Woot: A History of the Kuba Peoples*, Madison: The University of Wisconsin Press.

—— (1984), *Art History in Africa*, London and New York: Longman.

Vogel, S. (1980), '*Beauty in the Eyes of the Baule: Aesthetics and Cultural Values*', Working Papers in the Traditional Arts, no. 6, Philadelphia: Institute for the Study of Human Issues.

Wahab, B. (1997), personal communication, Ames, Iowa.

Walker, R.A. (1994), 'Anonymous Has a Name: Olowe of Ise', in R. Abiodun, H. J. Drewal and J. Pemberton III (eds), *The Yoruba Artist*, Washington, DC: Smithsonian Institution Press, pp. 91–106.

Warren, M. (1991), personal communication.

Warren, D.M. (1975), 'Bono Royal Regalia', *African Arts*, vol. VIII, no. 2, pp. 18–21.

Weiner, A.B. (1992), *Inalienable Possessions*, Berkeley: University of California Press.

Werewere-Liking (1987), *Statues Colons*, Paris: Les Nouvelles Editions Africaines.

Whitford, J. (1967, orig. 1877), *Trading Life in West And Central Africa*, London: Cass.

Winter, E.H. (1959), *Beyond the Mountains of the Moon: The Lives of Four Africans*, Urbana: The University of Illinois Press.

Wolff, N.H. (1981), 'Headdress', in S. Vogel (ed.), *For Spirits and Kings*, New York: Metropolitan Museum of Art, pp. 110–12.

—— (1982), 'Egungun Costuming in Abeokuta', *African Arts*, vol. XV, no. 3, pp. 66–70.

—— (1985), 'Dress and social identity in Nigeria: The women's wrapper', in *West African Textiles*, Raleigh: Student Center Gallery, North Carolina State University, pp. 26–9.

—— (1986), 'A Hausa Aluminum Spoon Industry', *African Arts*, vol. XIX, no. 3, pp. 40–4.

—— and Wahab, B. (1995), 'Learning from Craft Taxonomies: Development and the Yoruba Handwoven Textile Tradition', *Indigenous Knowledge and Development Monitor*, vol. 3, no. 3, pp. 10–12.

—— and Wahab, B. (1996), 'The Importance of Indigenous Organizations to the Sustainability of Contemporary Yoruba Strip-weaving Industries in Iseyin, Nigeria', in P. Blunt and D.M. Warren (eds), *Indigenous Organizations and Development*, London: Intermediate Technology Publications, pp. 67–87.

Yahaya, I.Y. (1984), 'Cultural Development in Kano State', *Nigeria Magazine*, no. 150, pp. 77–83.

Zarruk, R.M. (1978), 'The Study of Colour Terms in the Hausa Language', *Harsunan Nigeria*, no. 8, pp. 51–78.

Index

(Page numbers in *italics* refer to illustrations)